DARK ENGINE

RYAN BURTON
STORY

JOHN BIVENS
ART

KELLY FITZPATRICK
COLORS

CRANK!
LETTERS

IMAGE COMICS, INC.
Robert Kirkman – Chief Operating Officer
Erik Larsen – Chief Financial Officer
Todd McFarlane – President
Marc Silvestri – Chief Executive Officer
Jim Valentino – Vice-President

Eric Stephenson – Publisher
Ron Richards – Director of Business Development
Jennifer de Guzman – Director of Trade Book Sales
Kat Salazar – Director of PR & Marketing
Jeremy Sullivan – Director of Digital Sales
Emilio Bautista – Sales Assistant
Branwyn Bigglestone – Senior Accounts Manager
Emily Miller – Accounts Manager
Jessica Ambriz – Administrative Assistant
Tyler Shainline – Events Coordinator
David Brothers – Content Manager
Jonathan Chan – Production Manager
Drew Gill – Art Director
Meredith Wallace – Print Manager
Monica Garcia – Senior Production Artist
Jenna Savage – Production Artist
Addison Duke – Production Artist
Tricia Ramos – Production Assistant
IMAGECOMICS.COM

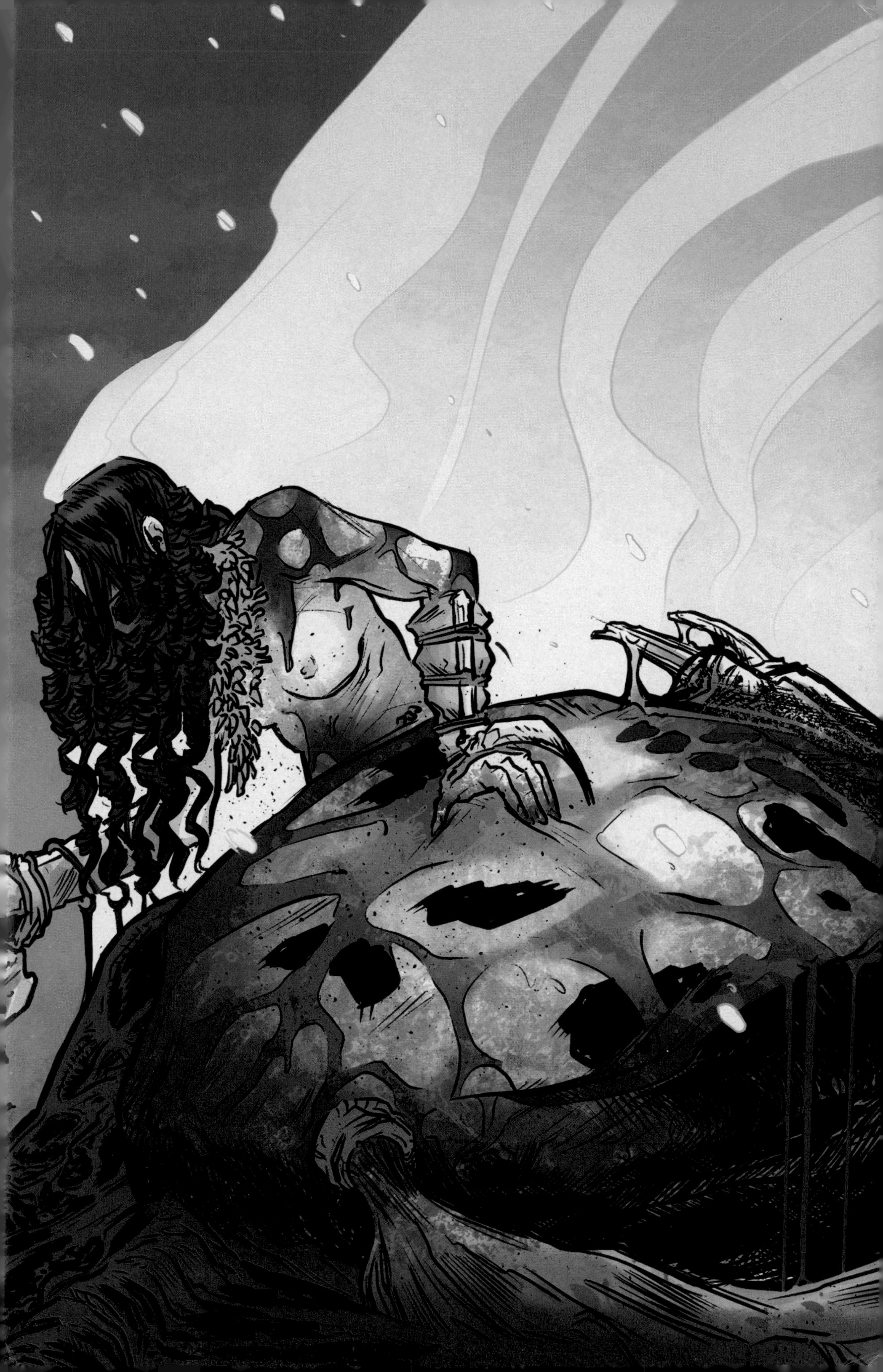

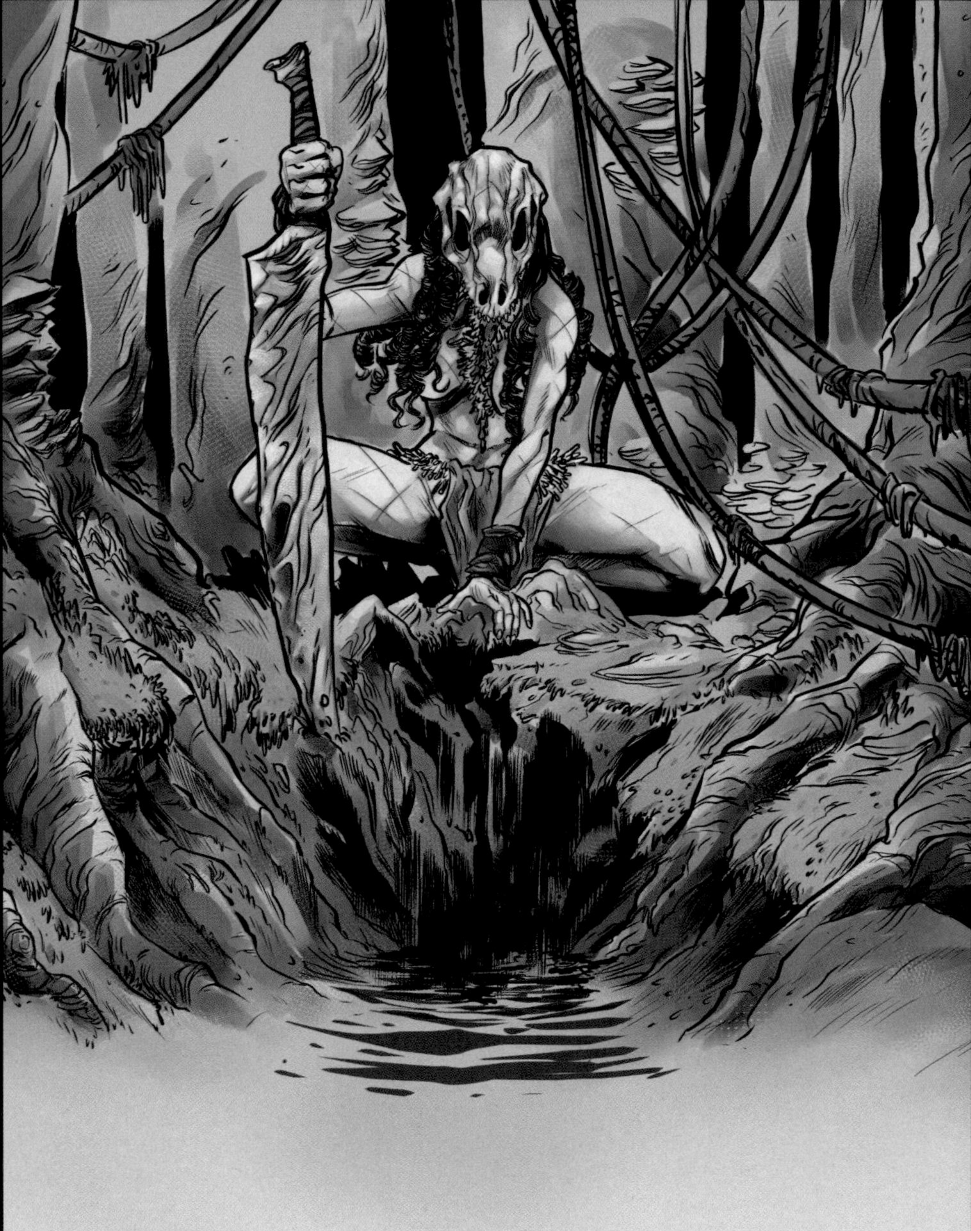

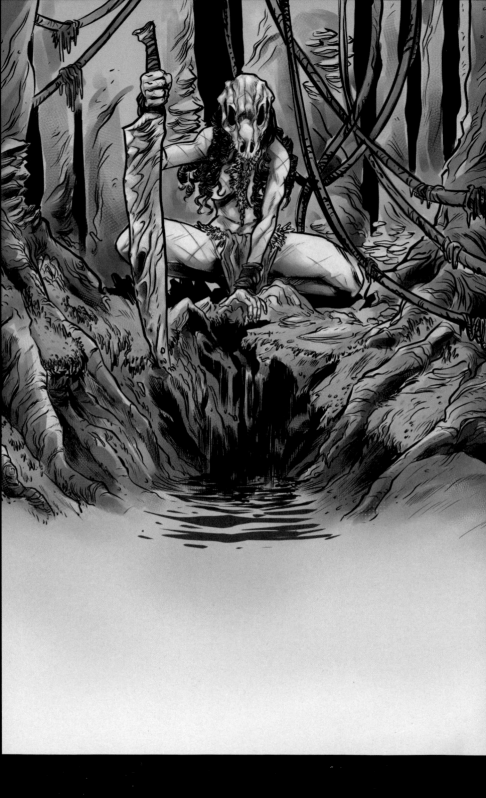

CHAPTER ONE

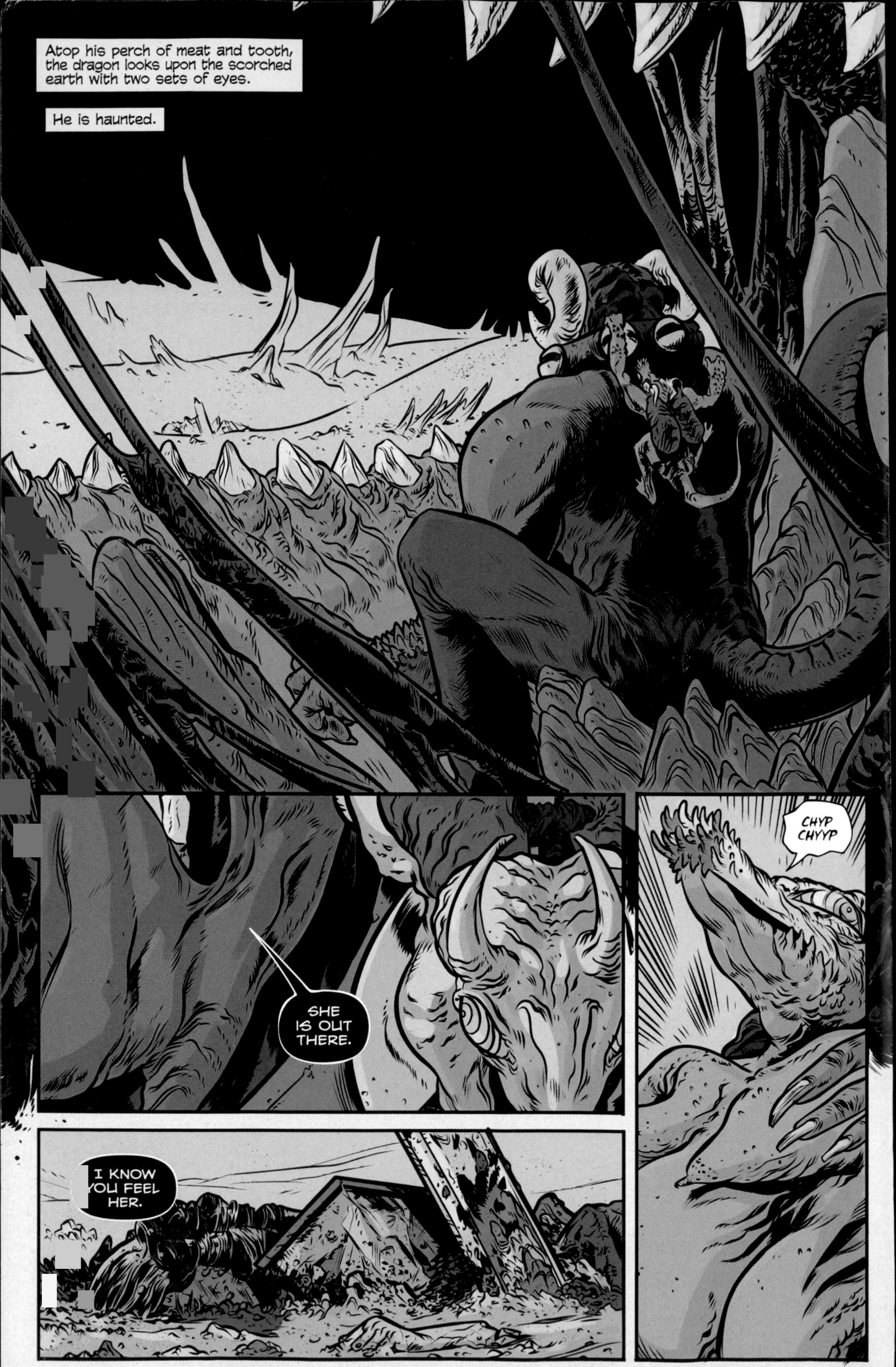
Atop his perch of meat and tooth, the dragon looks upon the scorched earth with two sets of eyes.
He is haunted.
SHE IS OUT THERE.
CHYP CHYYP
I KNOW YOU FEEL HER.

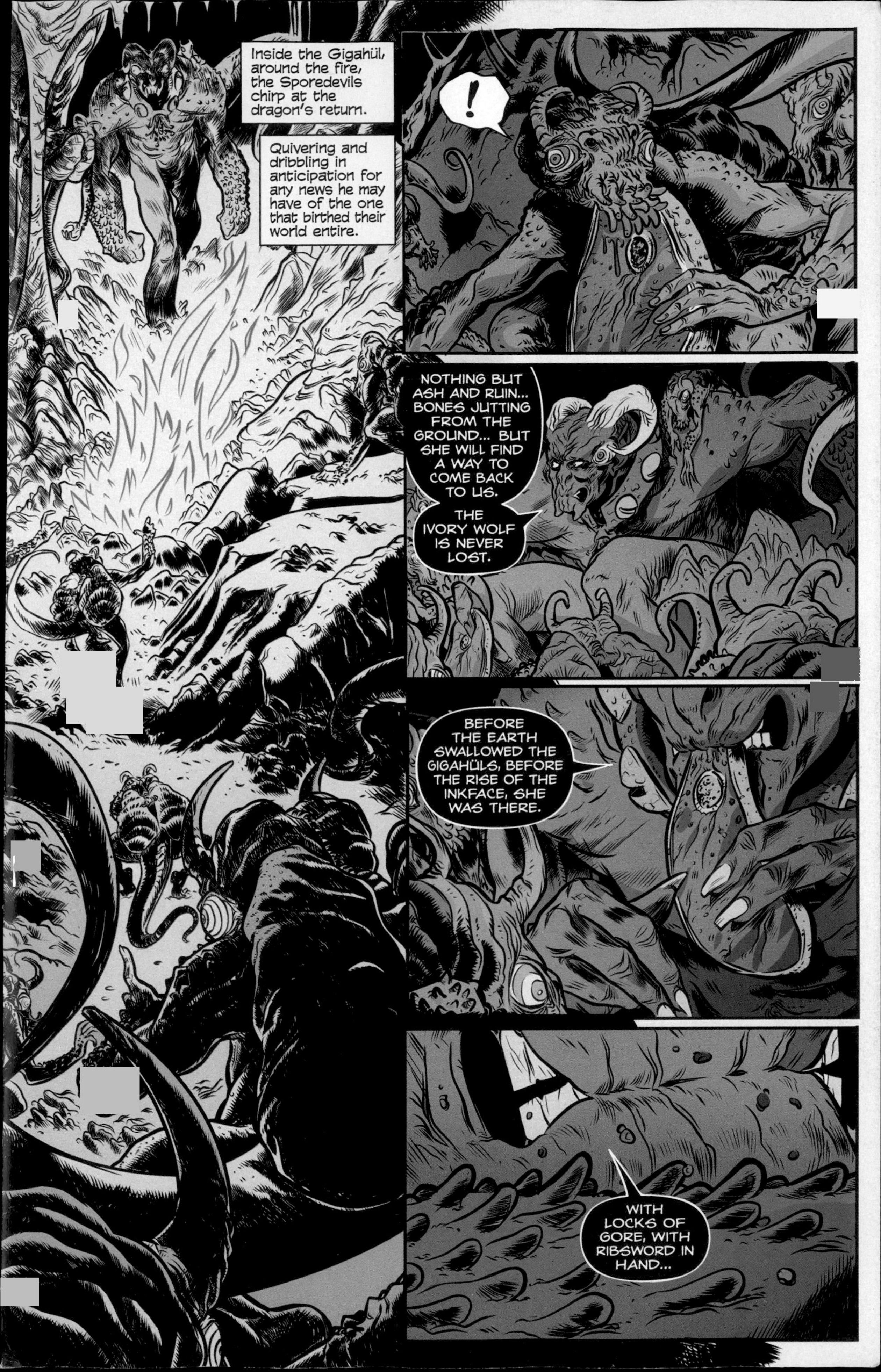
Inside the Gigahül, around the fire, the Sporedevils chirp at the dragon's return.
Quivering and dribbling in anticipation for any news he may have of the one that birthed their world entire.
!
NOTHING BUT ASH AND RUIN... BONES JUTTING FROM THE GROUND... BUT SHE WILL FIND A WAY TO COME BACK TO US.
THE IVORY WOLF IS NEVER LOST.
BEFORE THE EARTH SWALLOWED THE GIGAHÜLS, BEFORE THE RISE OF THE INKFACE, SHE WAS THERE.
WITH LOCKS OF GORE, WITH RIBSWORD IN HAND...

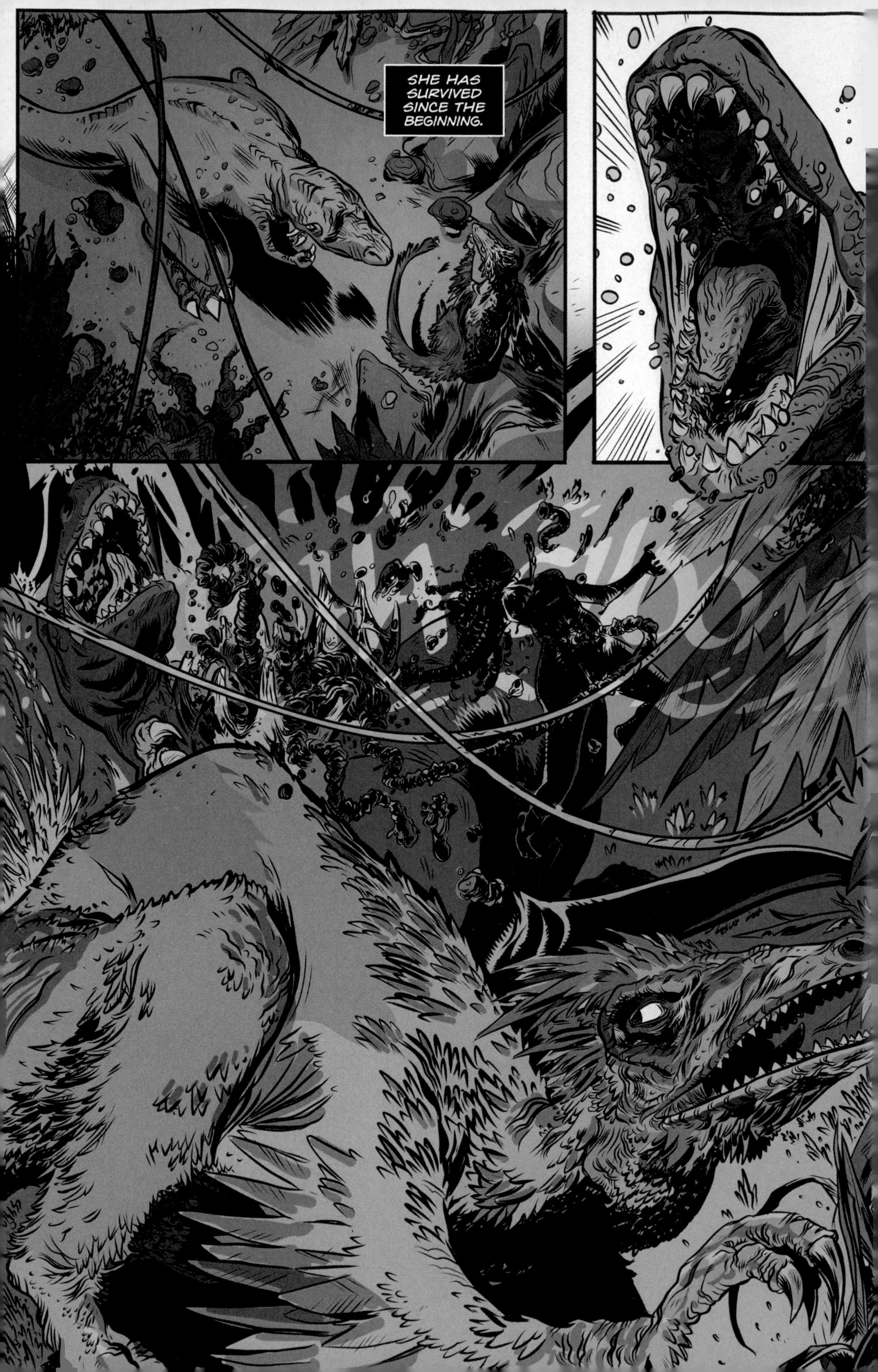
SHE HAS SURVIVED SINCE THE BEGINNING.

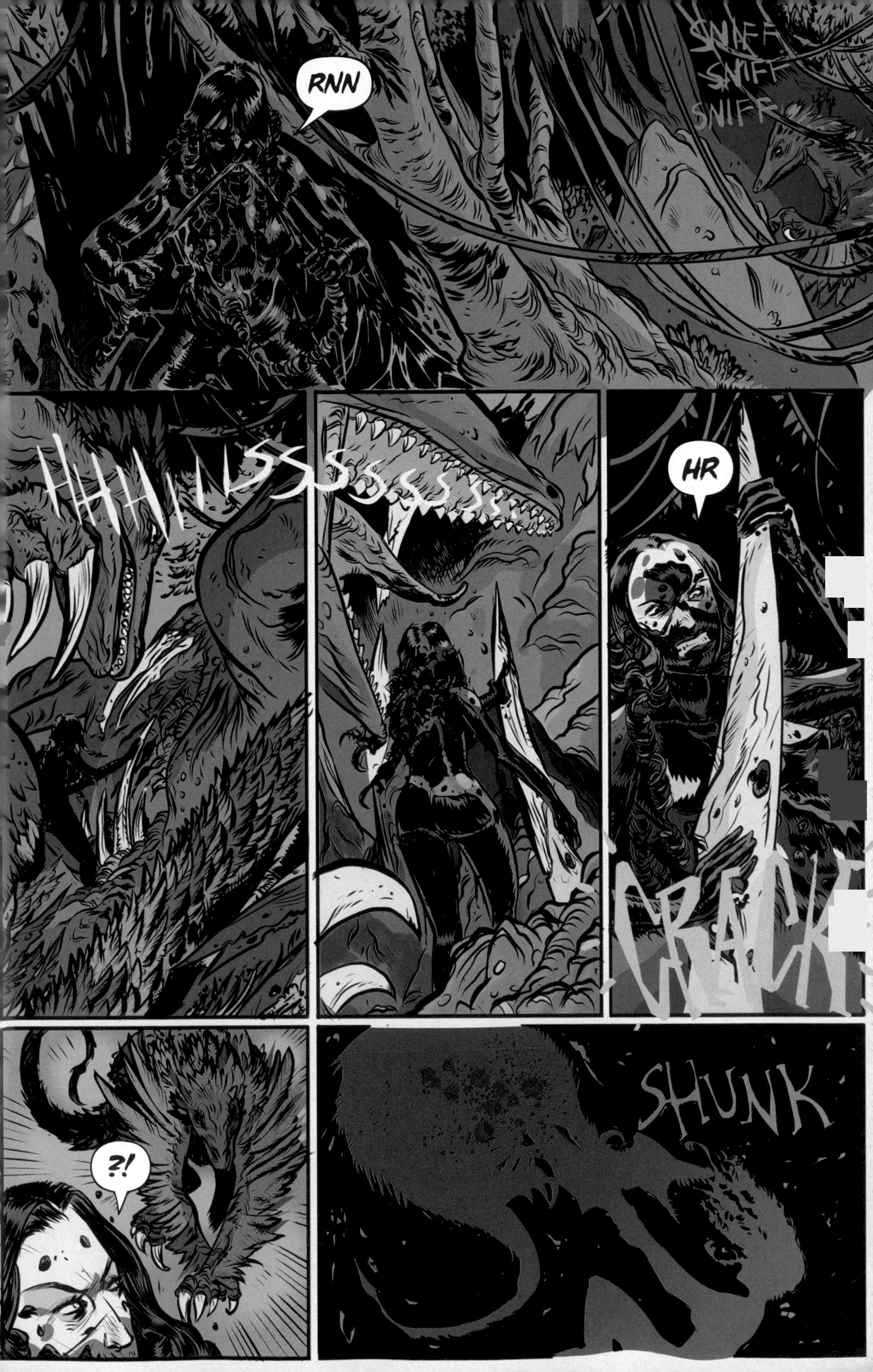
RNN
SNIFF
SNIFF
SNIFF
HHHHISSSSSSSSS
HR
CRACK
?!
SHUNK

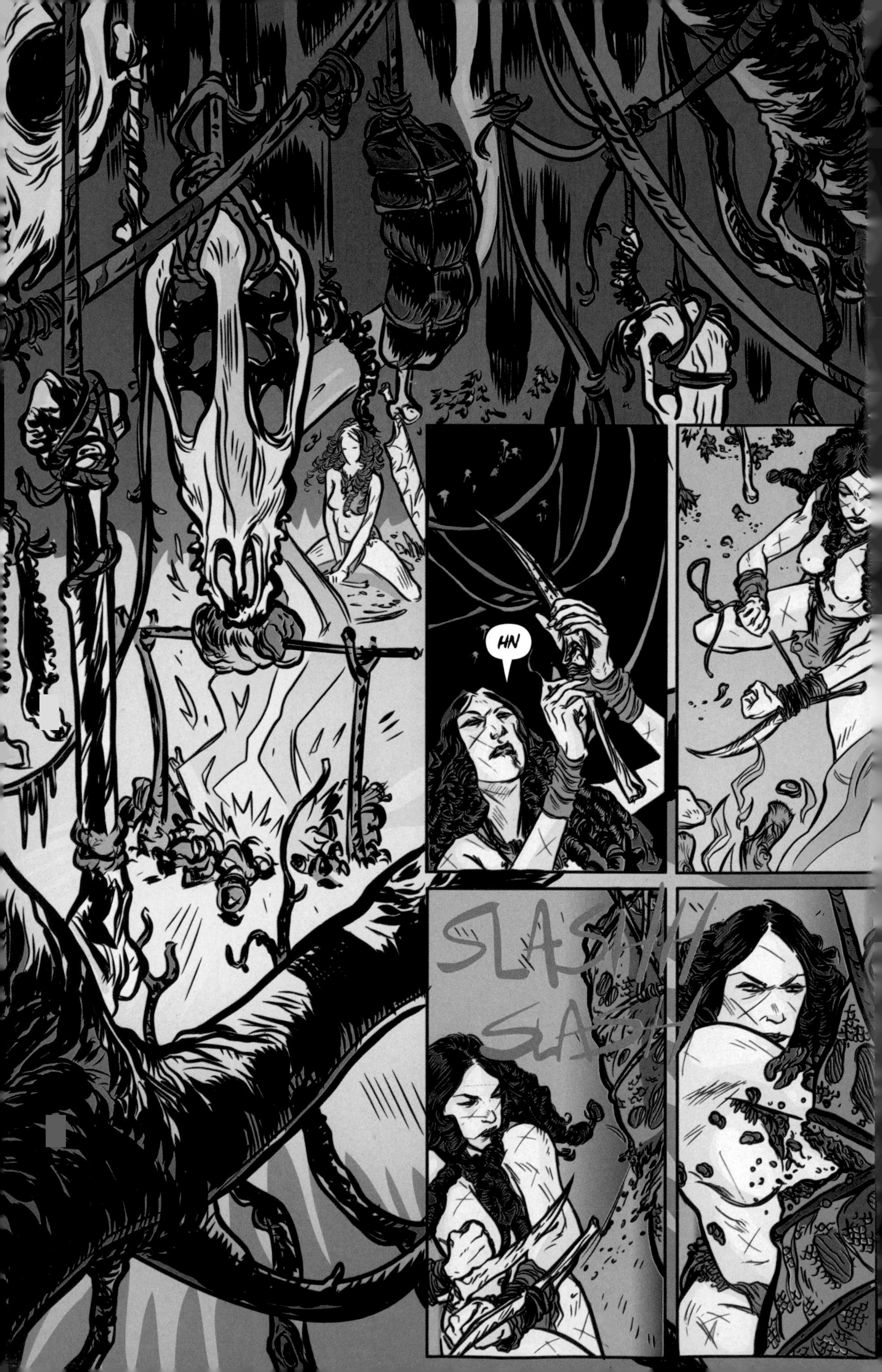
HN
SLASHH
SLASH

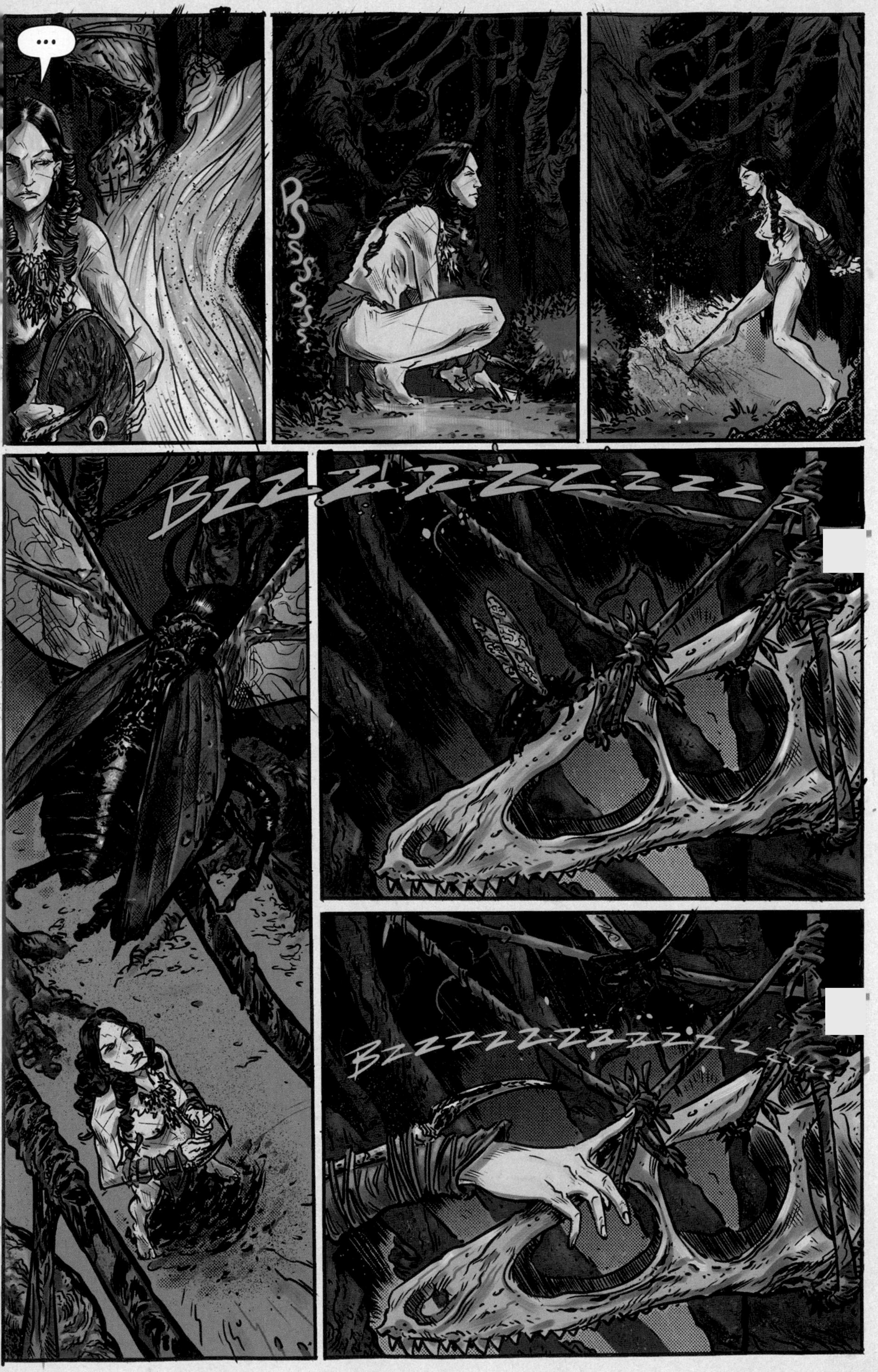
...
PSSSSSSS
BZZZZZZZZZZZZZ
BZZZZZZZZZZZZZZZZ

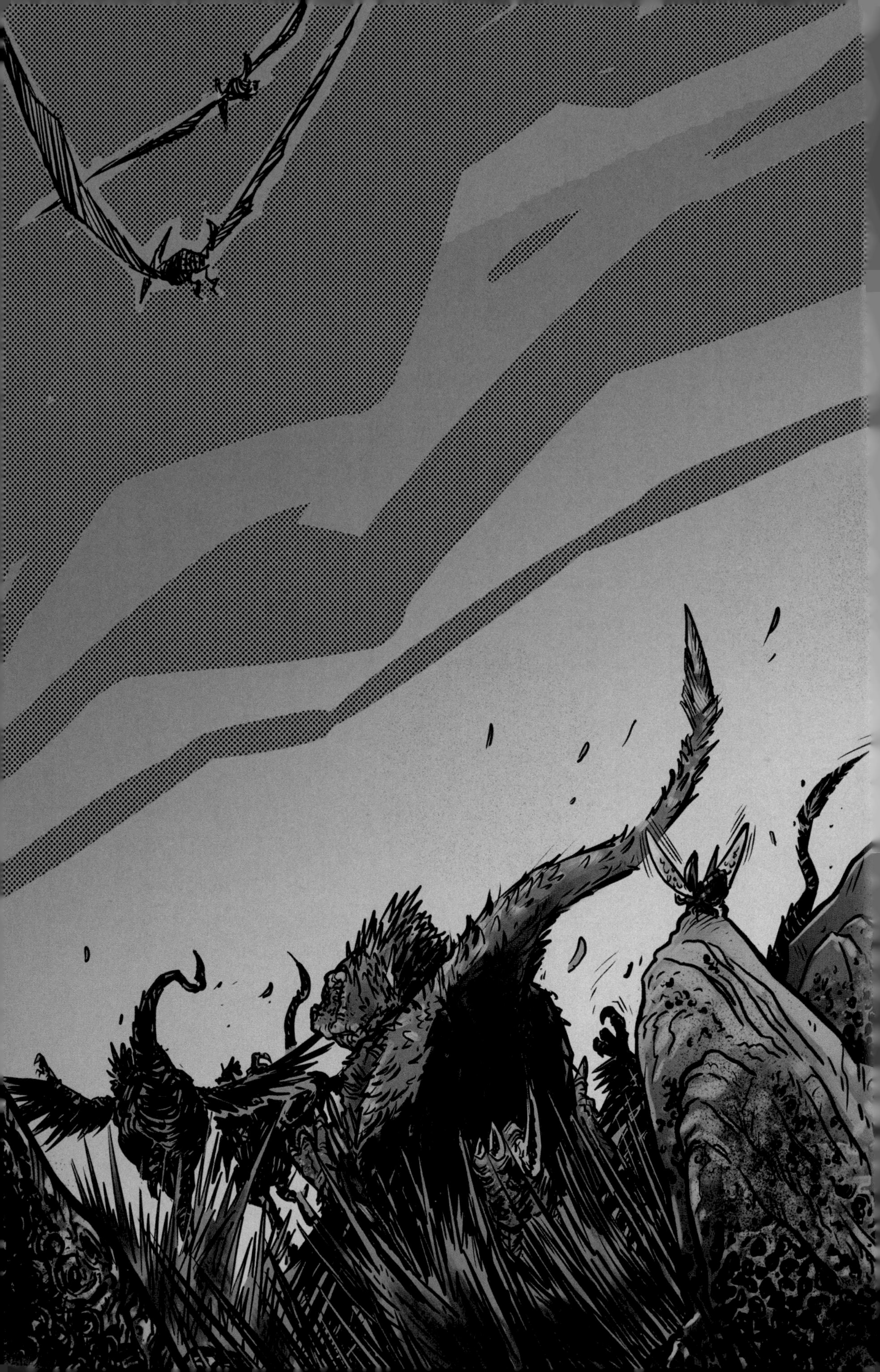

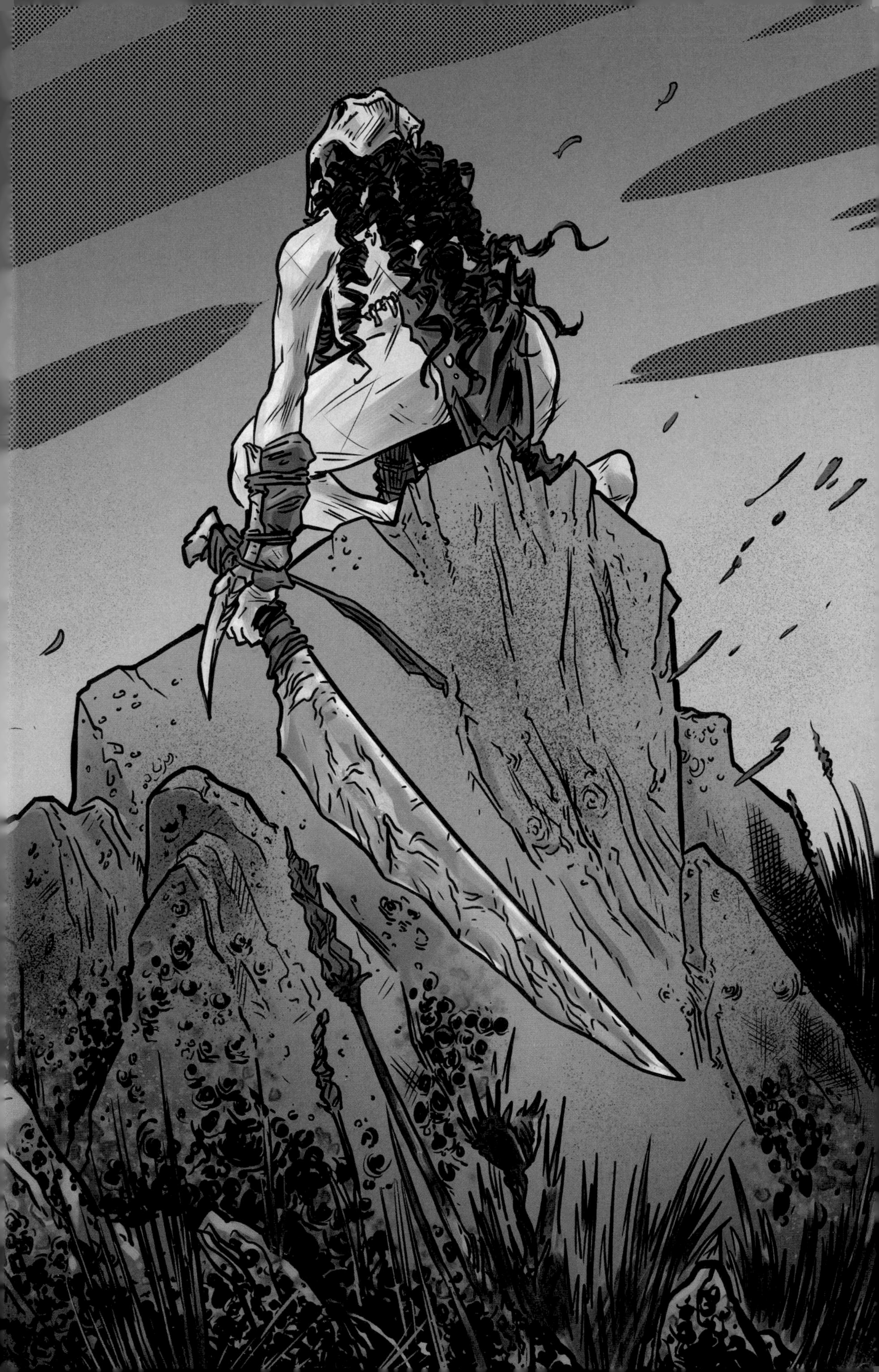

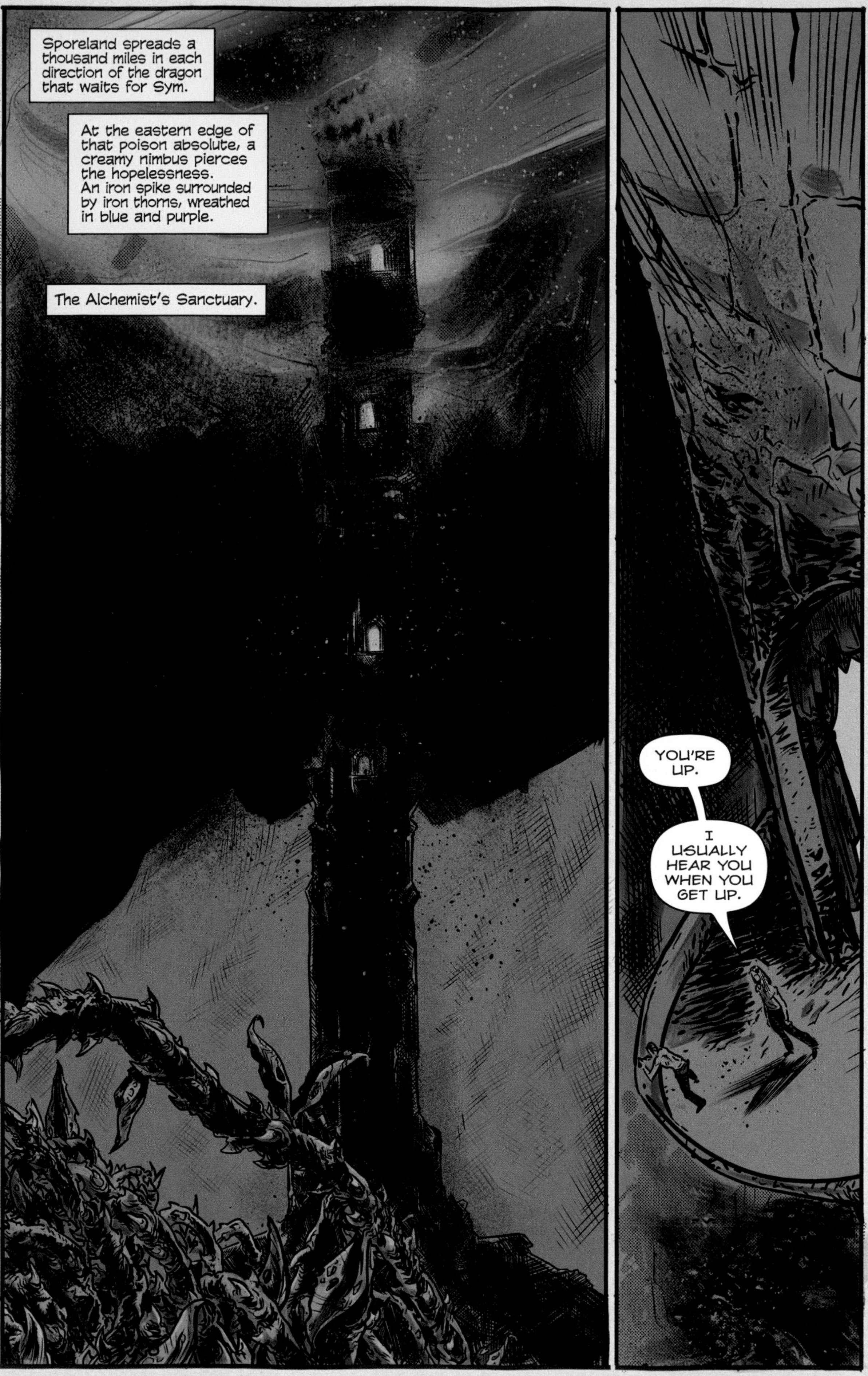
Sporeland spreads a thousand miles in each direction of the dragon that waits for Sym.
At the eastern edge of that poison absolute, a creamy nimbus pierces the hopelessness.
An iron spike surrounded by iron thorns, wreathed in blue and purple.
The Alchemist's Sanctuary.
YOU'RE UP.
I USUALLY HEAR YOU WHEN YOU GET UP.

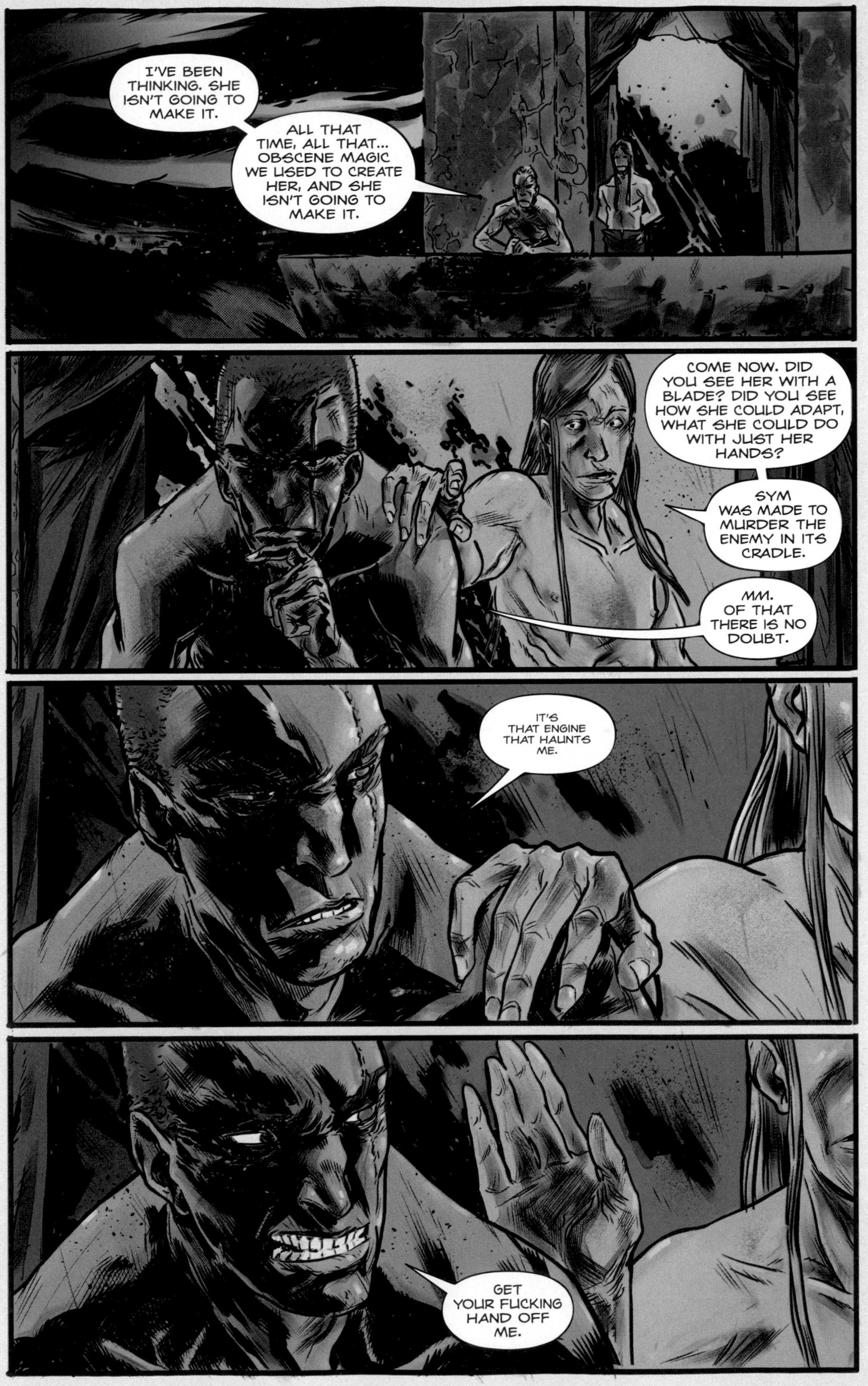
I'VE BEEN THINKING. SHE ISN'T GOING TO MAKE IT.
ALL THAT TIME, ALL THAT... OBSCENE MAGIC WE USED TO CREATE HER, AND SHE ISN'T GOING TO MAKE IT.
COME NOW. DID YOU SEE HER WITH A BLADE? DID YOU SEE HOW SHE COULD ADAPT, WHAT SHE COULD DO WITH JUST HER HANDS?
SYM WAS MADE TO MURDER THE ENEMY IN ITS CRADLE.
MM. OF THAT THERE IS NO DOUBT.
IT'S THAT ENGINE THAT HAUNTS ME.
GET YOUR FUCKING HAND OFF ME.

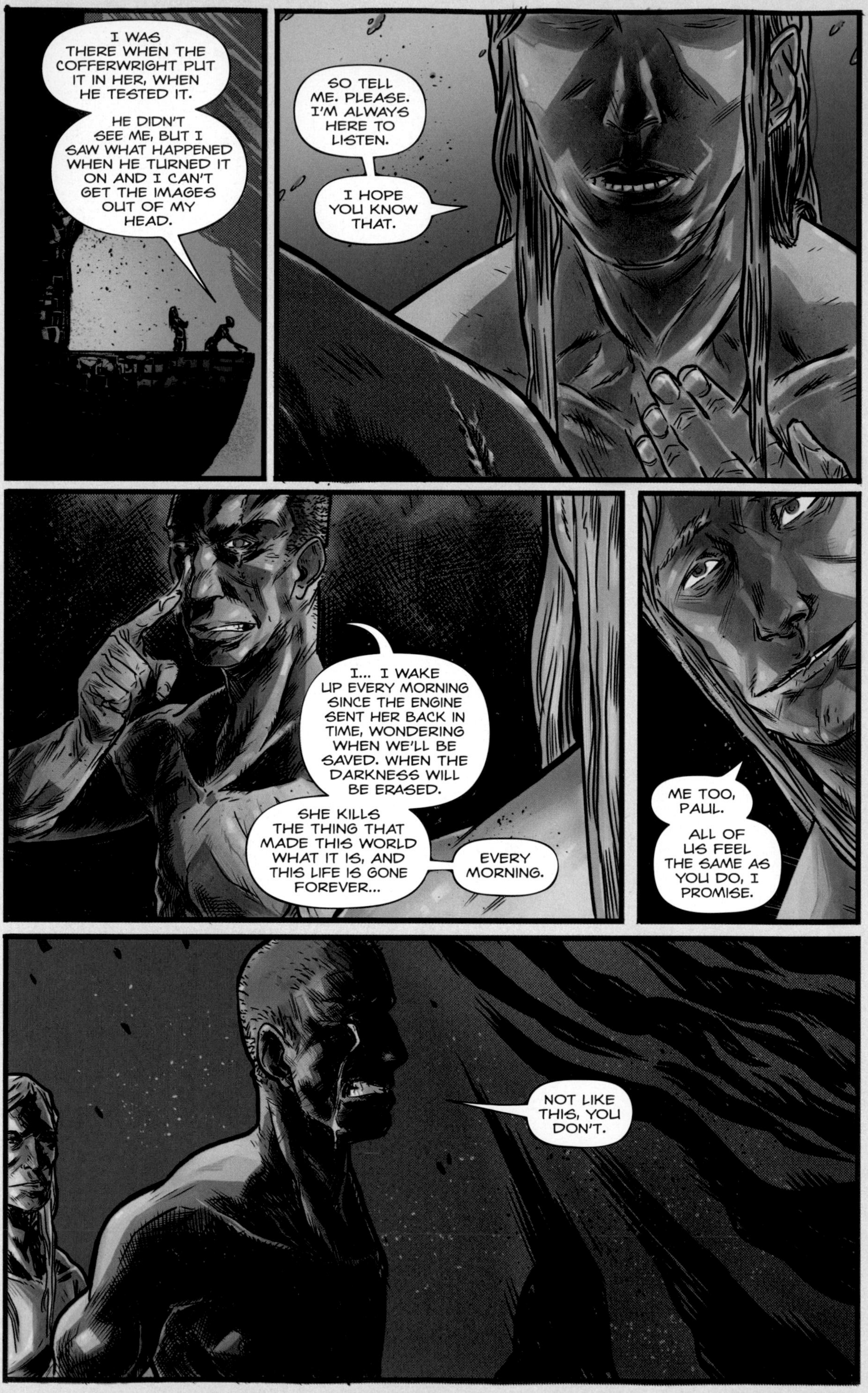
I WAS THERE WHEN THE COFFERWRIGHT PUT IT IN HER, WHEN HE TESTED IT.
HE DIDN'T SEE ME, BUT I SAW WHAT HAPPENED WHEN HE TURNED IT ON AND I CAN'T GET THE IMAGES OUT OF MY HEAD.
SO TELL ME. PLEASE. I'M ALWAYS HERE TO LISTEN.
I HOPE YOU KNOW THAT.
I... I WAKE UP EVERY MORNING SINCE THE ENGINE SENT HER BACK IN TIME, WONDERING WHEN WE'LL BE SAVED. WHEN THE DARKNESS WILL BE ERASED.
SHE KILLS THE THING THAT MADE THIS WORLD WHAT IT IS, AND THIS LIFE IS GONE FOREVER...
EVERY MORNING.
ME TOO, PAUL.
ALL OF US FEEL THE SAME AS YOU DO, I PROMISE.
NOT LIKE THIS, YOU DON'T.

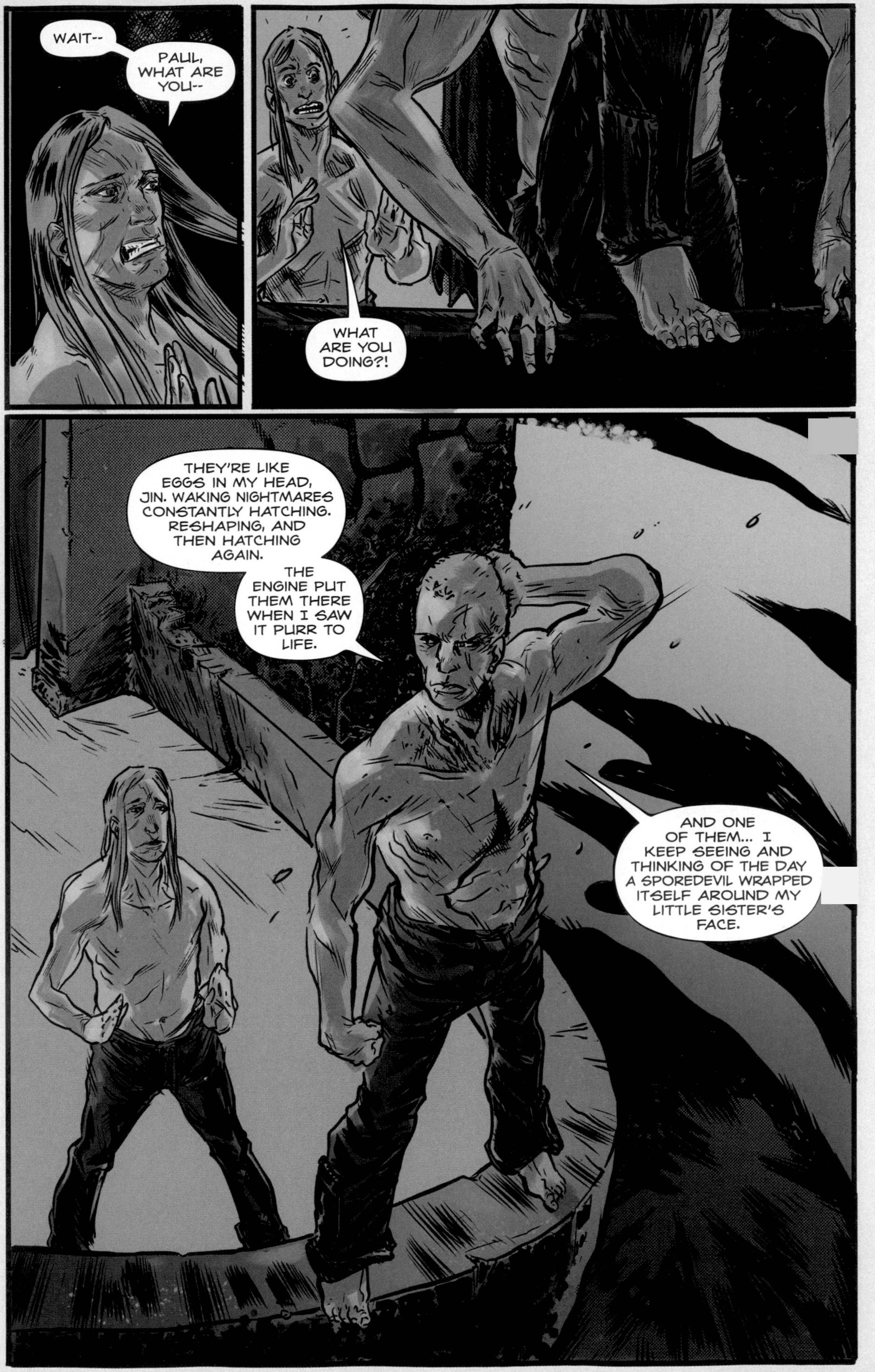
WAIT--
PAUL, WHAT ARE YOU--
WHAT ARE YOU DOING?!
THEY'RE LIKE EGGS IN MY HEAD, JIN. WAKING NIGHTMARES CONSTANTLY HATCHING. RESHAPING, AND THEN HATCHING AGAIN.
THE ENGINE PUT THEM THERE WHEN I SAW IT PURR TO LIFE.
AND ONE OF THEM... I KEEP SEEING AND THINKING OF THE DAY A SPOREDEVIL WRAPPED ITSELF AROUND MY LITTLE SISTER'S FACE.

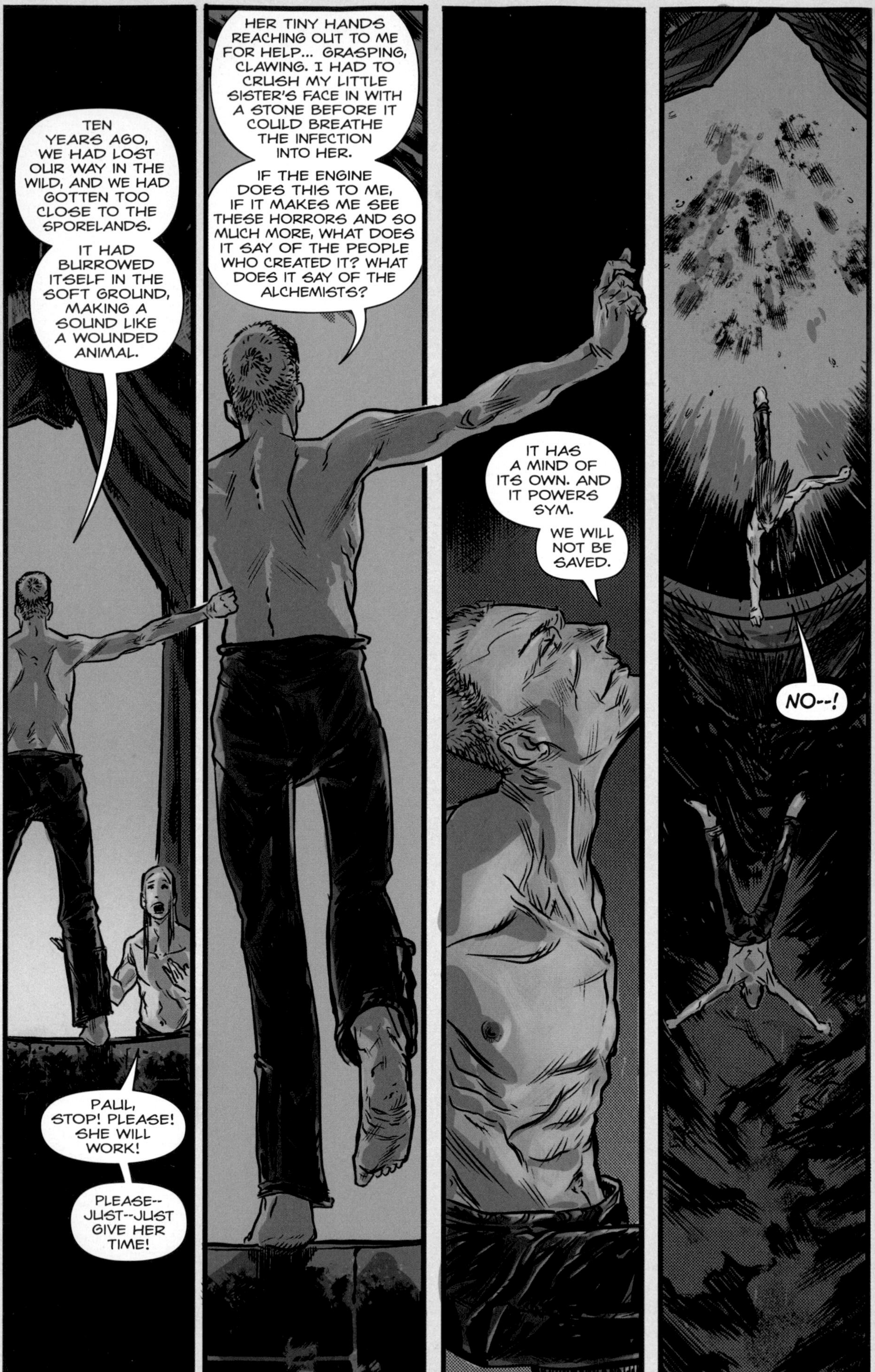
TEN YEARS AGO, WE HAD LOST OUR WAY IN THE WILD, AND WE HAD GOTTEN TOO CLOSE TO THE SPORELANDS.
IT HAD BURROWED ITSELF IN THE SOFT GROUND, MAKING A SOUND LIKE A WOUNDED ANIMAL.
PAUL, STOP! PLEASE! SHE WILL WORK!
PLEASE-- JUST--JUST GIVE HER TIME!
HER TINY HANDS REACHING OUT TO ME FOR HELP... GRASPING, CLAWING. I HAD TO CRUSH MY LITTLE SISTER'S FACE IN WITH A STONE BEFORE IT COULD BREATHE THE INFECTION INTO HER.
IF THE ENGINE DOES THIS TO ME, IF IT MAKES ME SEE THESE HORRORS AND SO MUCH MORE, WHAT DOES IT SAY OF THE PEOPLE WHO CREATED IT? WHAT DOES IT SAY OF THE ALCHEMISTS?
IT HAS A MIND OF ITS OWN. AND IT POWERS SYM.
WE WILL NOT BE SAVED.
NO--!

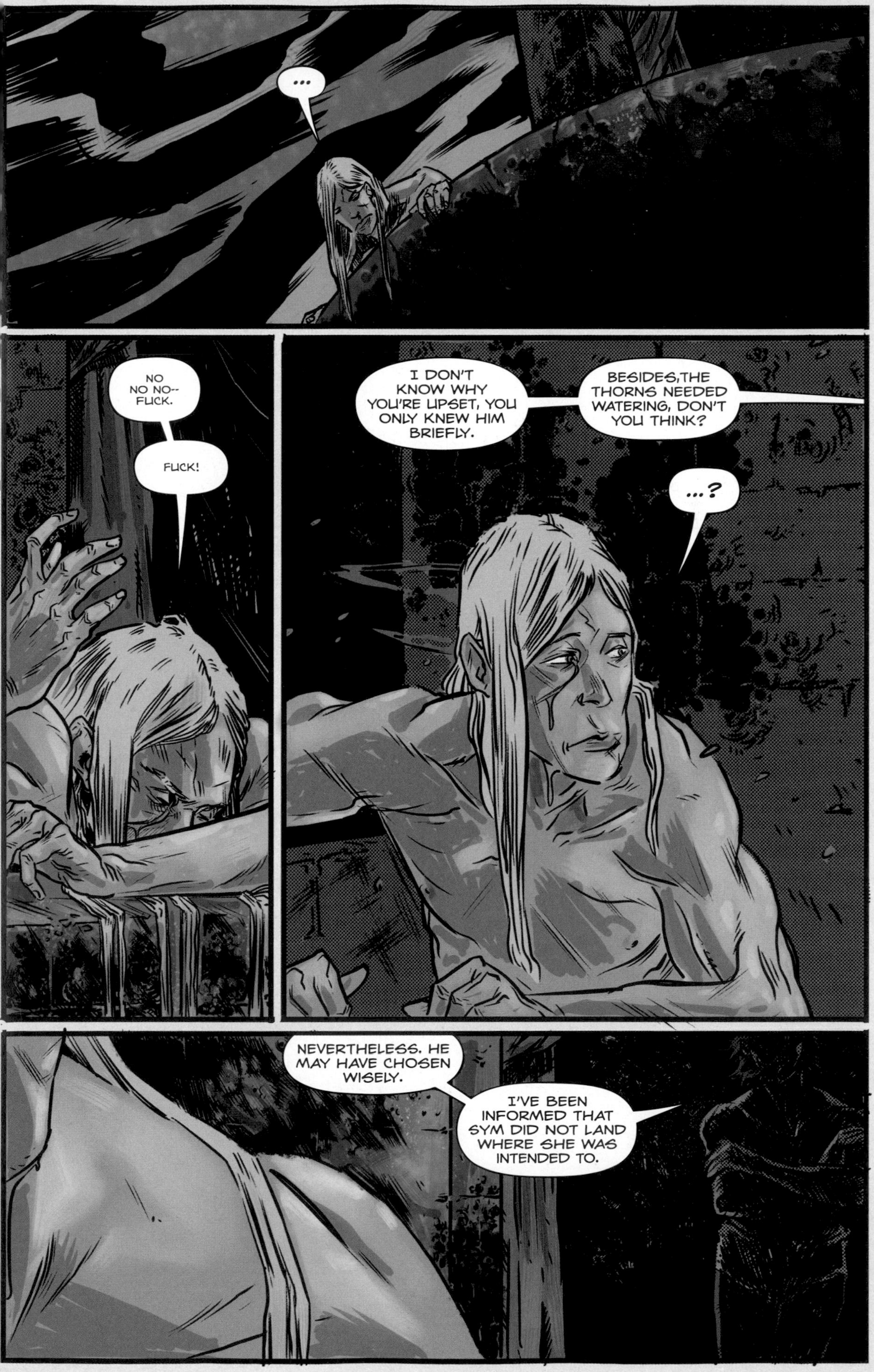
...
NO NO NO-- FUCK.
FUCK!
I DON'T KNOW WHY YOU'RE UPSET, YOU ONLY KNEW HIM BRIEFLY.
BESIDES, THE THORNS NEEDED WATERING, DON'T YOU THINK?
...?
NEVERTHELESS. HE MAY HAVE CHOSEN WISELY.
I'VE BEEN INFORMED THAT SYM DID NOT LAND WHERE SHE WAS INTENDED TO.

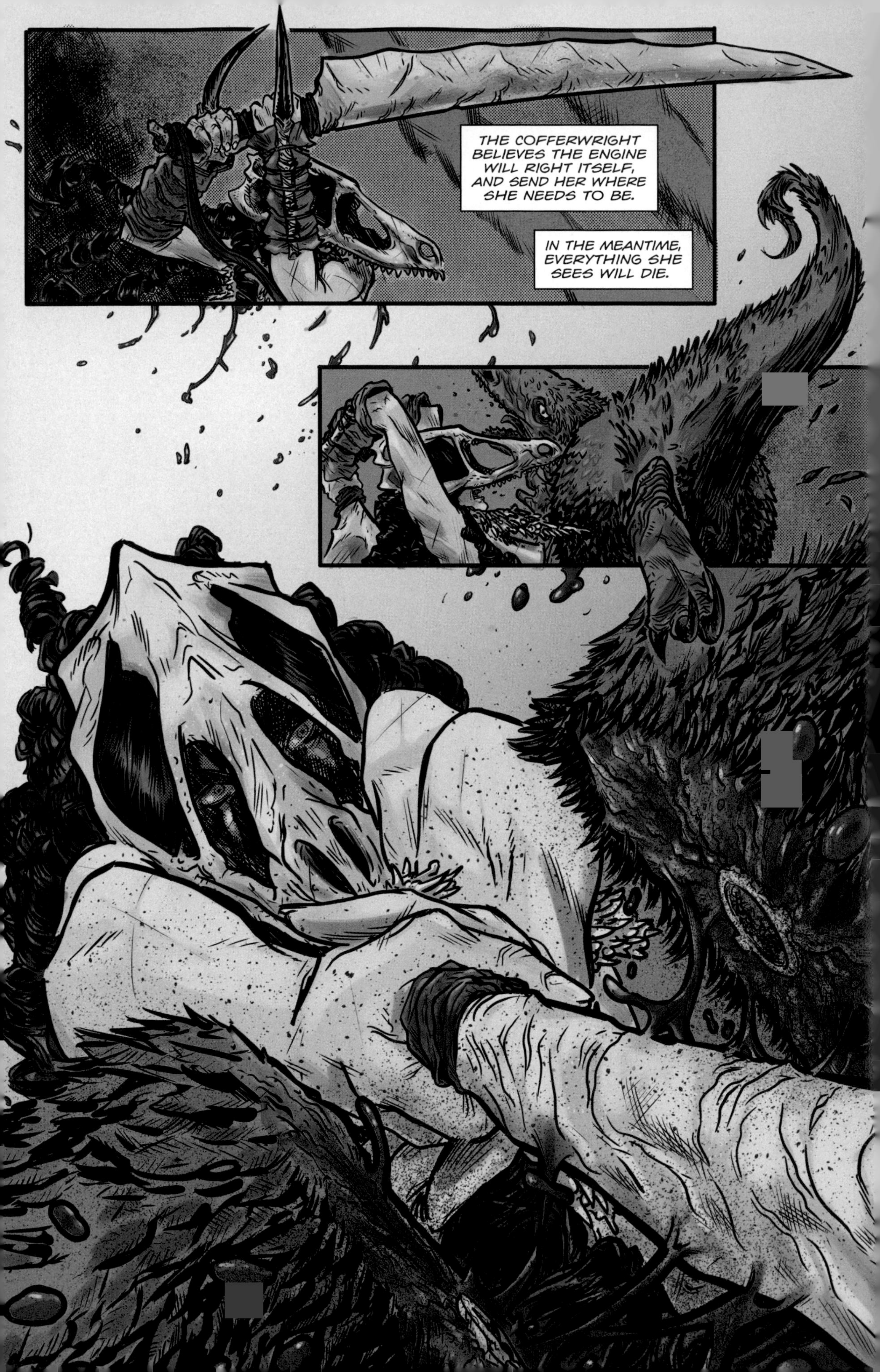
THE COFFERWRIGHT BELIEVES THE ENGINE WILL RIGHT ITSELF, AND SEND HER WHERE SHE NEEDS TO BE.
IN THE MEANTIME, EVERYTHING SHE SEES WILL DIE.

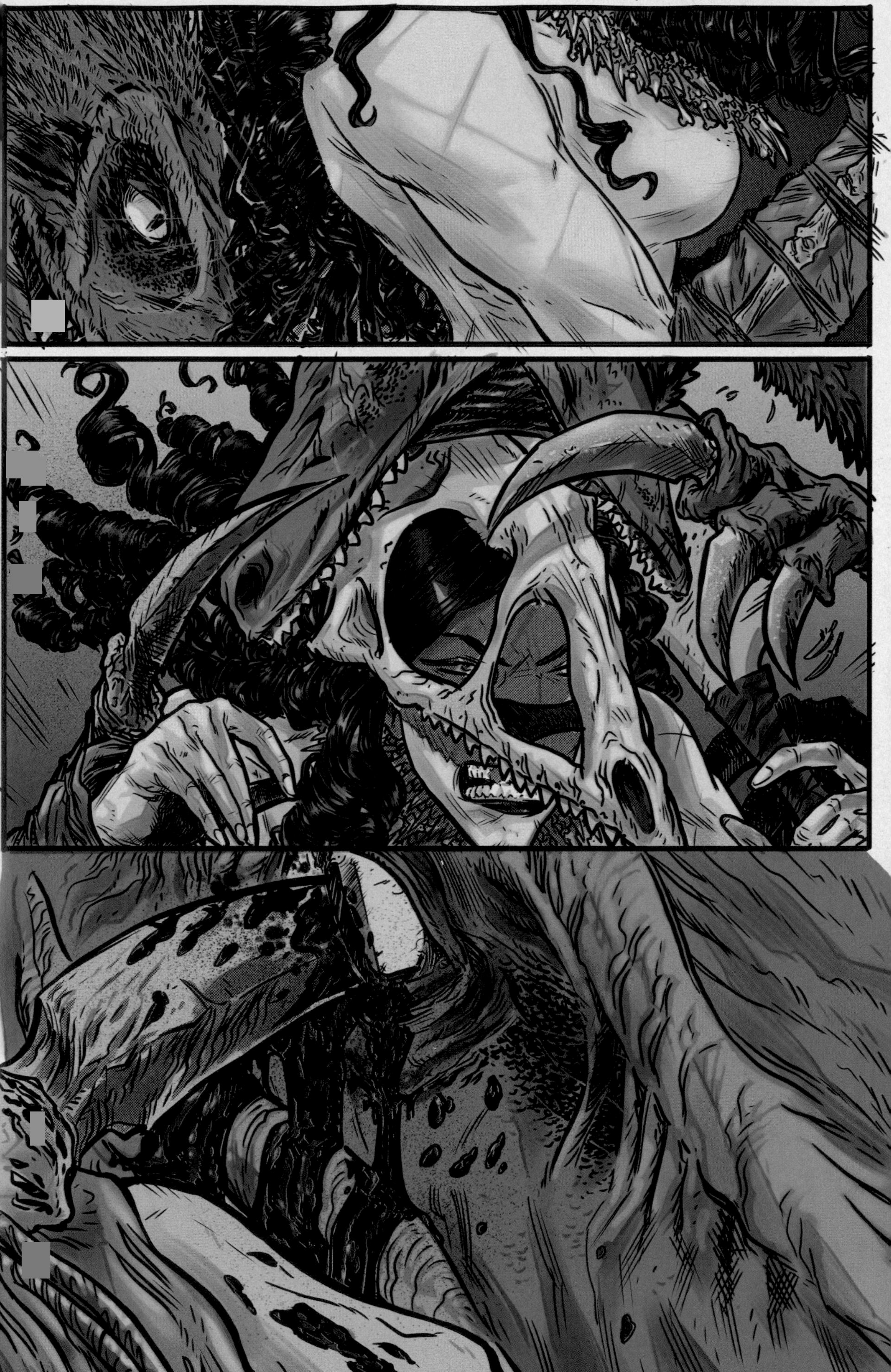

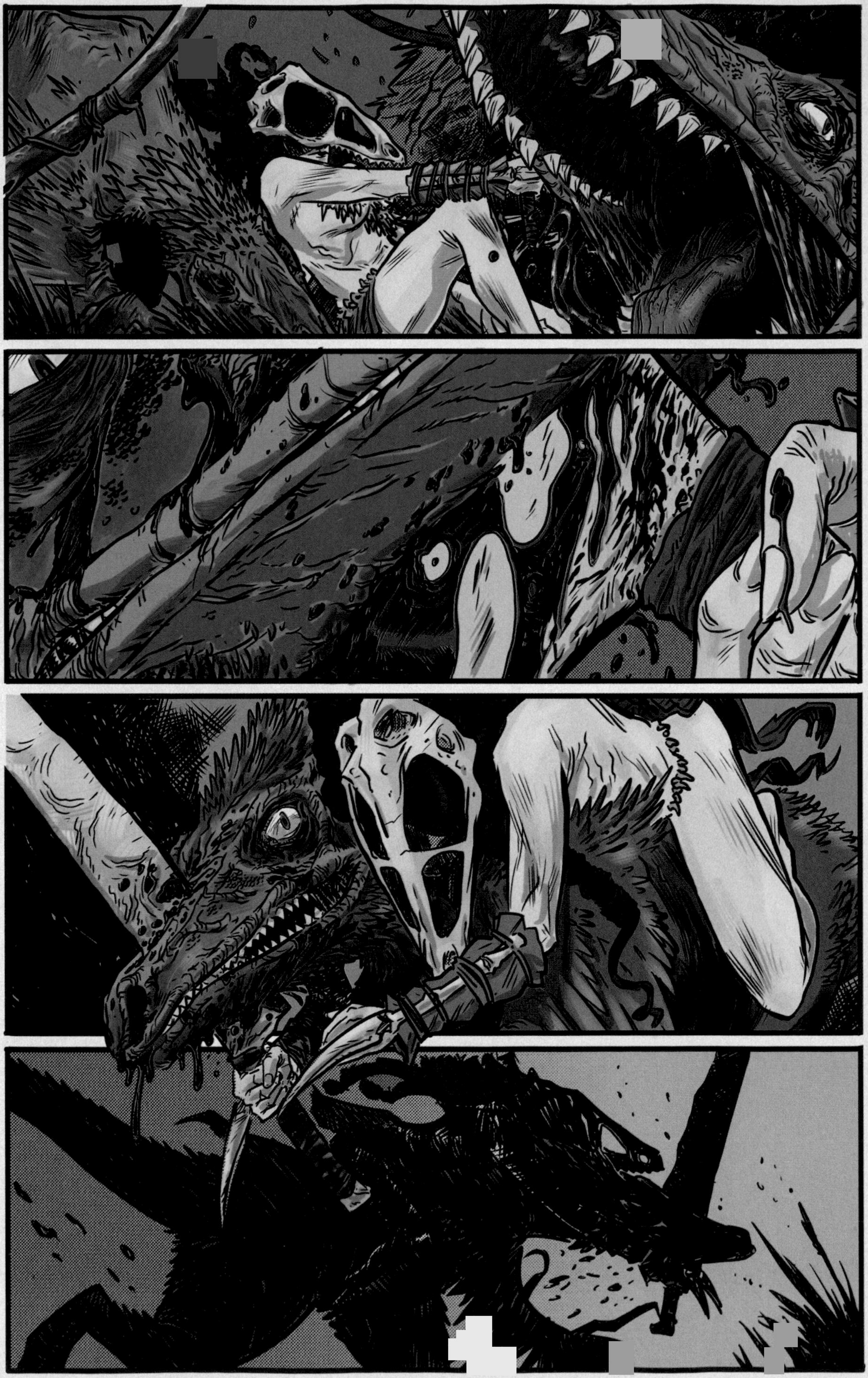

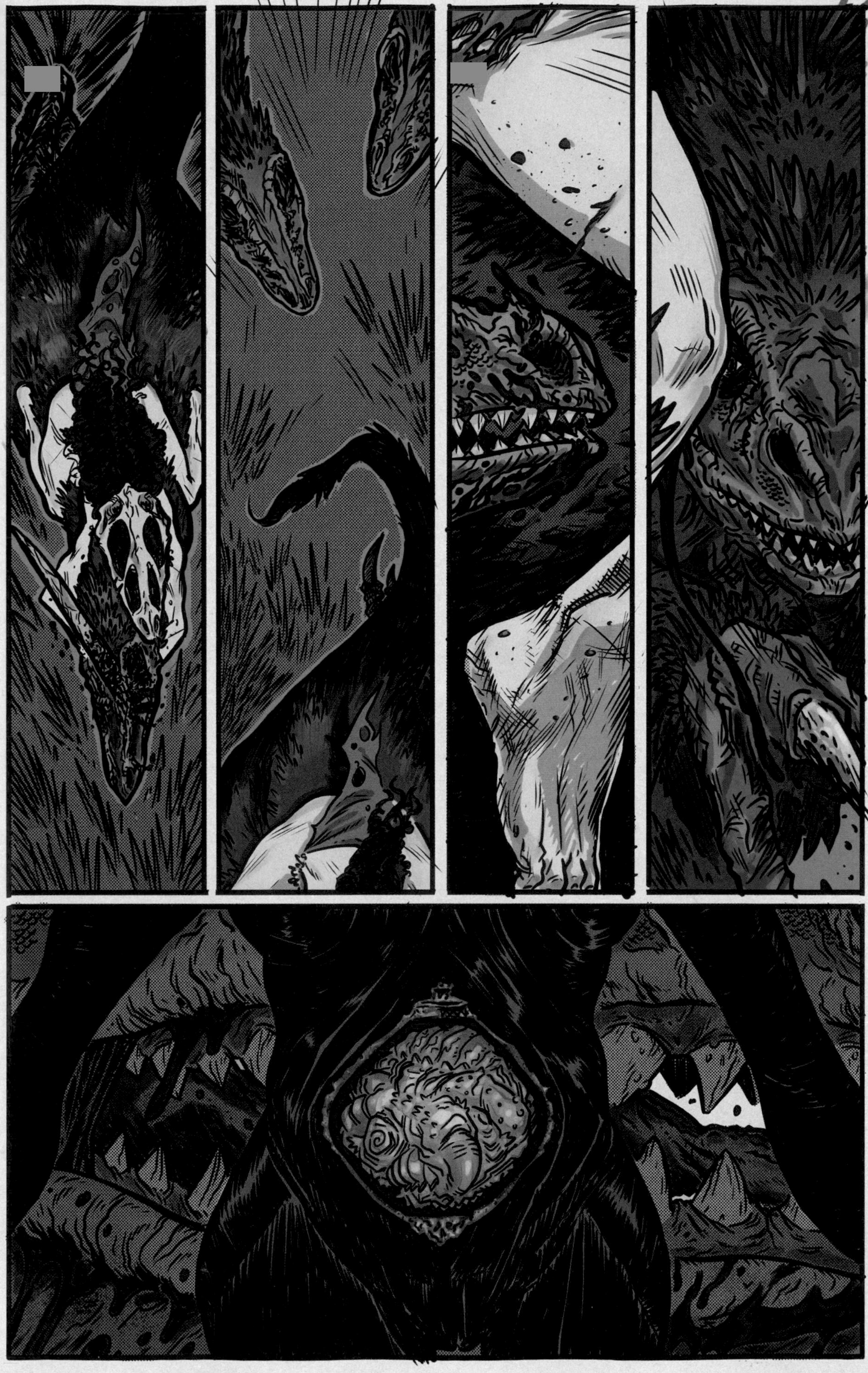

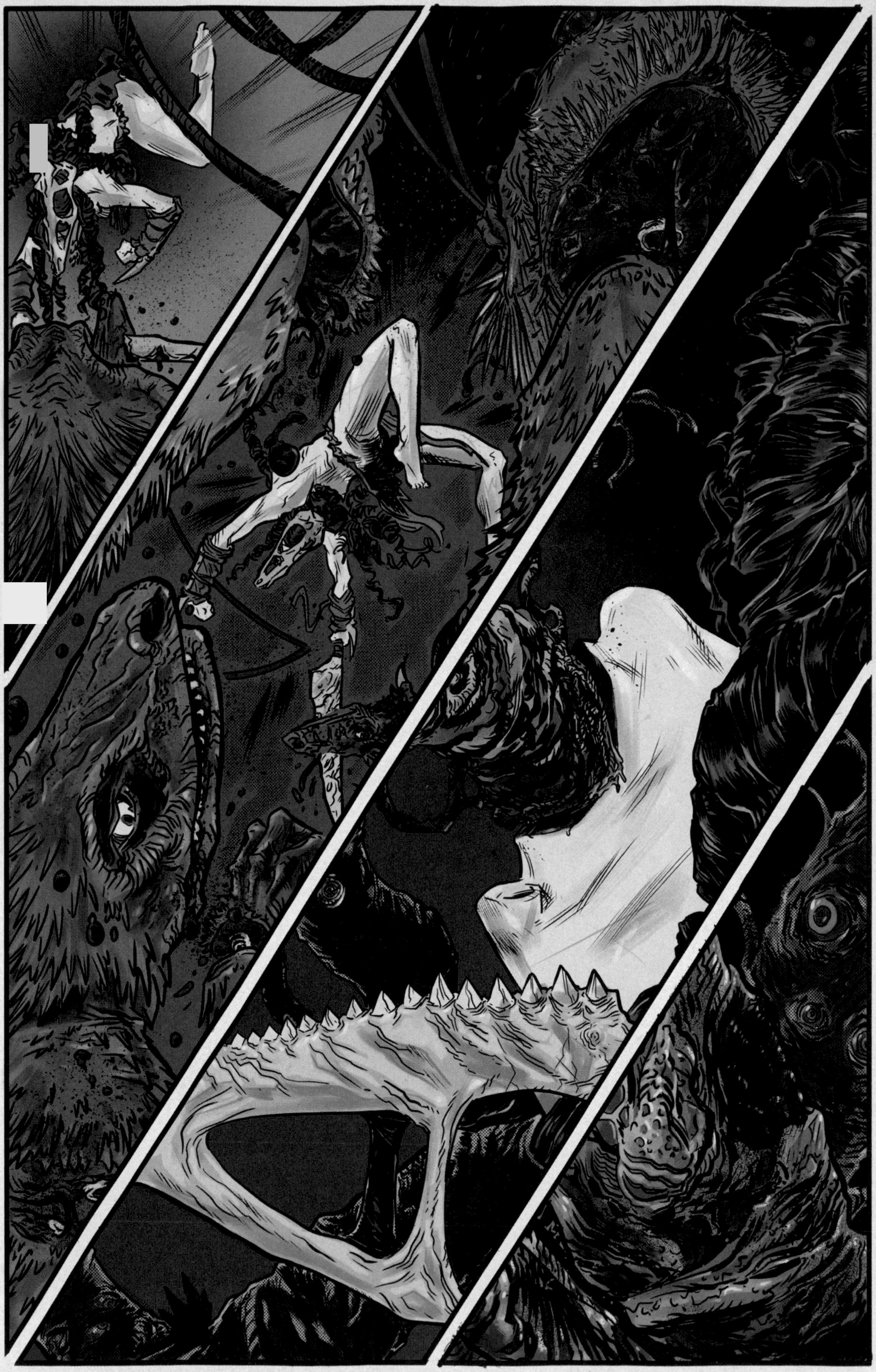

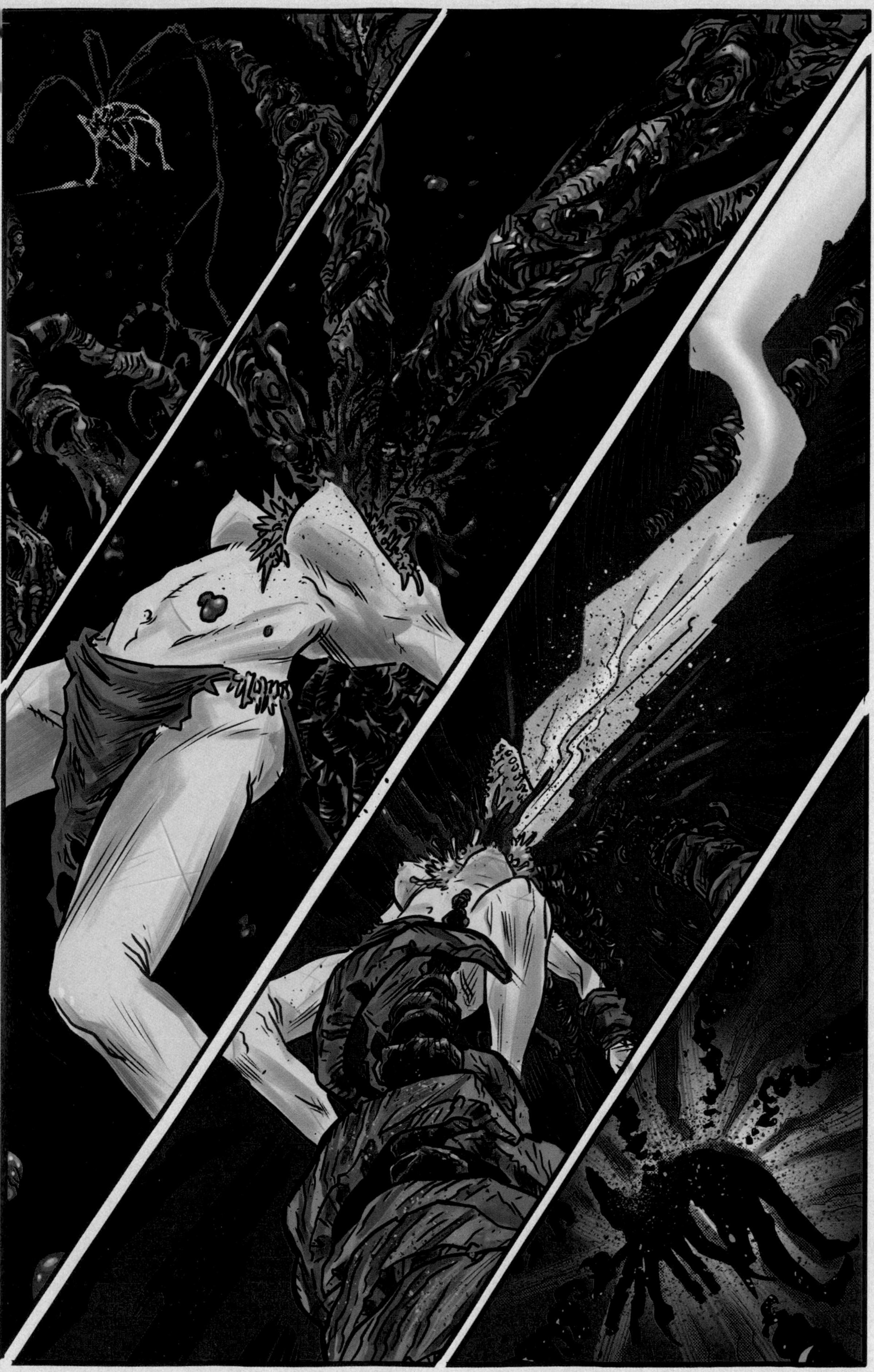

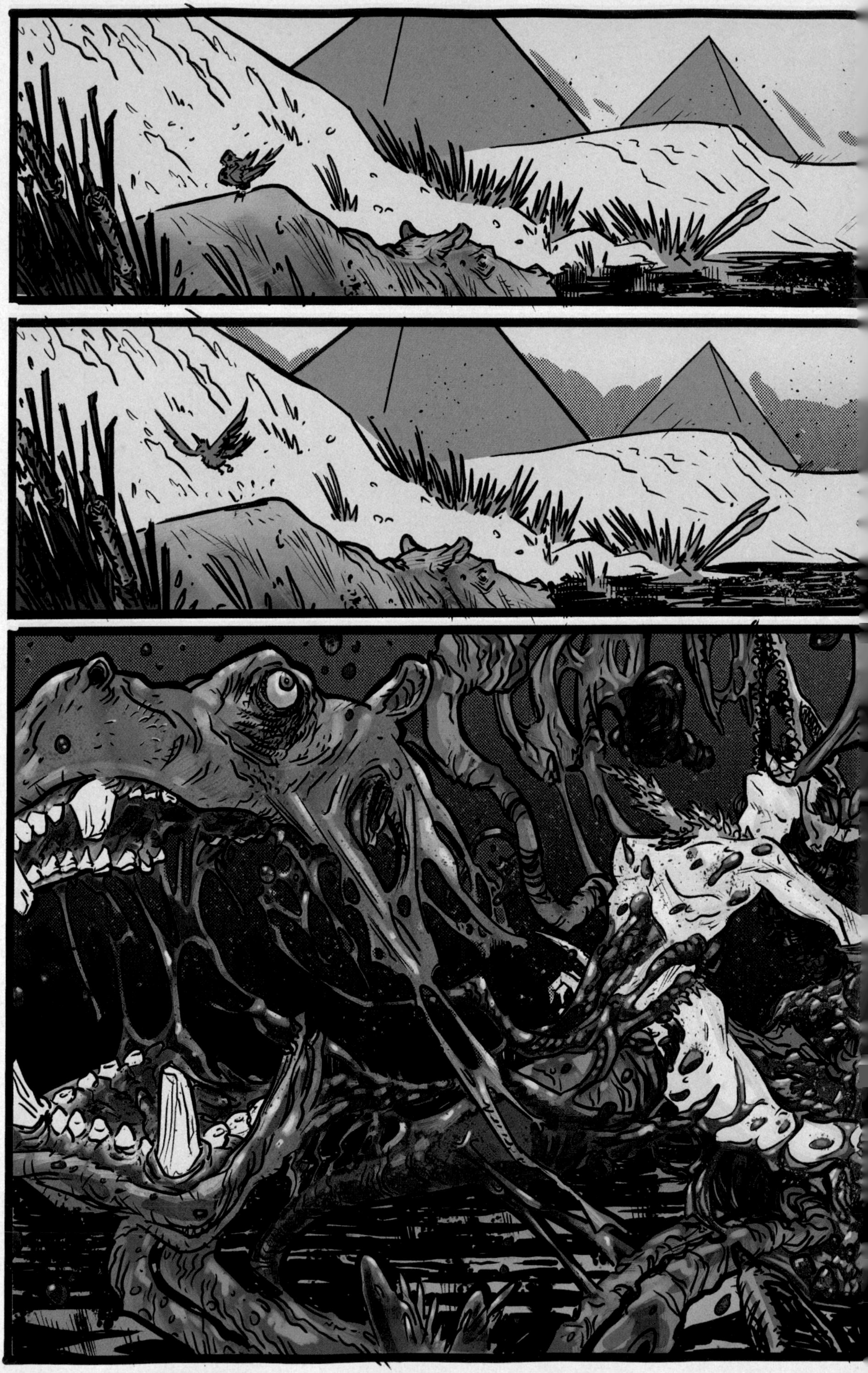

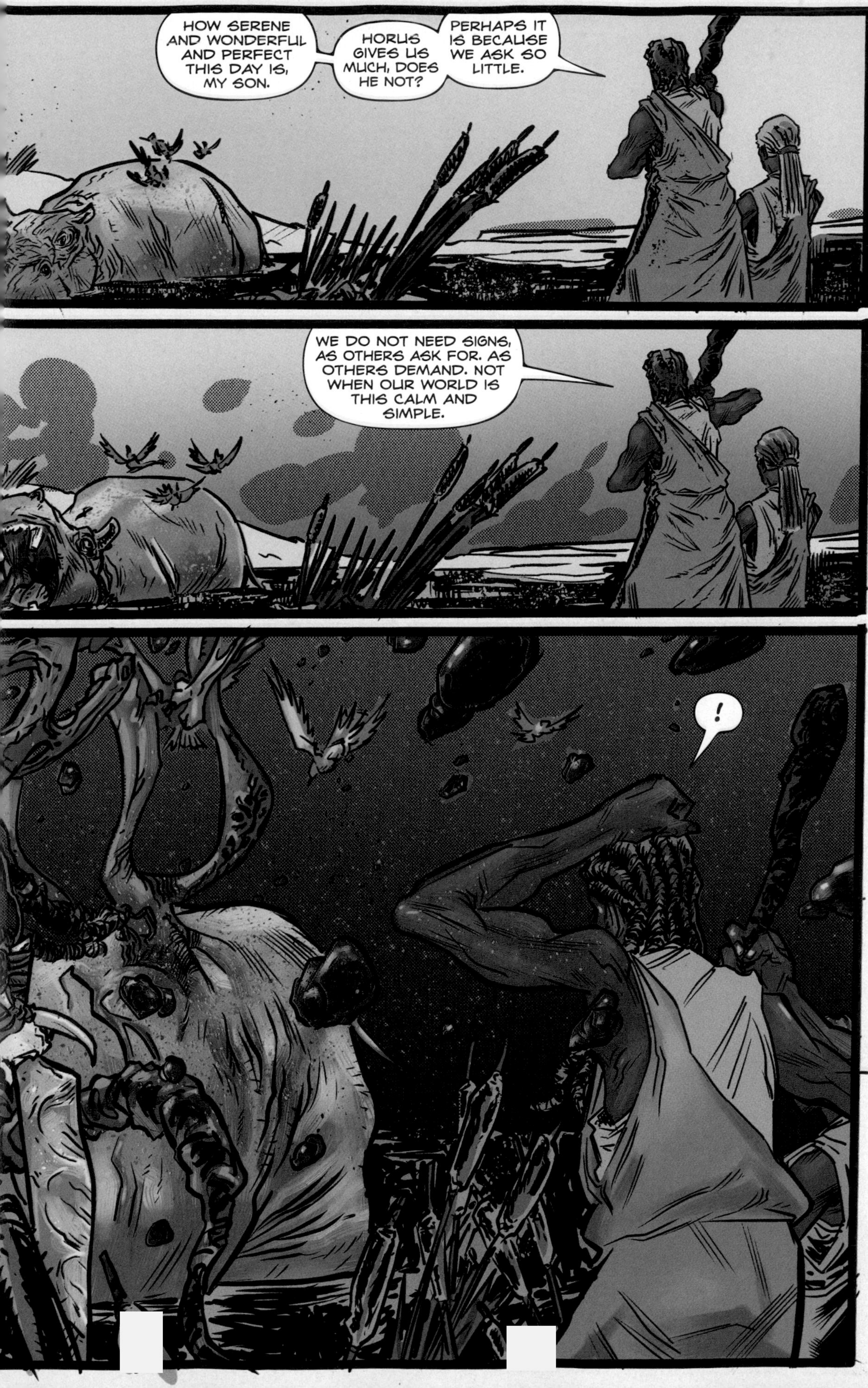
HOW SERENE AND WONDERFUL AND PERFECT THIS DAY IS, MY SON.
HORUS GIVES US MUCH, DOES HE NOT?
PERHAPS IT IS BECAUSE WE ASK SO LITTLE.
WE DO NOT NEED SIGNS, AS OTHERS ASK FOR. AS OTHERS DEMAND. NOT WHEN OUR WORLD IS THIS CALM AND SIMPLE.
!

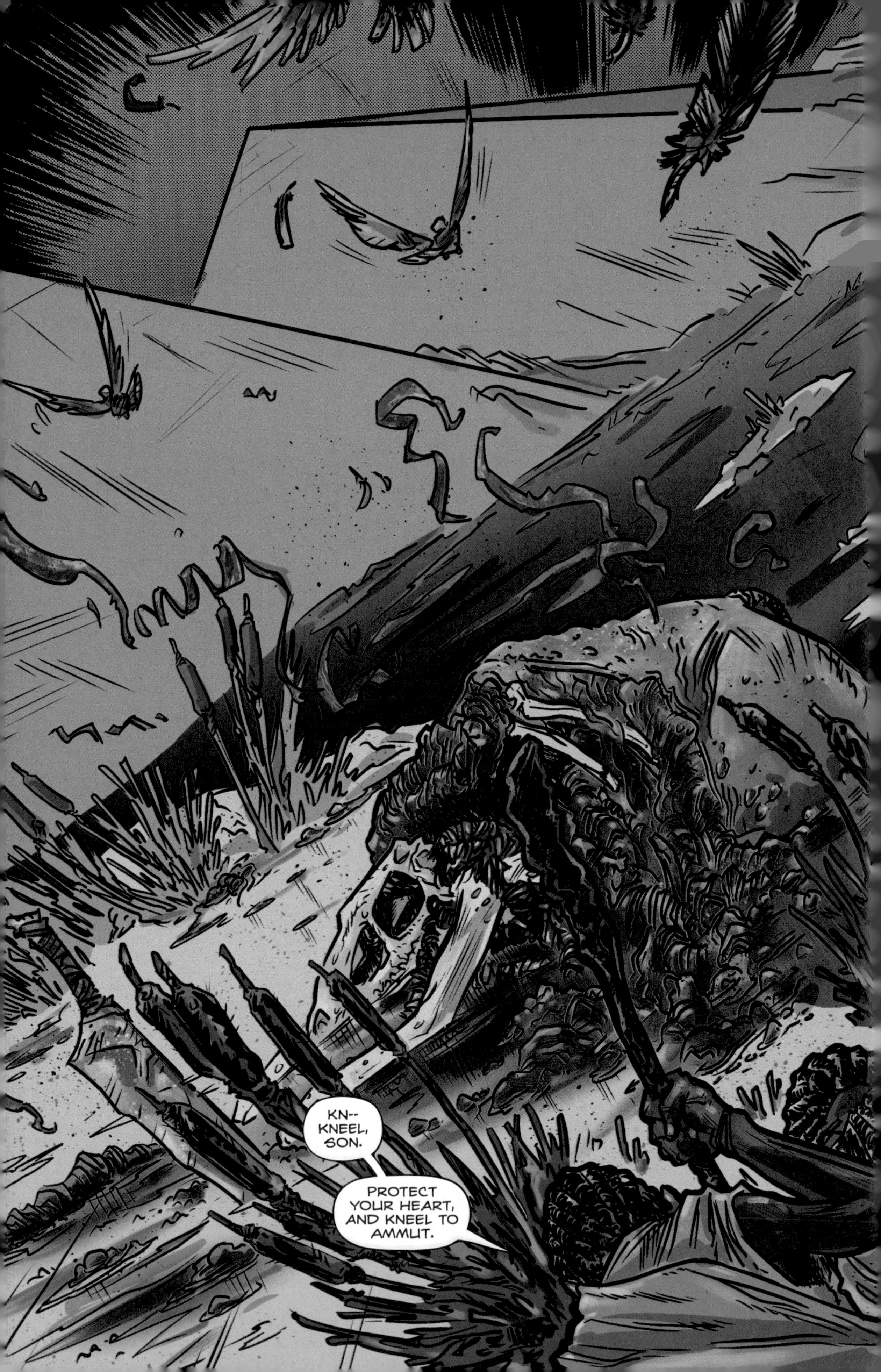
KN--
KNEEL,
SON.
PROTECT
YOUR HEART,
AND KNEEL TO
AMMUT.

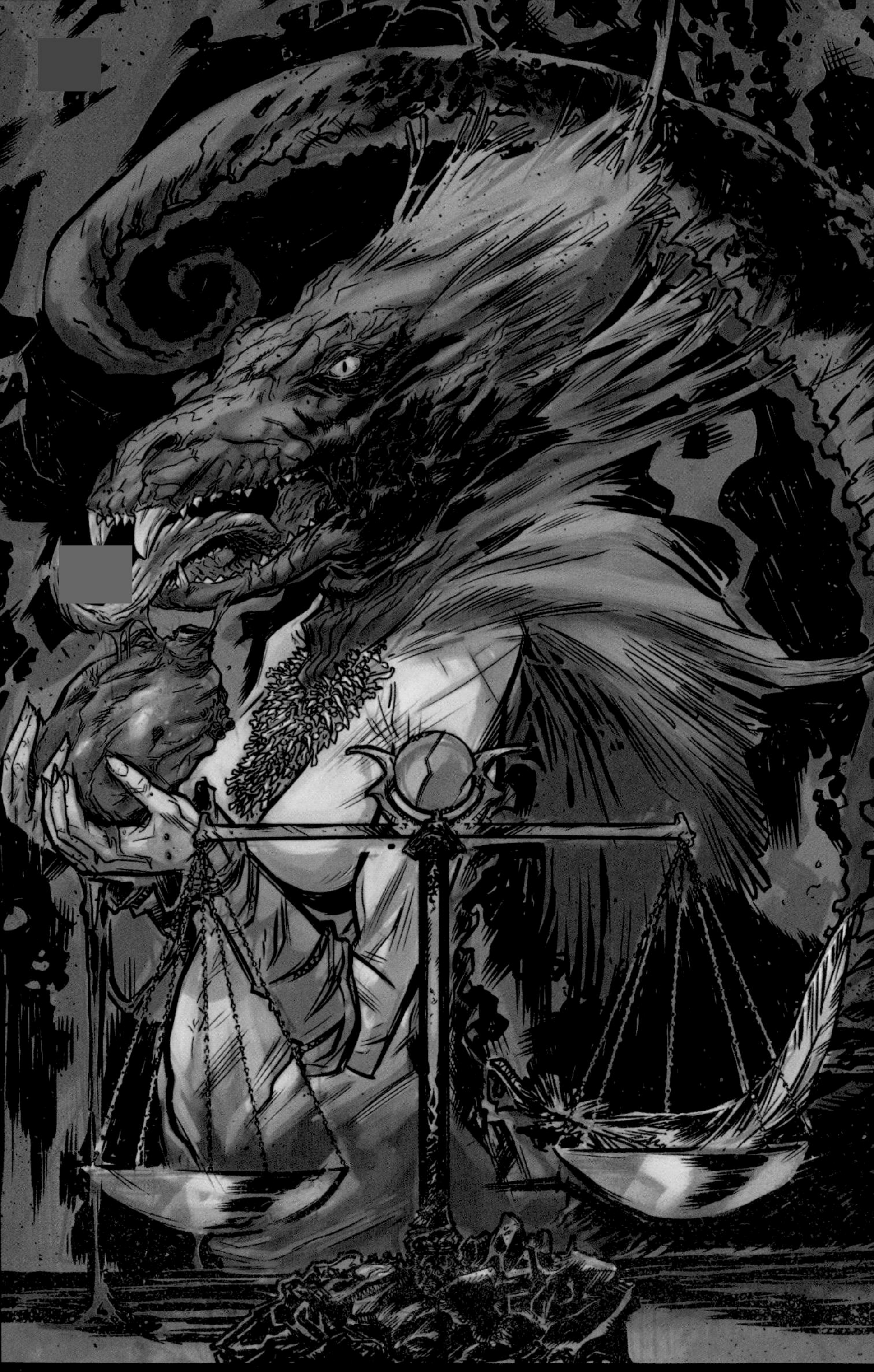

CHAPTER TWO

Its pilot was old and the Gigahül was smaller than the other twelve that roamed the sky and the sea and the earth.

For a brief time it sailed the sands of the Sporeland, a nightmare among the dunes. When it was piloted past that familiar country, a greater predator was waiting.

Now the carcass of that nightmare is preserved by the corruption that fills the air.

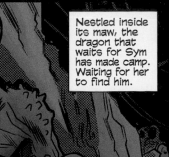

Nestled inside its maw, the dragon that waits for Sym has made camp. Waiting for her to find him.

But something stronger beckons him.

A need to see how the pilot met its end.

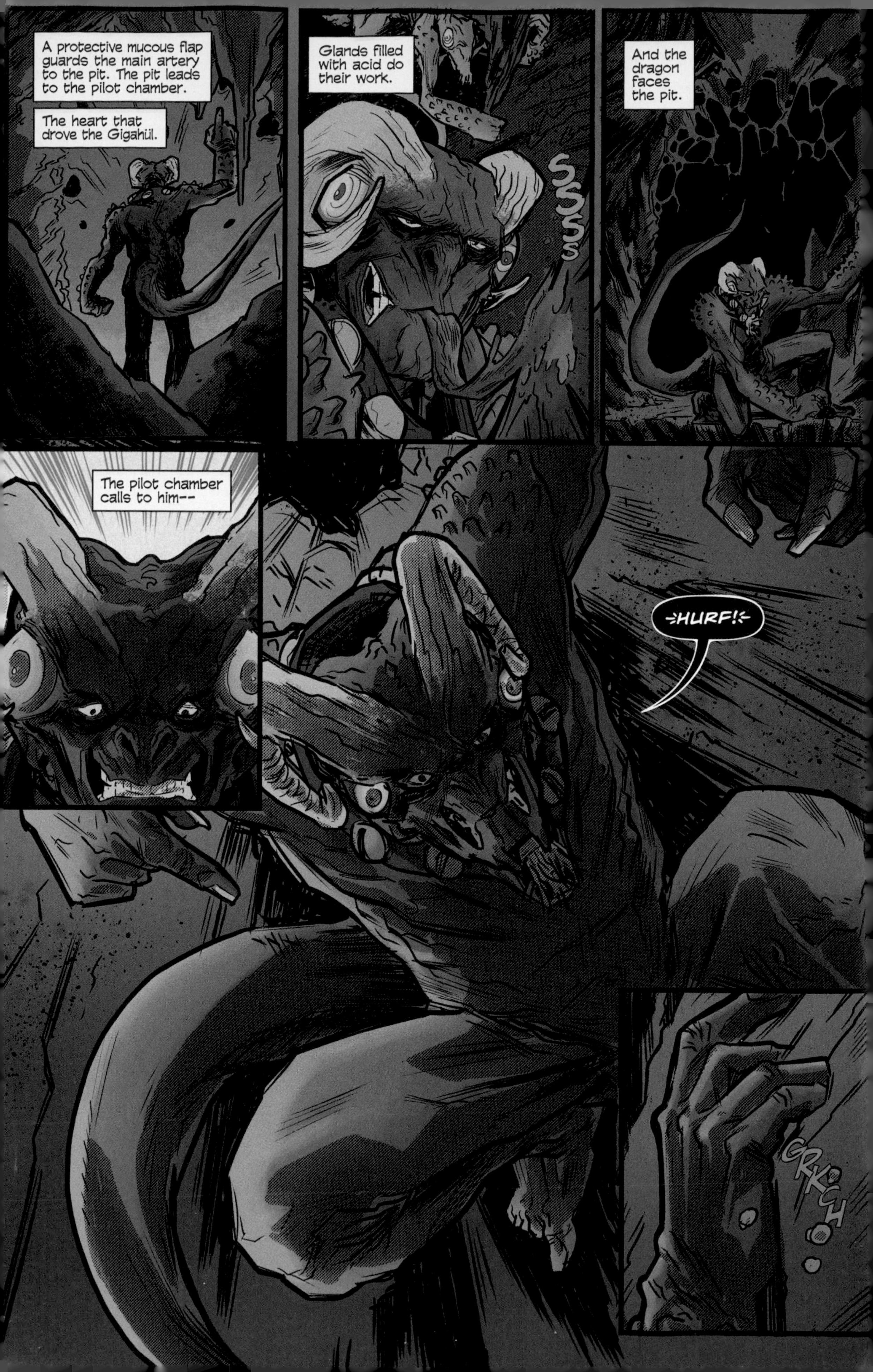
A protective mucous flap guards the main artery to the pit. The pit leads to the pilot chamber.
The heart that drove the Gigahül.
Glands filled with acid do their work.
SSSSS
And the dragon faces the pit.
The pilot chamber calls to him--
HURF!
GRKCH

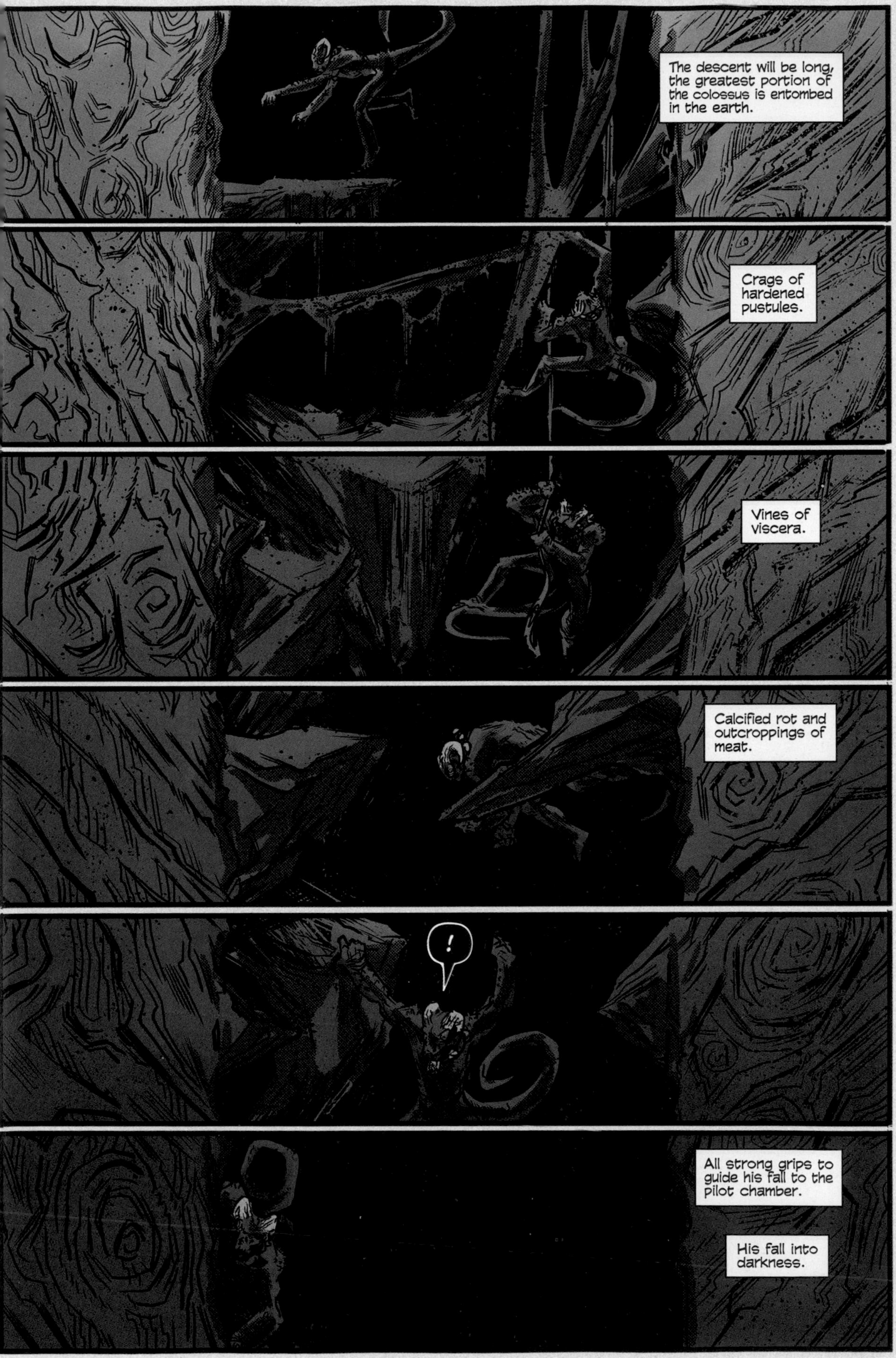
The descent will be long, the greatest portion of the colossus is entombed in the earth.
Crags of hardened pustules.
Vines of viscera.
Calcified rot and outcroppings of meat.
!
All strong grips to guide his fall to the pilot chamber.
His fall into darkness.

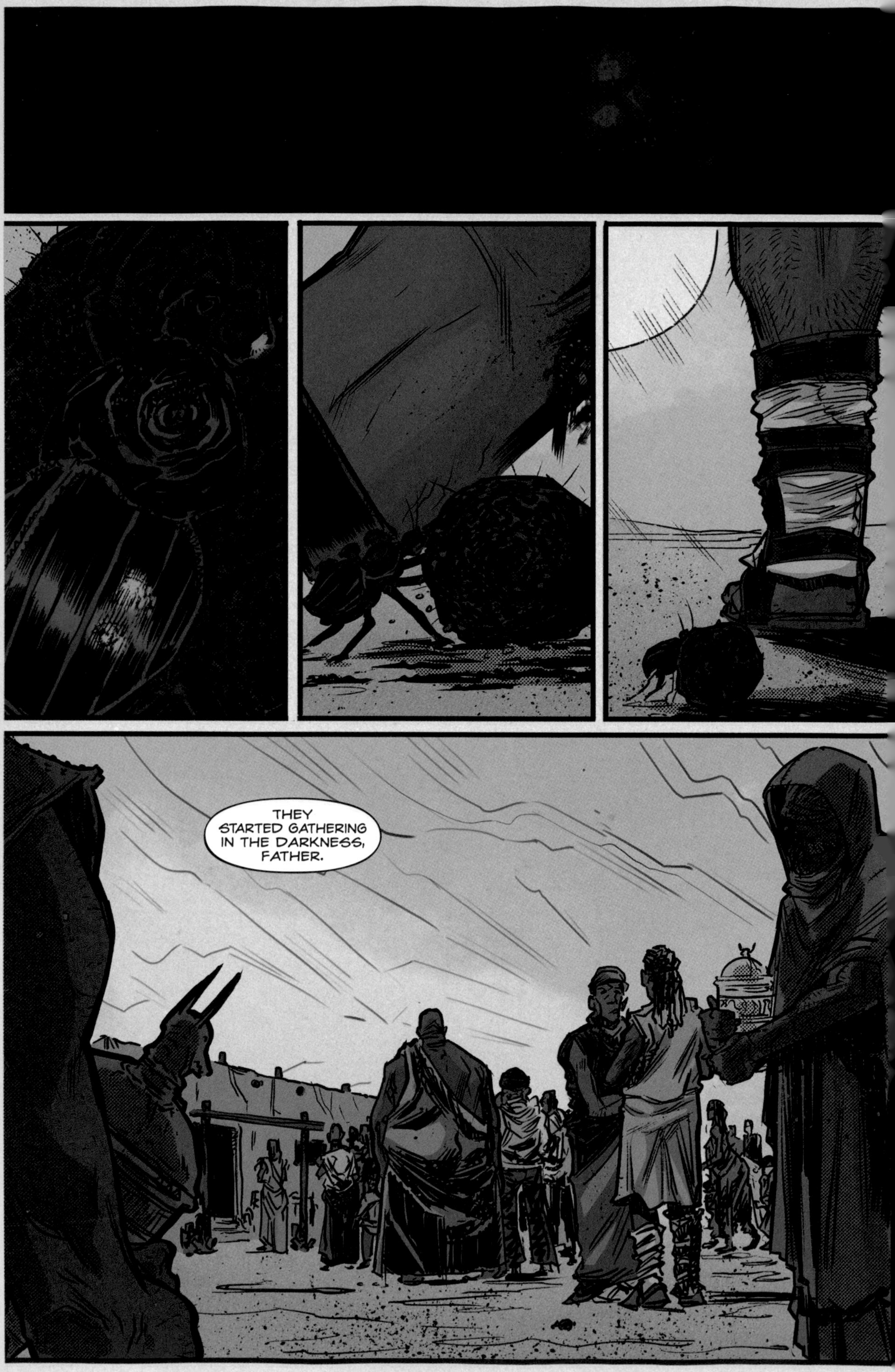
THEY STARTED GATHERING IN THE DARKNESS, FATHER.

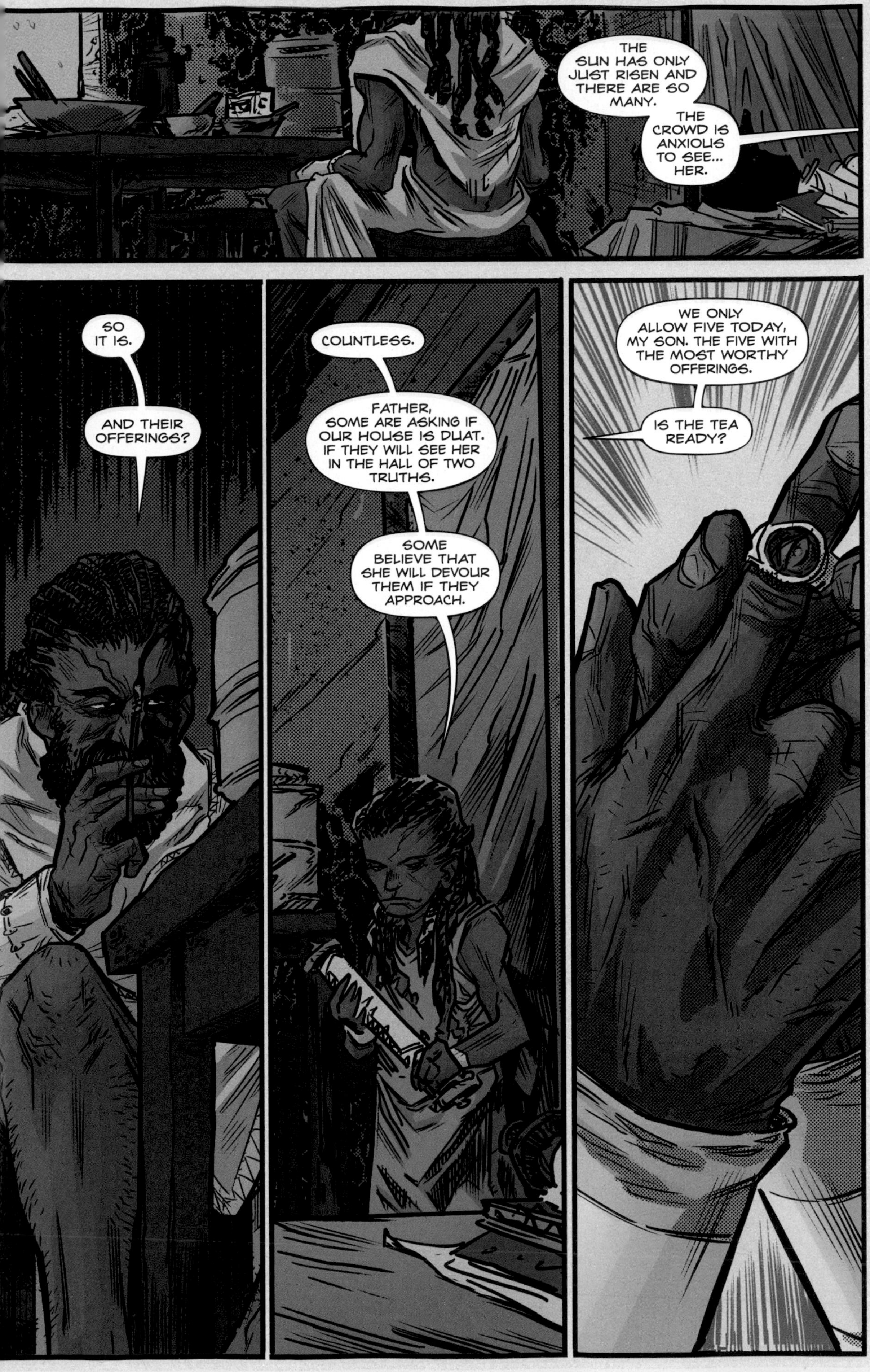
THE SUN HAS ONLY JUST RISEN AND THERE ARE SO MANY.
THE CROWD IS ANXIOUS TO SEE... HER.
SO IT IS.
AND THEIR OFFERINGS?
COUNTLESS.
FATHER, SOME ARE ASKING IF OUR HOUSE IS DUAT. IF THEY WILL SEE HER IN THE HALL OF TWO TRUTHS.
SOME BELIEVE THAT SHE WILL DEVOUR THEM IF THEY APPROACH.
WE ONLY ALLOW FIVE TODAY, MY SON. THE FIVE WITH THE MOST WORTHY OFFERINGS.
IS THE TEA READY?

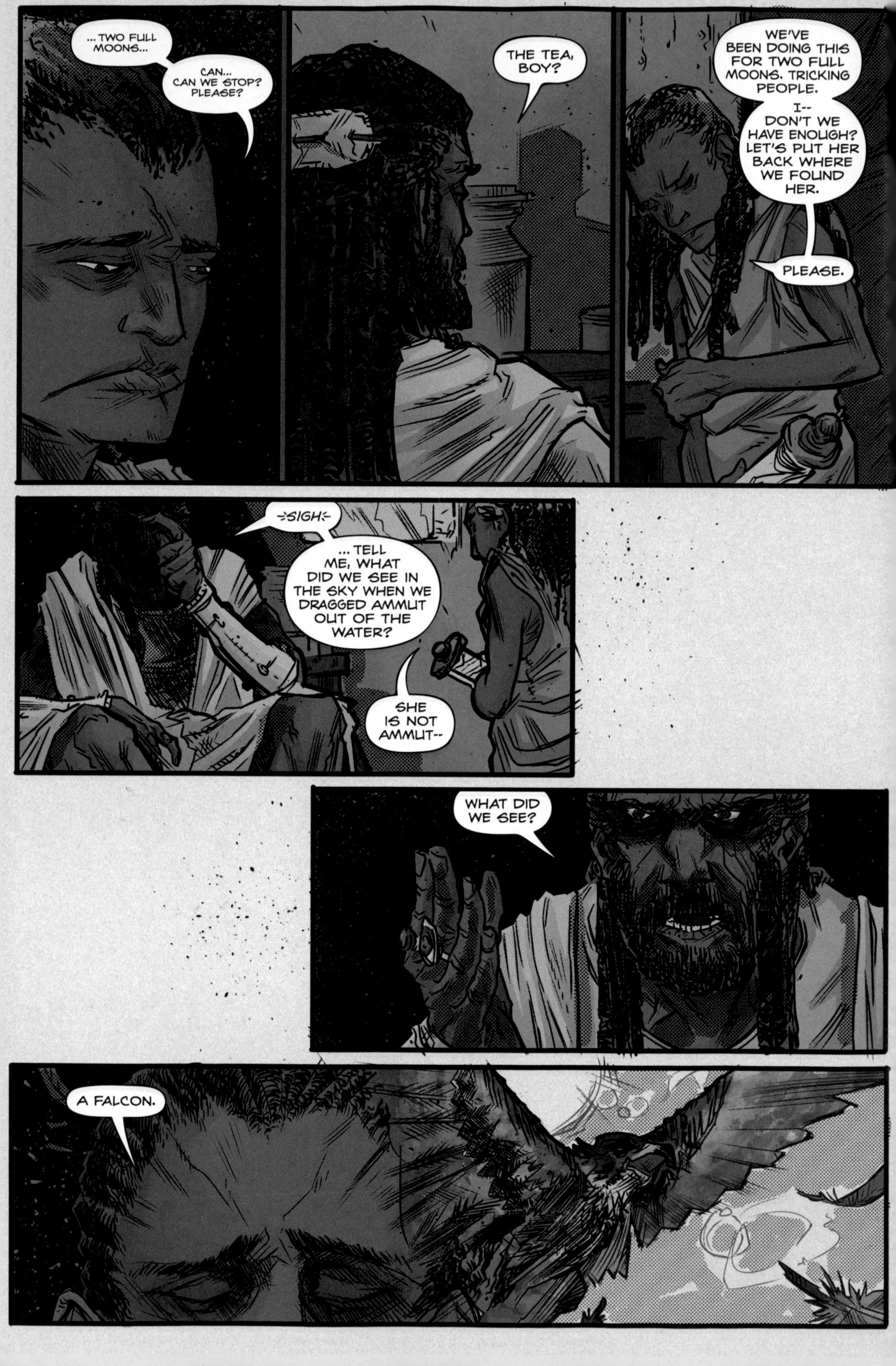
...TWO FULL MOONS...
CAN... CAN WE STOP? PLEASE?
THE TEA, BOY?
WE'VE BEEN DOING THIS FOR TWO FULL MOONS. TRICKING PEOPLE.
I-- DON'T WE HAVE ENOUGH? LET'S PUT HER BACK WHERE WE FOUND HER.
PLEASE.
-SIGH-
...TELL ME, WHAT DID WE SEE IN THE SKY WHEN WE DRAGGED AMMUT OUT OF THE WATER?
SHE IS NOT AMMUT--
WHAT DID WE SEE?
A FALCON.

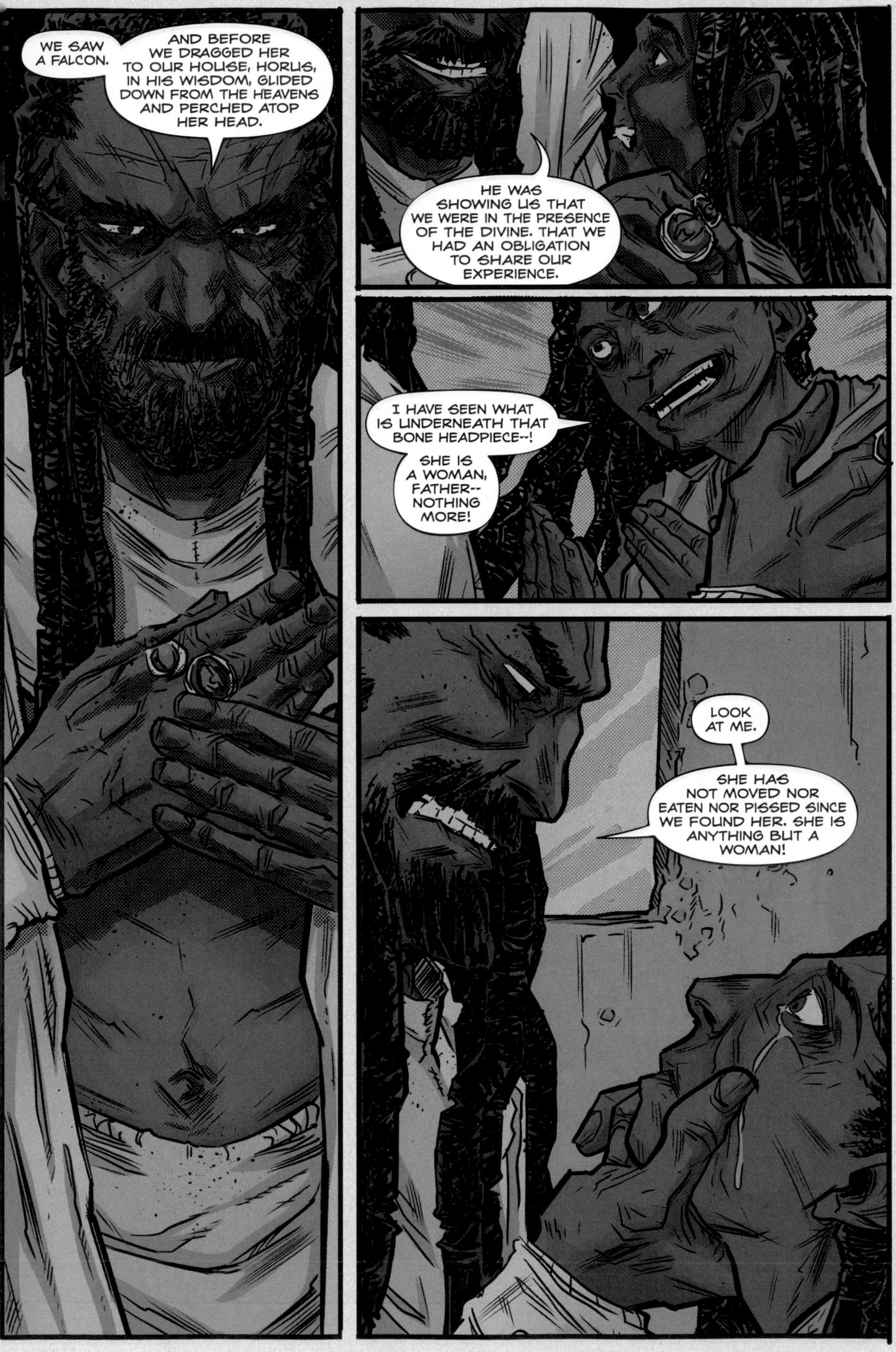
WE SAW A FALCON.
AND BEFORE WE DRAGGED HER TO OUR HOUSE, HORUS, IN HIS WISDOM, GLIDED DOWN FROM THE HEAVENS AND PERCHED ATOP HER HEAD.
HE WAS SHOWING US THAT WE WERE IN THE PRESENCE OF THE DIVINE. THAT WE HAD AN OBLIGATION TO SHARE OUR EXPERIENCE.
I HAVE SEEN WHAT IS UNDERNEATH THAT BONE HEADPIECE--!
SHE IS A WOMAN, FATHER-- NOTHING MORE!
LOOK AT ME.
SHE HAS NOT MOVED NOR EATEN NOR PISSED SINCE WE FOUND HER. SHE IS ANYTHING BUT A WOMAN!

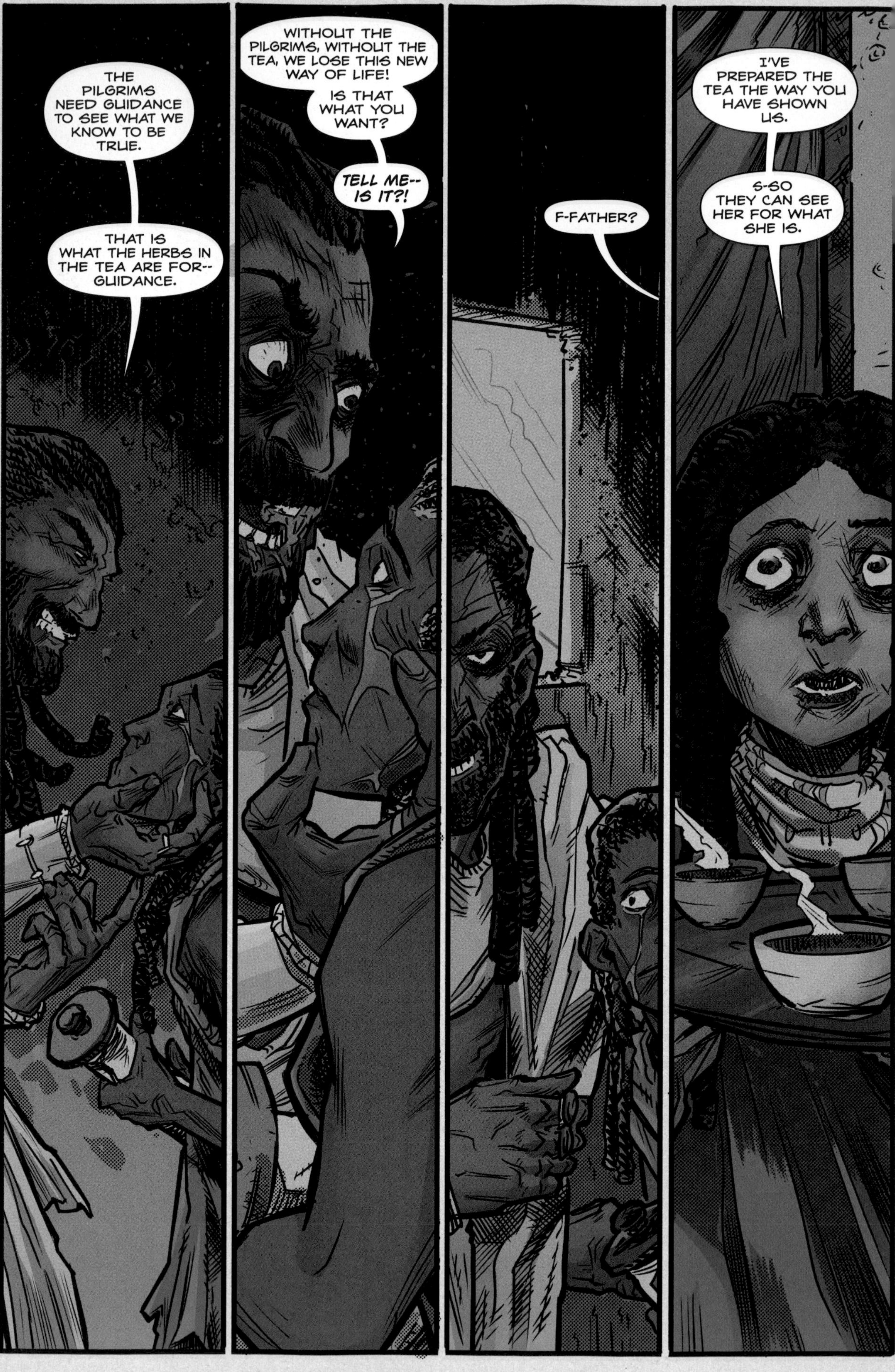
THE PILGRIMS NEED GUIDANCE TO SEE WHAT WE KNOW TO BE TRUE.
THAT IS WHAT THE HERBS IN THE TEA ARE FOR-- GUIDANCE.
WITHOUT THE PILGRIMS, WITHOUT THE TEA, WE LOSE THIS NEW WAY OF LIFE!
IS THAT WHAT YOU WANT?
TELL ME-- IS IT?!
F-FATHER?
I'VE PREPARED THE TEA THE WAY YOU HAVE SHOWN US.
S-SO THEY CAN SEE HER FOR WHAT SHE IS.

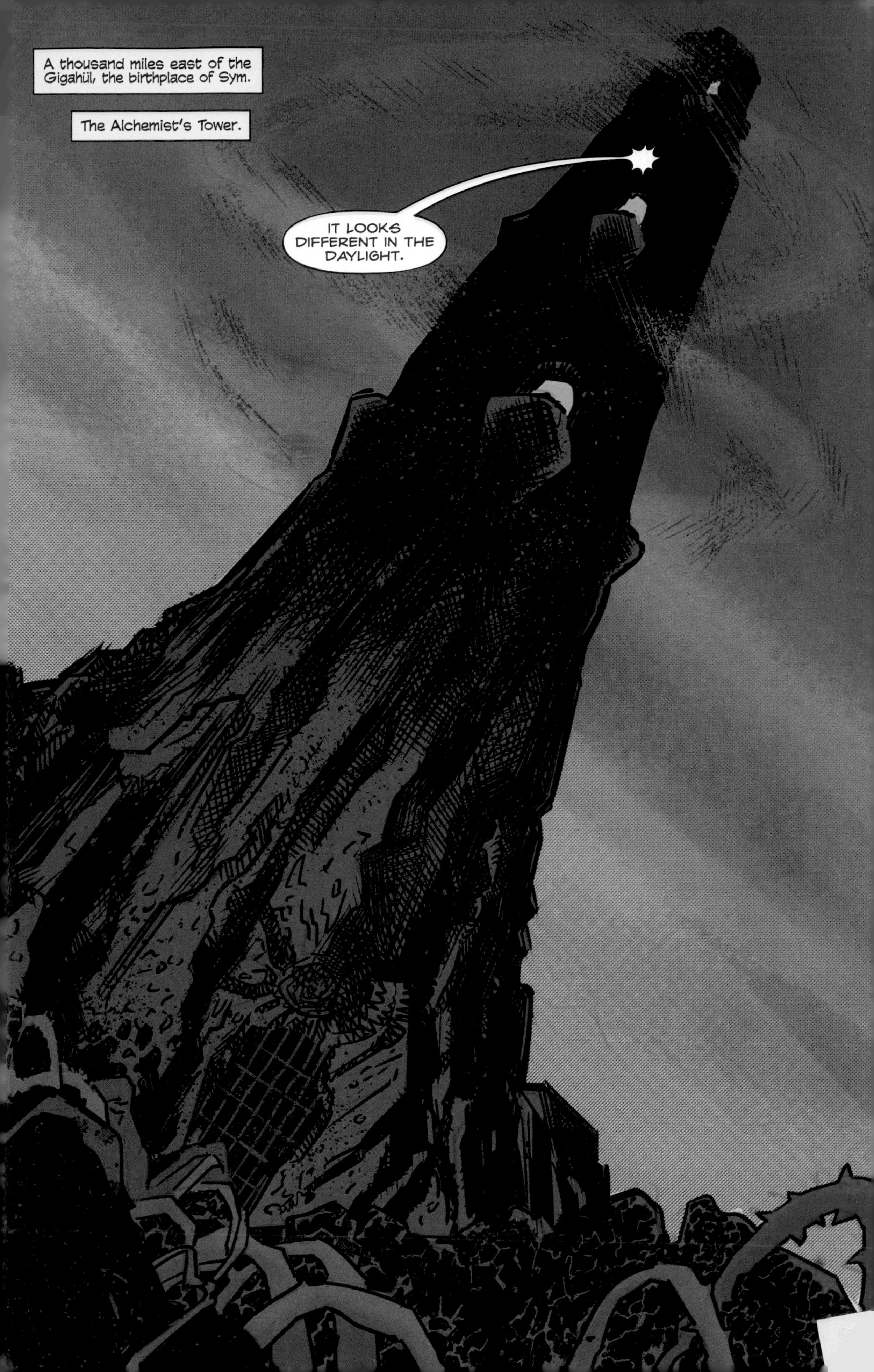
A thousand miles east of the Gigahül, the birthplace of Sym.
The Alchemist's Tower.
IT LOOKS DIFFERENT IN THE DAYLIGHT.

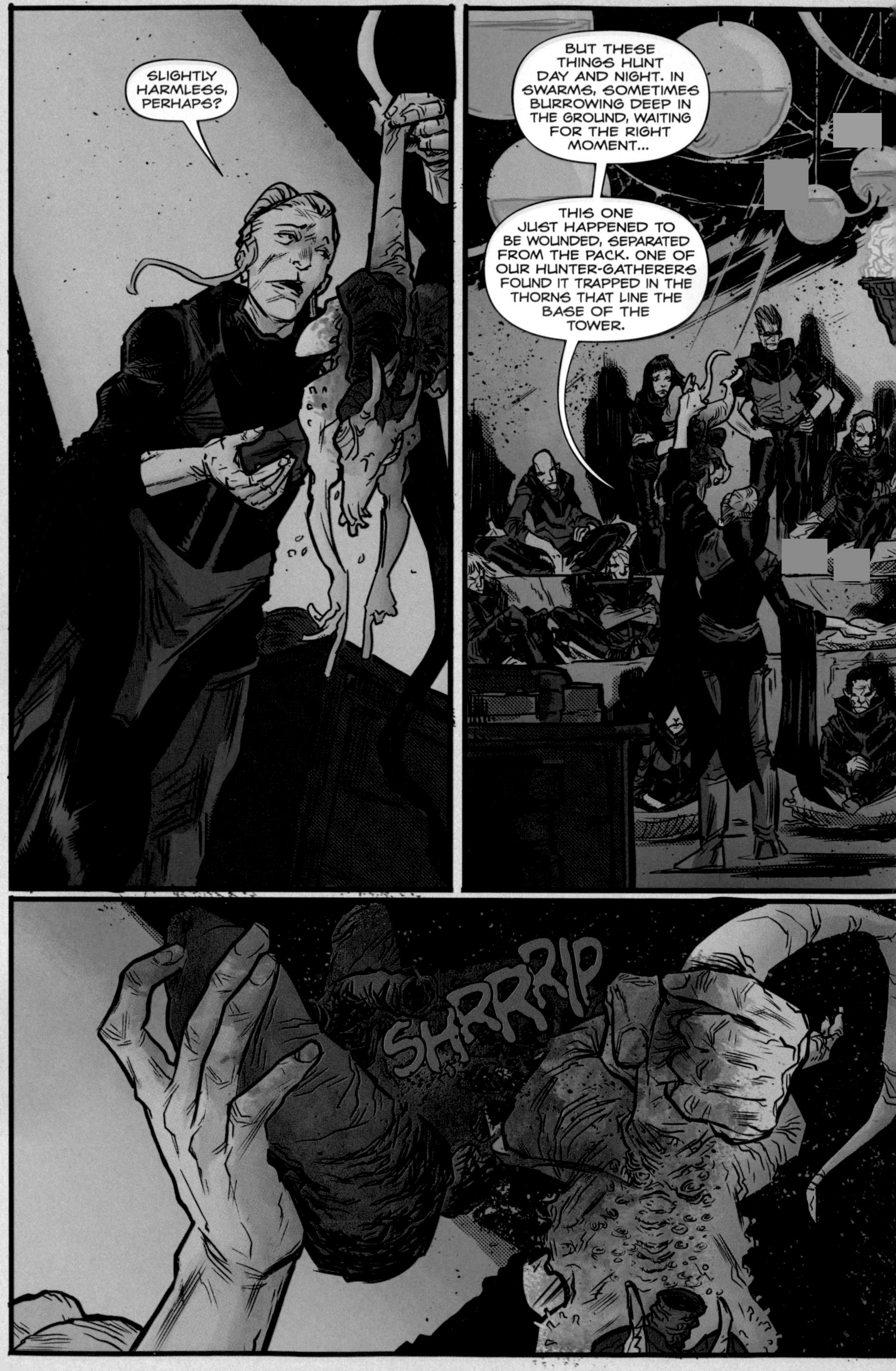
SLIGHTLY HARMLESS, PERHAPS?
BUT THESE THINGS HUNT DAY AND NIGHT. IN SWARMS, SOMETIMES BURROWING DEEP IN THE GROUND, WAITING FOR THE RIGHT MOMENT...
THIS ONE JUST HAPPENED TO BE WOUNDED, SEPARATED FROM THE PACK. ONE OF OUR HUNTER-GATHERERS FOUND IT TRAPPED IN THE THORNS THAT LINE THE BASE OF THE TOWER.
SHRRRIP

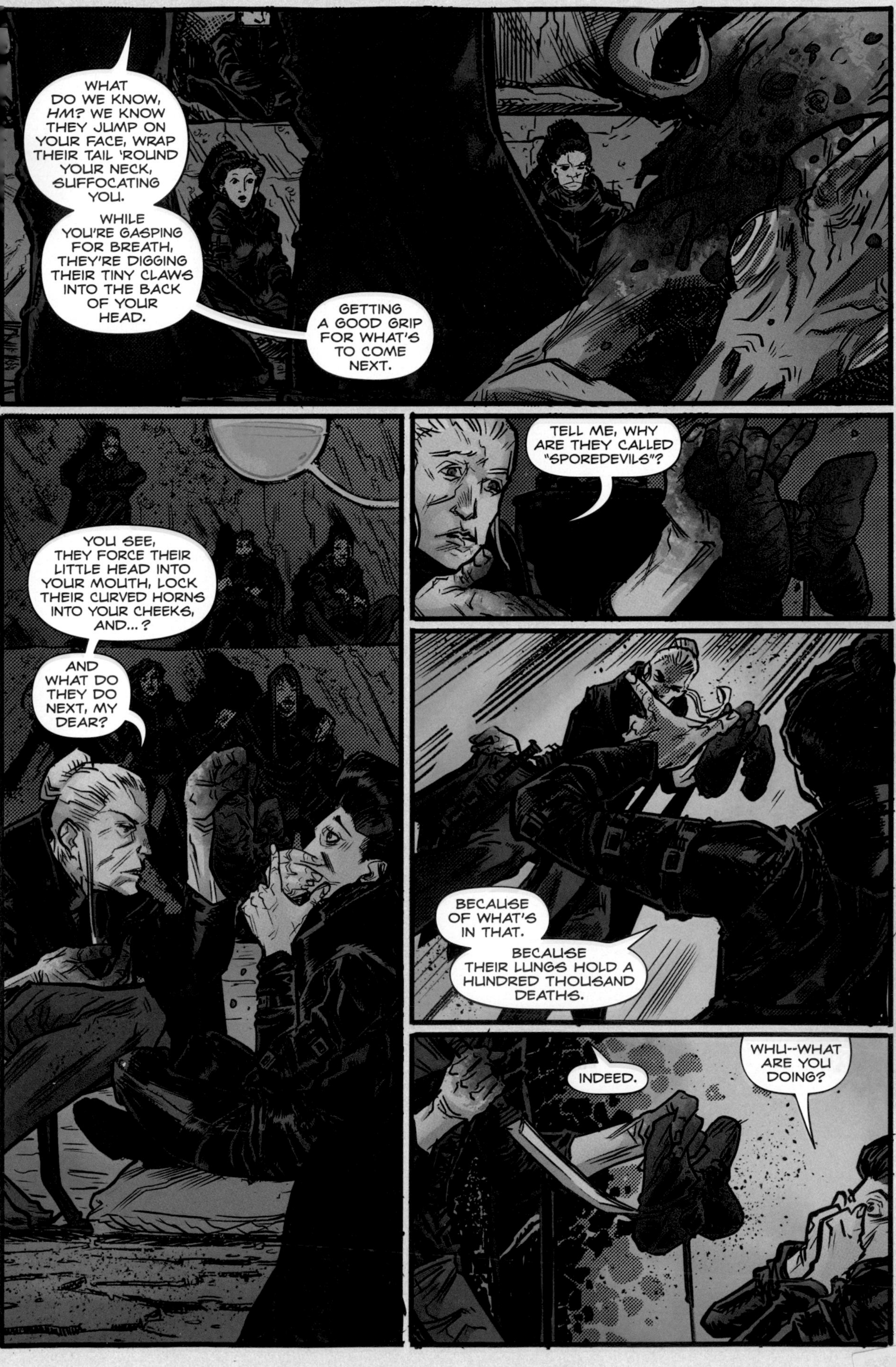
WHAT DO WE KNOW, *HM*? WE KNOW THEY JUMP ON YOUR FACE, WRAP THEIR TAIL 'ROUND YOUR NECK, SUFFOCATING YOU.
WHILE YOU'RE GASPING FOR BREATH, THEY'RE DIGGING THEIR TINY CLAWS INTO THE BACK OF YOUR HEAD.
GETTING A GOOD GRIP FOR WHAT'S TO COME NEXT.
YOU SEE, THEY FORCE THEIR LITTLE HEAD INTO YOUR MOUTH, LOCK THEIR CURVED HORNS INTO YOUR CHEEKS, AND...?
AND WHAT DO THEY DO NEXT, MY DEAR?
TELL ME, WHY ARE THEY CALLED "SPOREDEVILS"?
BECAUSE OF WHAT'S IN THAT.
BECAUSE THEIR LUNGS HOLD A HUNDRED THOUSAND DEATHS.
INDEED.
WHU--WHAT ARE YOU DOING?

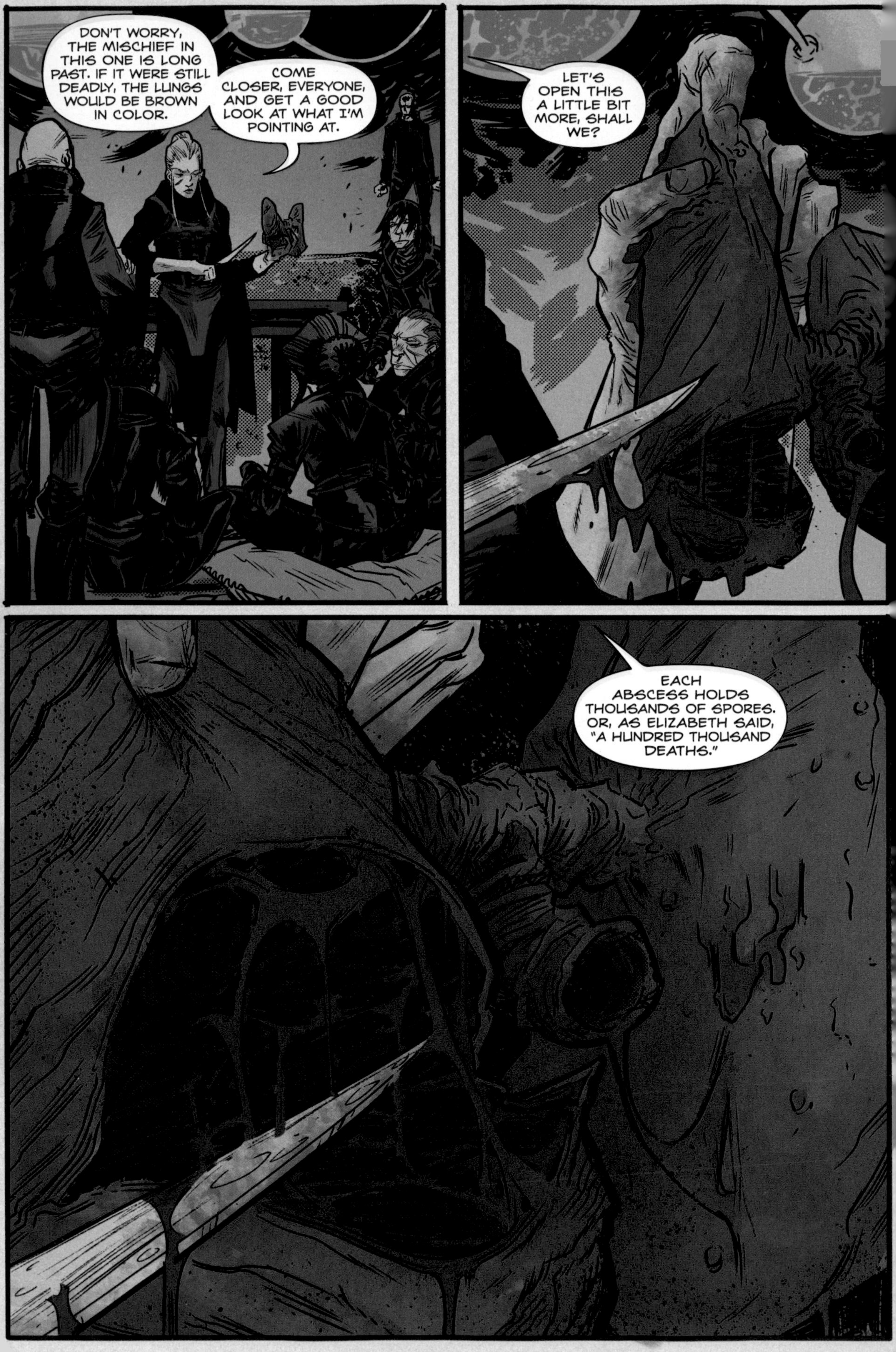
DON'T WORRY, THE MISCHIEF IN THIS ONE IS LONG PAST. IF IT WERE STILL DEADLY, THE LUNGS WOULD BE BROWN IN COLOR.
COME CLOSER, EVERYONE, AND GET A GOOD LOOK AT WHAT I'M POINTING AT.
LET'S OPEN THIS A LITTLE BIT MORE, SHALL WE?
EACH ABSCESS HOLDS THOUSANDS OF SPORES. OR, AS ELIZABETH SAID, "A HUNDRED THOUSAND DEATHS."

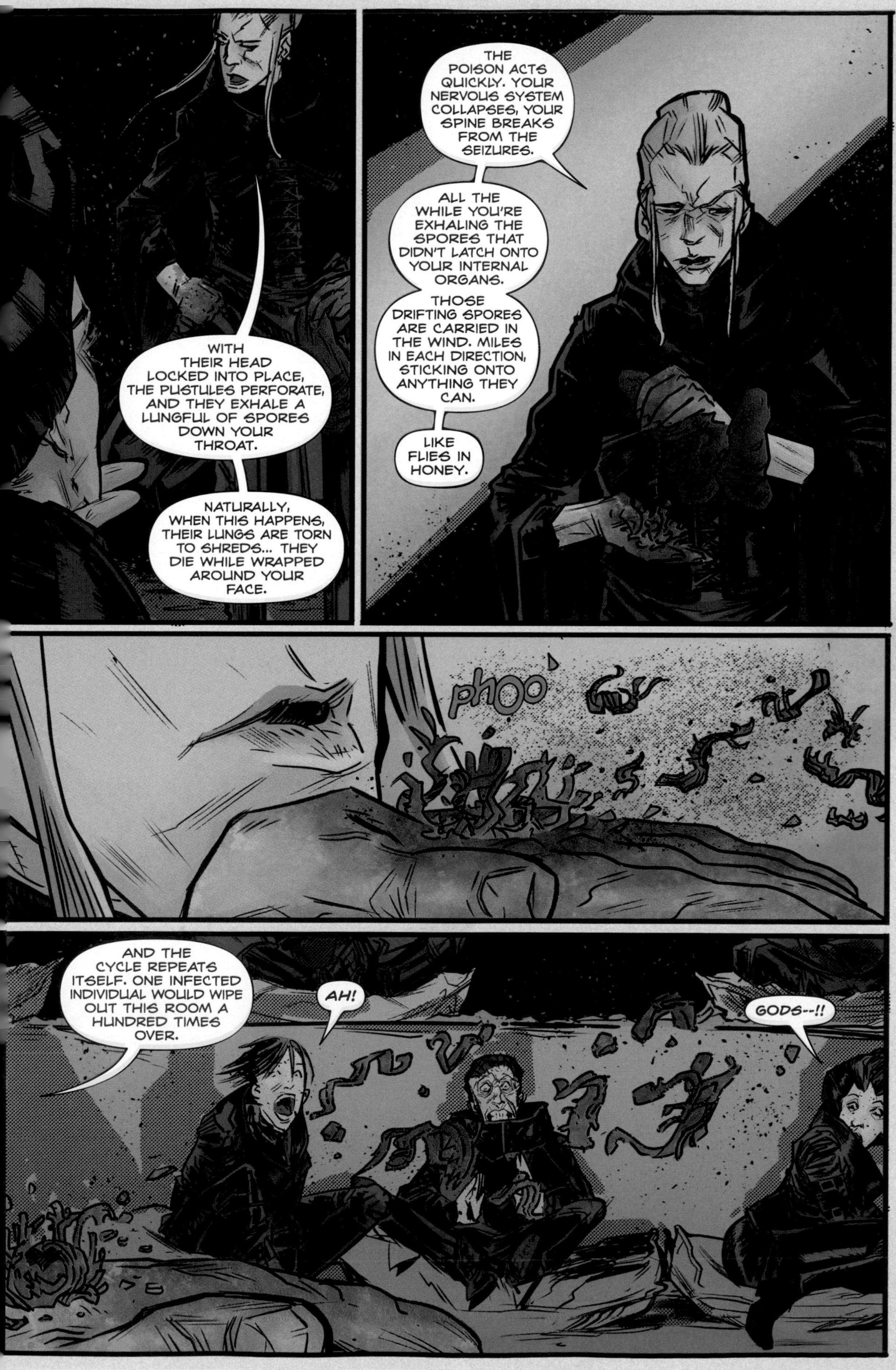
WITH THEIR HEAD LOCKED INTO PLACE, THE PUSTULES PERFORATE, AND THEY EXHALE A LUNGFUL OF SPORES DOWN YOUR THROAT.
NATURALLY, WHEN THIS HAPPENS, THEIR LUNGS ARE TORN TO SHREDS... THEY DIE WHILE WRAPPED AROUND YOUR FACE.
THE POISON ACTS QUICKLY. YOUR NERVOUS SYSTEM COLLAPSES, YOUR SPINE BREAKS FROM THE SEIZURES.
ALL THE WHILE YOU'RE EXHALING THE SPORES THAT DIDN'T LATCH ONTO YOUR INTERNAL ORGANS.
THOSE DRIFTING SPORES ARE CARRIED IN THE WIND. MILES IN EACH DIRECTION, STICKING ONTO ANYTHING THEY CAN.
LIKE FLIES IN HONEY.
phoo
AND THE CYCLE REPEATS ITSELF. ONE INFECTED INDIVIDUAL WOULD WIPE OUT THIS ROOM A HUNDRED TIMES OVER.
AH!
GODS--!!

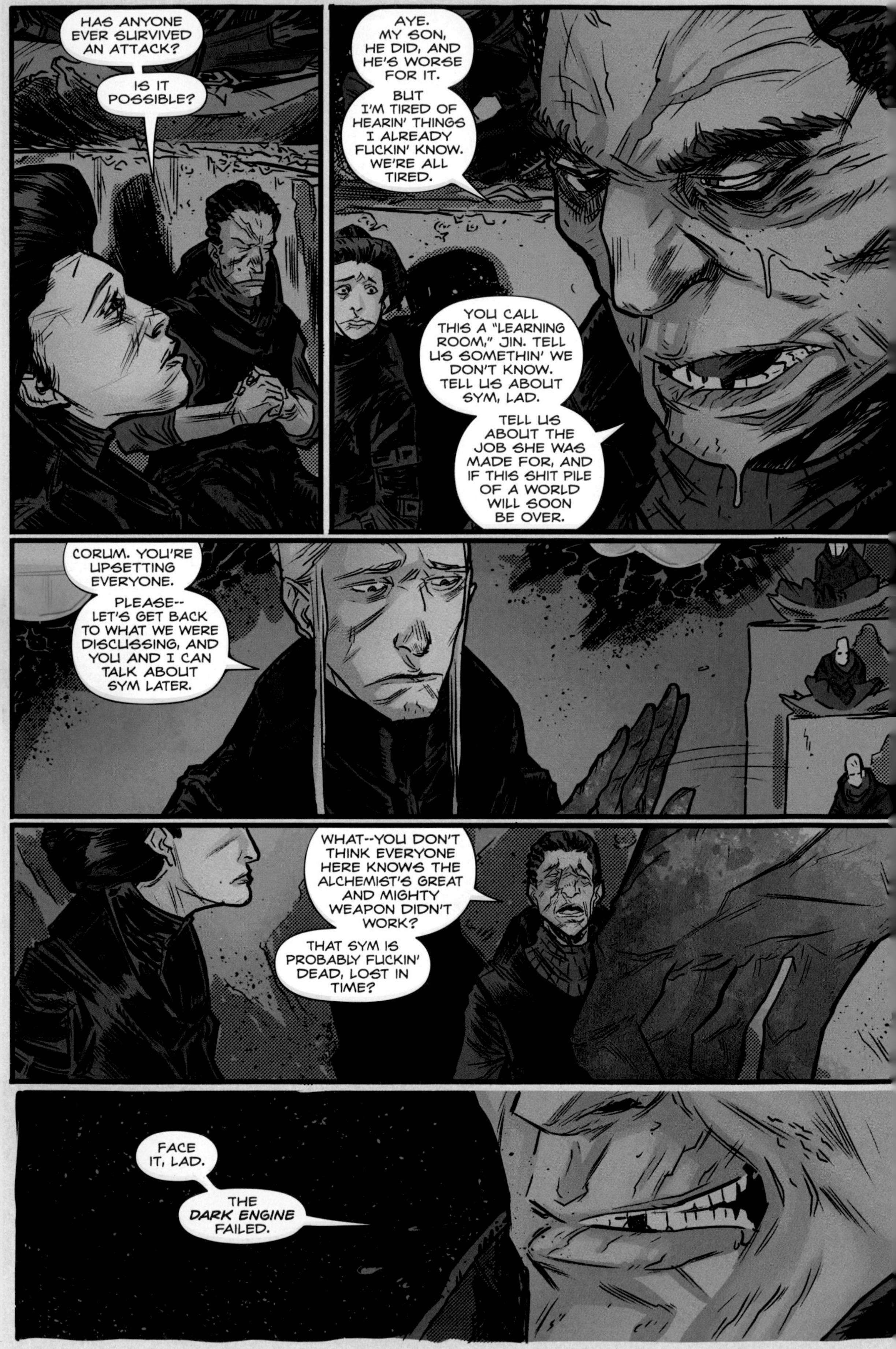
HAS ANYONE EVER SURVIVED AN ATTACK?
IS IT POSSIBLE?
AYE. MY SON, HE DID, AND HE'S WORSE FOR IT.
BUT I'M TIRED OF HEARIN' THINGS I ALREADY FUCKIN' KNOW. WE'RE ALL TIRED.
YOU CALL THIS A "LEARNING ROOM," JIN. TELL US SOMETHIN' WE DON'T KNOW. TELL US ABOUT SYM, LAD.
TELL US ABOUT THE JOB SHE WAS MADE FOR, AND IF THIS SHIT PILE OF A WORLD WILL SOON BE OVER.
CORUM. YOU'RE UPSETTING EVERYONE.
PLEASE-- LET'S GET BACK TO WHAT WE WERE DISCUSSING, AND YOU AND I CAN TALK ABOUT SYM LATER.
WHAT--YOU DON'T THINK EVERYONE HERE KNOWS THE ALCHEMIST'S GREAT AND MIGHTY WEAPON DIDN'T WORK?
THAT SYM IS PROBABLY FUCKIN' DEAD, LOST IN TIME?
FACE IT, LAD.
THE *DARK ENGINE* FAILED.

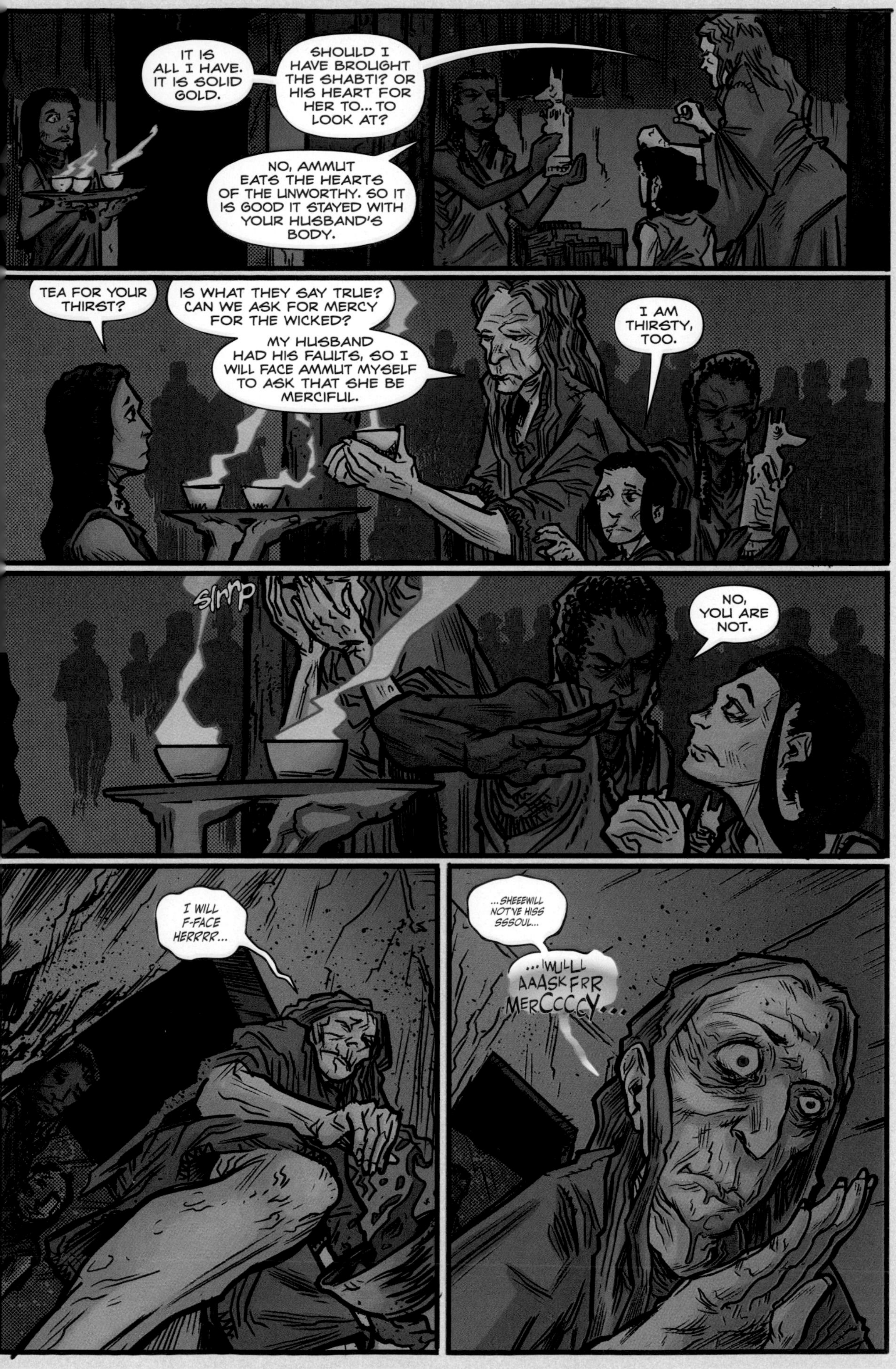
IT IS ALL I HAVE. IT IS SOLID GOLD.
SHOULD I HAVE BROUGHT THE SHABTI? OR HIS HEART FOR HER TO... TO LOOK AT?
NO, AMMUT EATS THE HEARTS OF THE UNWORTHY. SO IT IS GOOD IT STAYED WITH YOUR HUSBAND'S BODY.
TEA FOR YOUR THIRST?
IS WHAT THEY SAY TRUE? CAN WE ASK FOR MERCY FOR THE WICKED?
MY HUSBAND HAD HIS FAULTS, SO I WILL FACE AMMUT MYSELF TO ASK THAT SHE BE MERCIFUL.
I AM THIRSTY, TOO.
slrrp
NO, YOU ARE NOT.
I WILL F-FACE HERRRR...
...SHEEEWILL NOT'VE HISS SSSOUL...
...IWULLL AAASKFRR MERCCCCY...

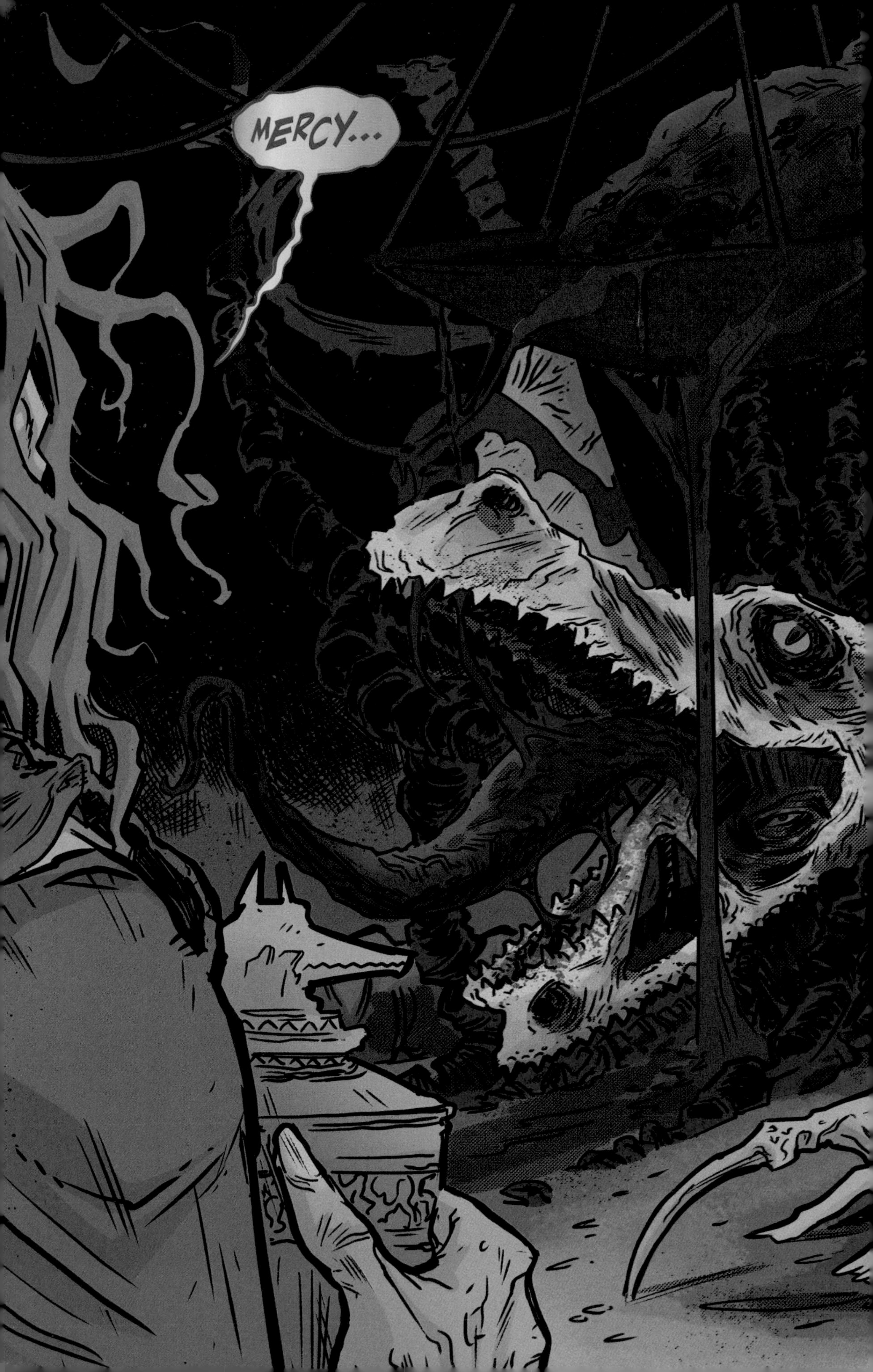
MERCY...

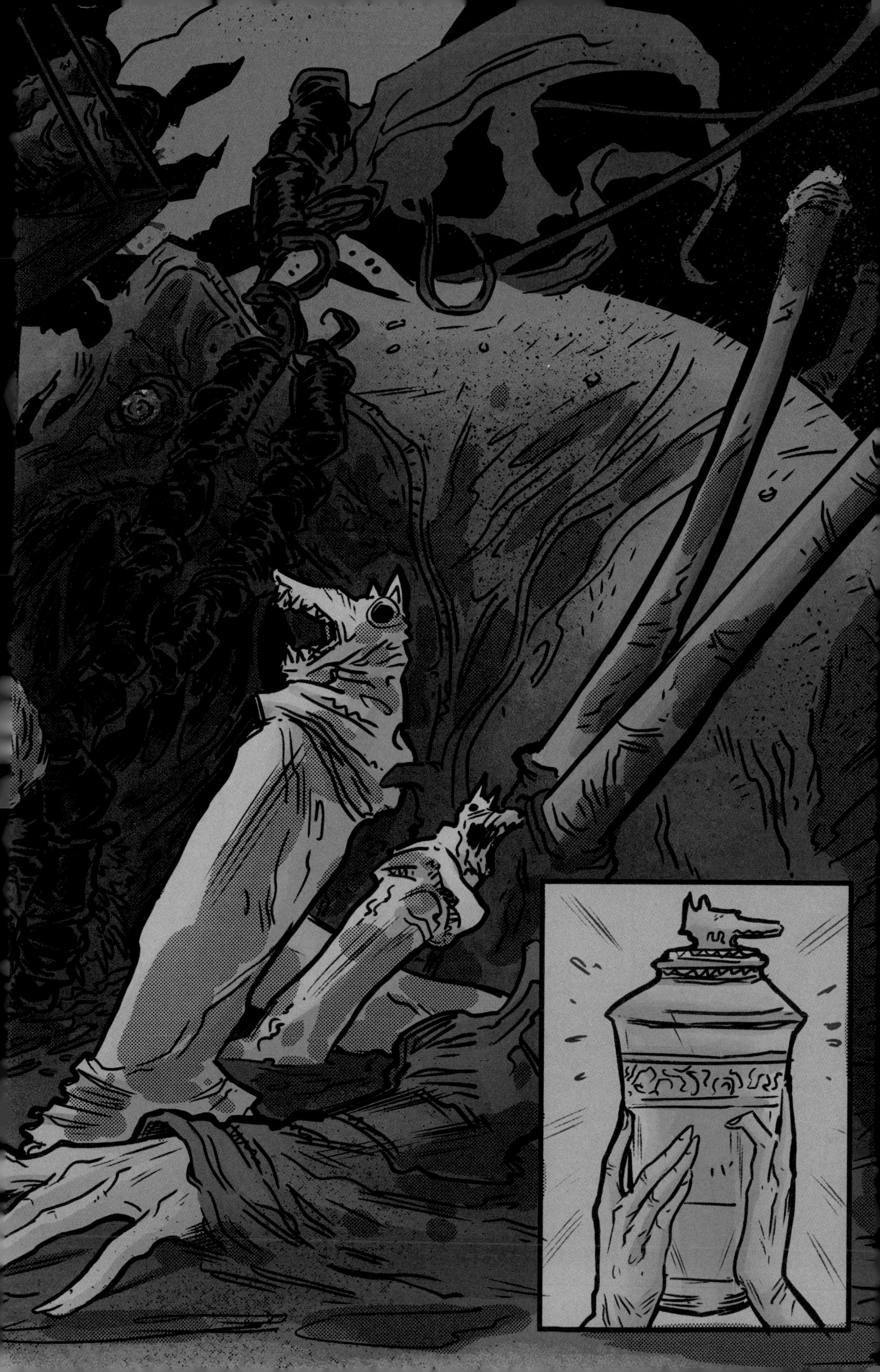

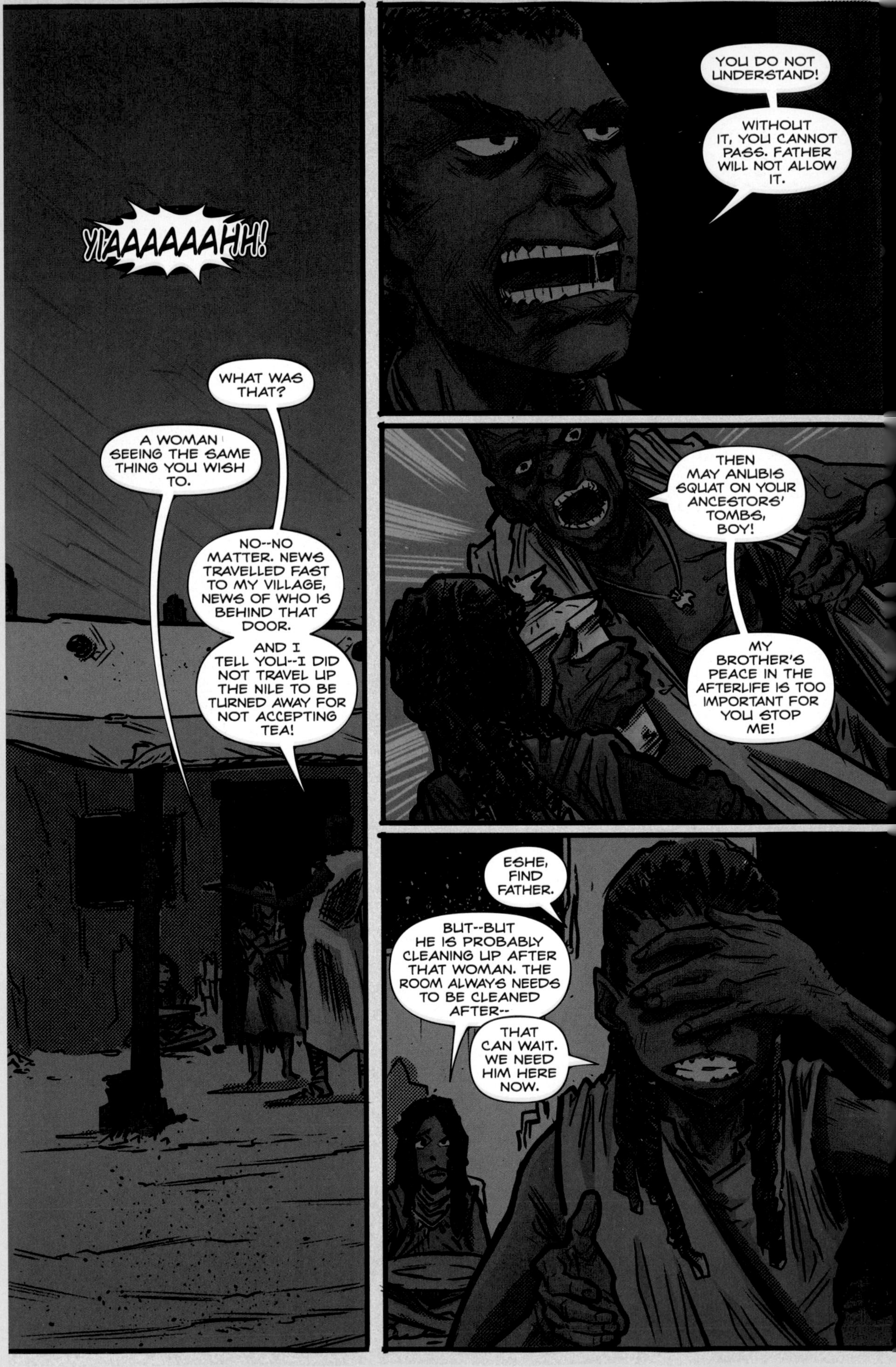

YIAAAAAAHH!
WHAT WAS THAT?
A WOMAN SEEING THE SAME THING YOU WISH TO.
NO--NO MATTER. NEWS TRAVELLED FAST TO MY VILLAGE, NEWS OF WHO IS BEHIND THAT DOOR.
AND I TELL YOU--I DID NOT TRAVEL UP THE NILE TO BE TURNED AWAY FOR NOT ACCEPTING TEA!
YOU DO NOT UNDERSTAND!
WITHOUT IT, YOU CANNOT PASS. FATHER WILL NOT ALLOW IT.
THEN MAY ANUBIS SQUAT ON YOUR ANCESTORS' TOMBS, BOY!
MY BROTHER'S PEACE IN THE AFTERLIFE IS TOO IMPORTANT FOR YOU STOP ME!
ESHE, FIND FATHER.
BUT--BUT HE IS PROBABLY CLEANING UP AFTER THAT WOMAN. THE ROOM ALWAYS NEEDS TO BE CLEANED AFTER--
THAT CAN WAIT. WE NEED HIM HERE NOW.

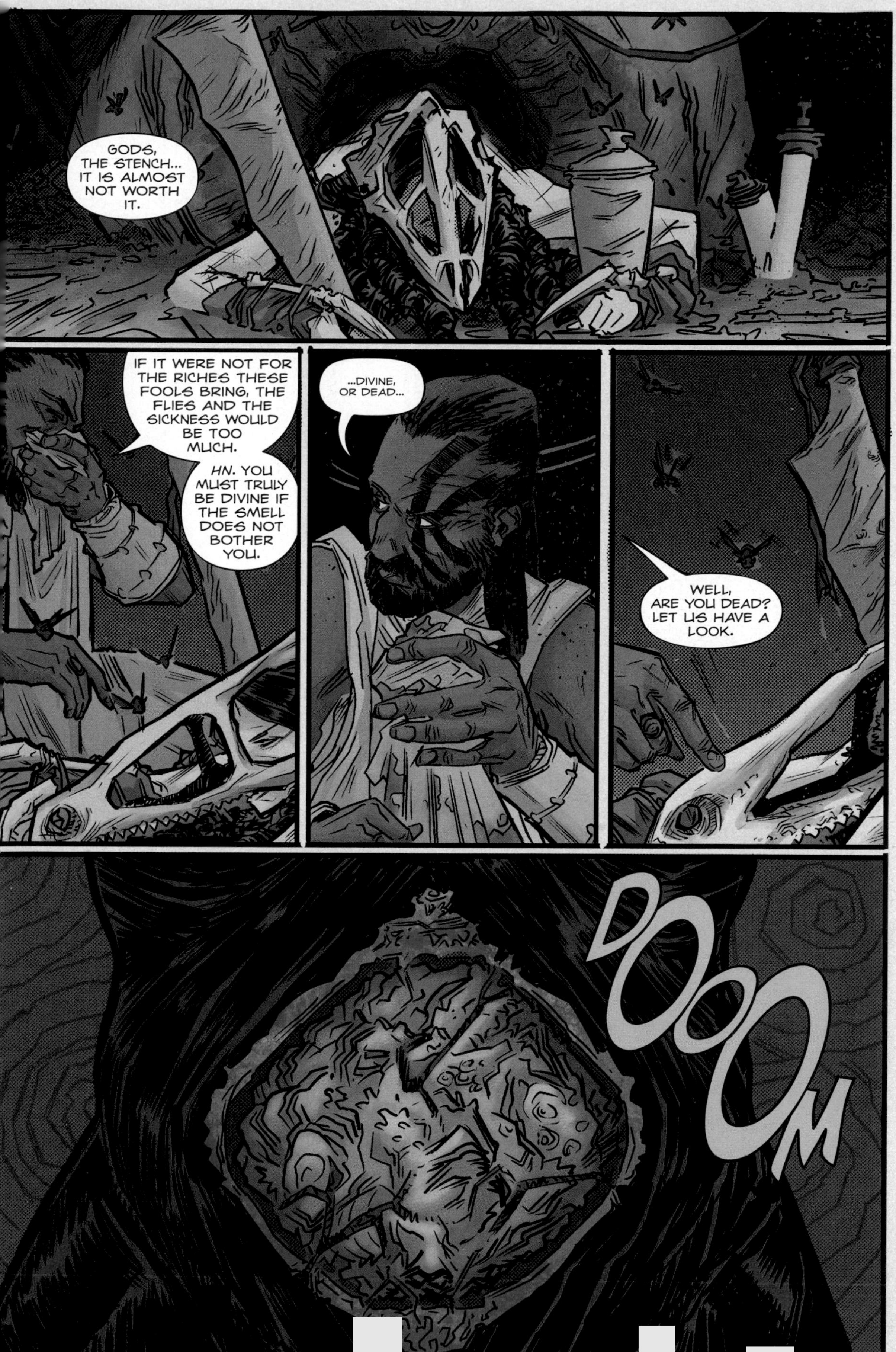
GODS, THE STENCH... IT IS ALMOST NOT WORTH IT.
IF IT WERE NOT FOR THE RICHES THESE FOOLS BRING, THE FLIES AND THE SICKNESS WOULD BE TOO MUCH.
HN. YOU MUST TRULY BE DIVINE IF THE SMELL DOES NOT BOTHER YOU.
...DIVINE, OR DEAD...
WELL, ARE YOU DEAD? LET US HAVE A LOOK.
DOOOOM

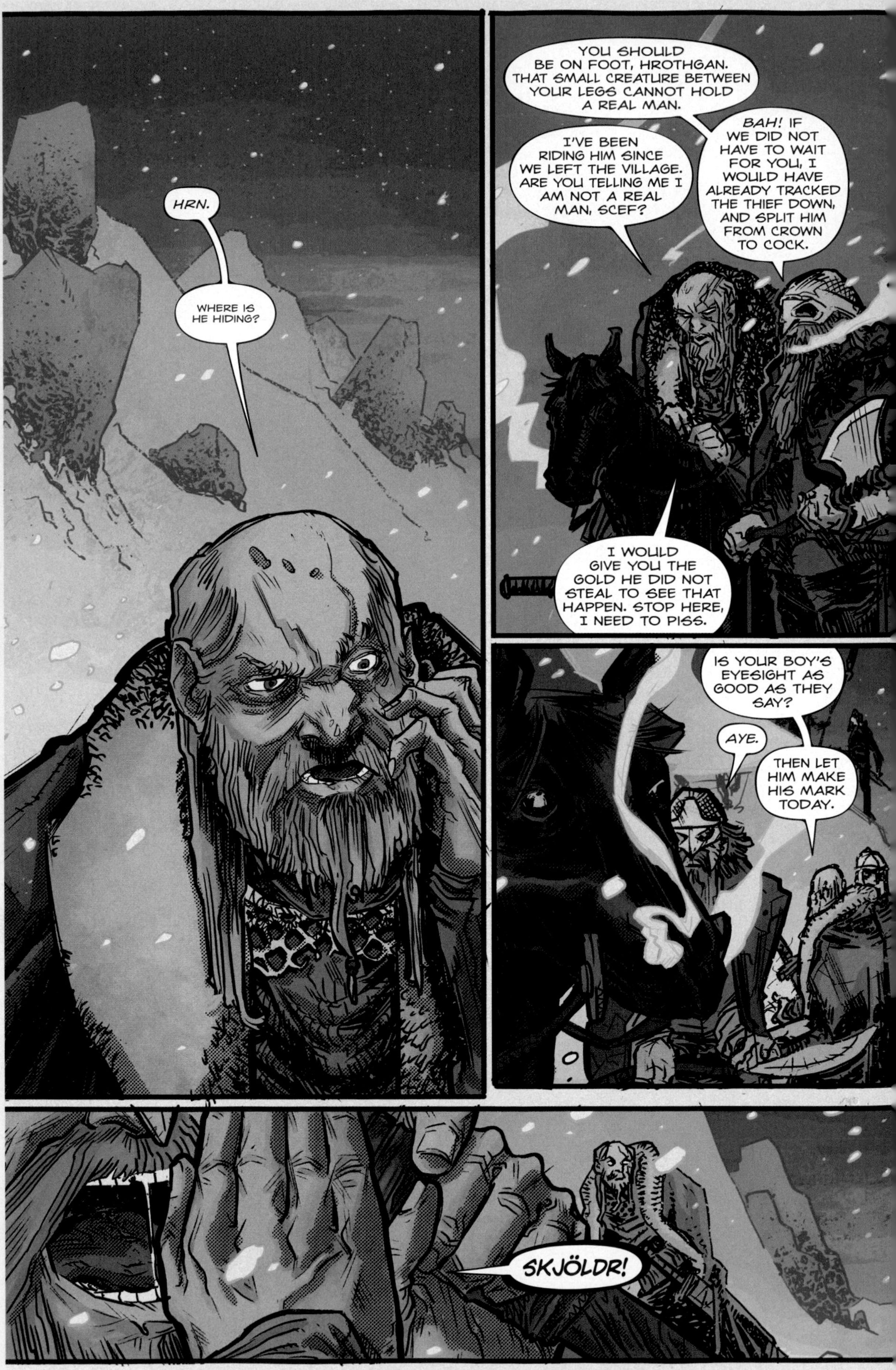

HRN.
WHERE IS HE HIDING?
YOU SHOULD BE ON FOOT, HROTHGAN. THAT SMALL CREATURE BETWEEN YOUR LEGS CANNOT HOLD A REAL MAN.
I'VE BEEN RIDING HIM SINCE WE LEFT THE VILLAGE. ARE YOU TELLING ME I AM NOT A REAL MAN, SCEF?
BAH! IF WE DID NOT HAVE TO WAIT FOR YOU, I WOULD HAVE ALREADY TRACKED THE THIEF DOWN, AND SPLIT HIM FROM CROWN TO COCK.
I WOULD GIVE YOU THE GOLD HE DID NOT STEAL TO SEE THAT HAPPEN. STOP HERE, I NEED TO PISS.
IS YOUR BOY'S EYESIGHT AS GOOD AS THEY SAY?
AYE.
THEN LET HIM MAKE HIS MARK TODAY.
SKJÖLDR!

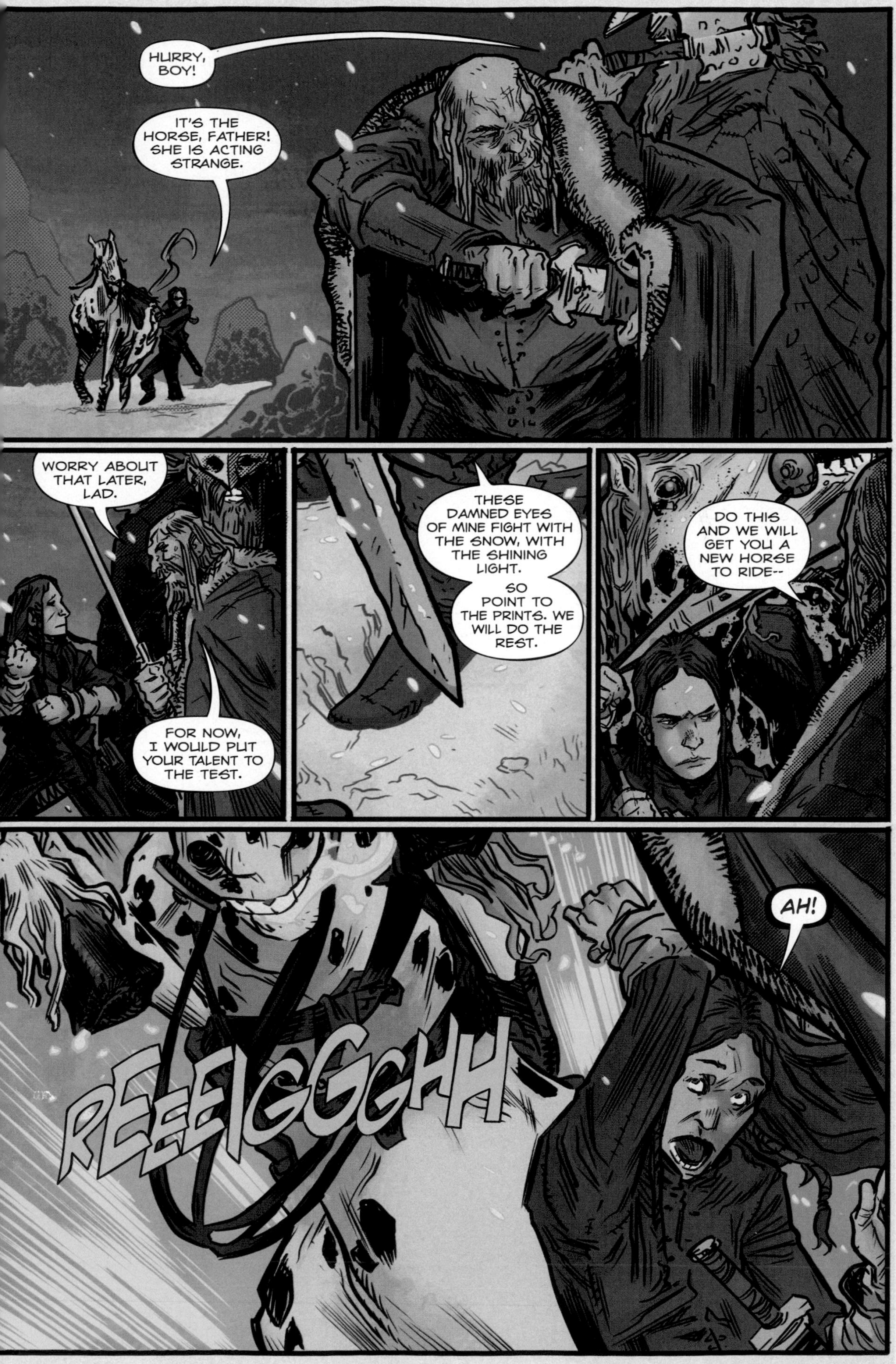
HURRY, BOY!
IT'S THE HORSE, FATHER! SHE IS ACTING STRANGE.
WORRY ABOUT THAT LATER, LAD.
FOR NOW, I WOULD PUT YOUR TALENT TO THE TEST.
THESE DAMNED EYES OF MINE FIGHT WITH THE SNOW, WITH THE SHINING LIGHT.
SO POINT TO THE PRINTS. WE WILL DO THE REST.
DO THIS AND WE WILL GET YOU A NEW HORSE TO RIDE--
REEEIGGGHH
AH!

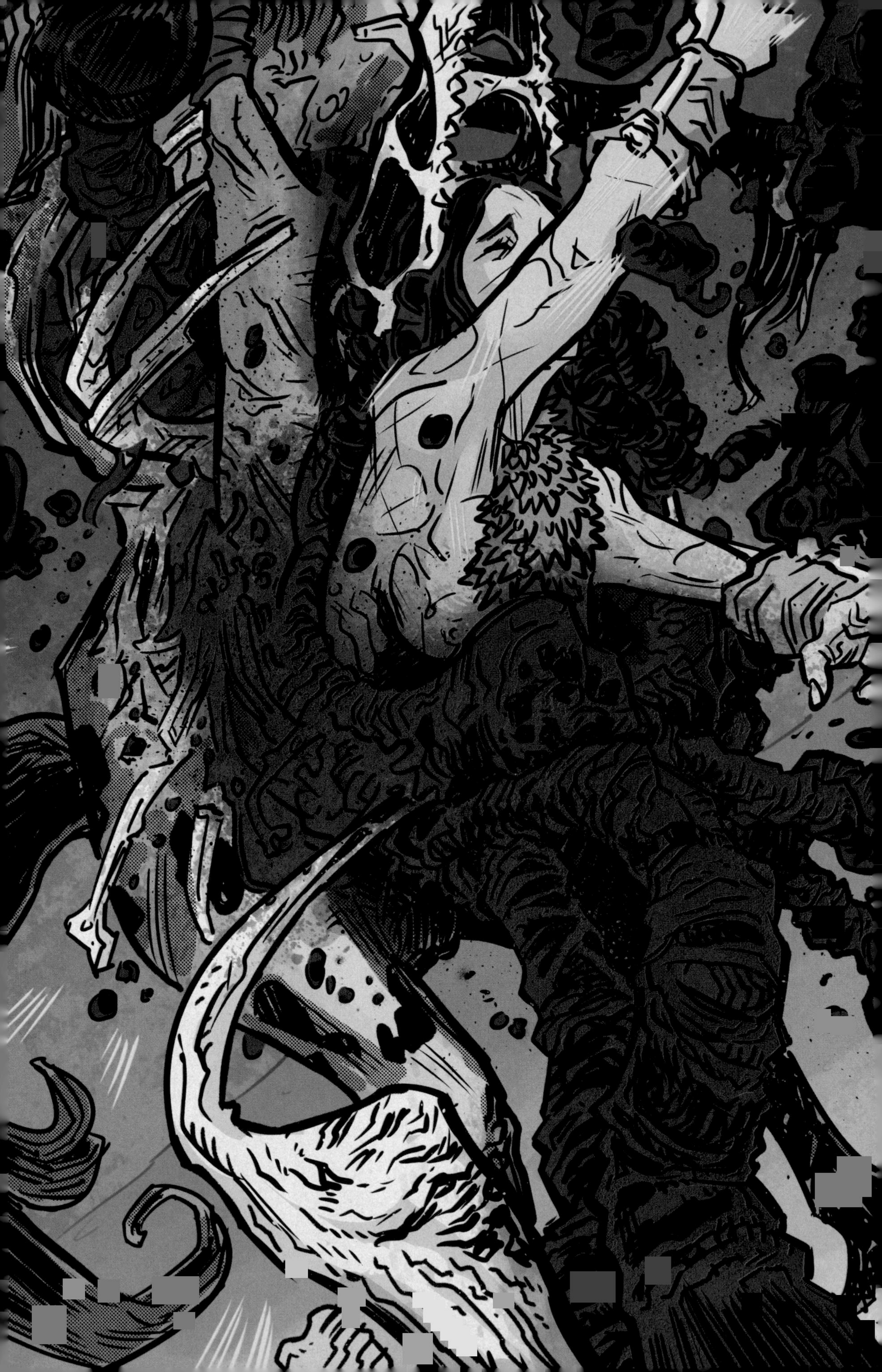

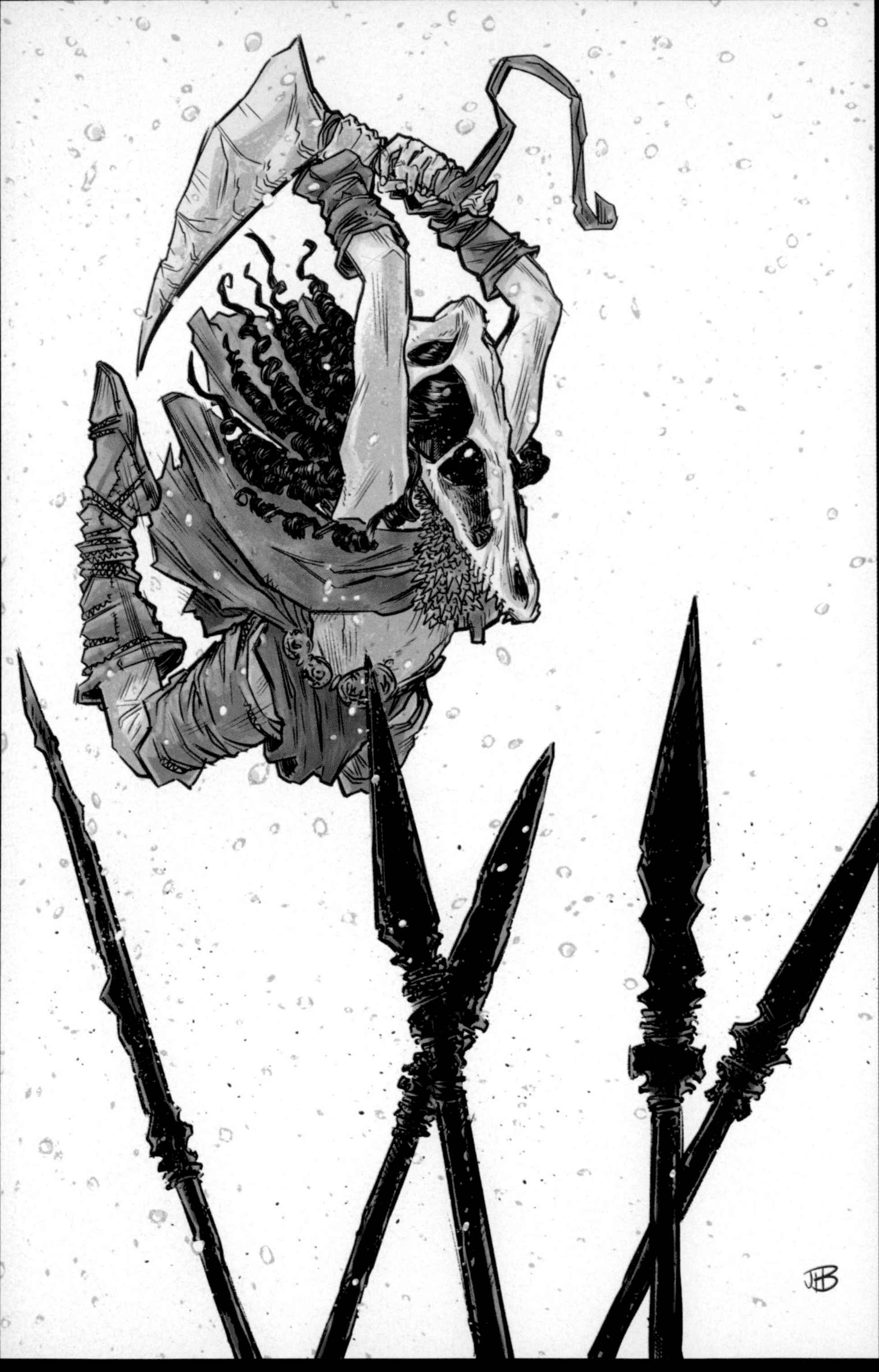

CHAPTER THREE

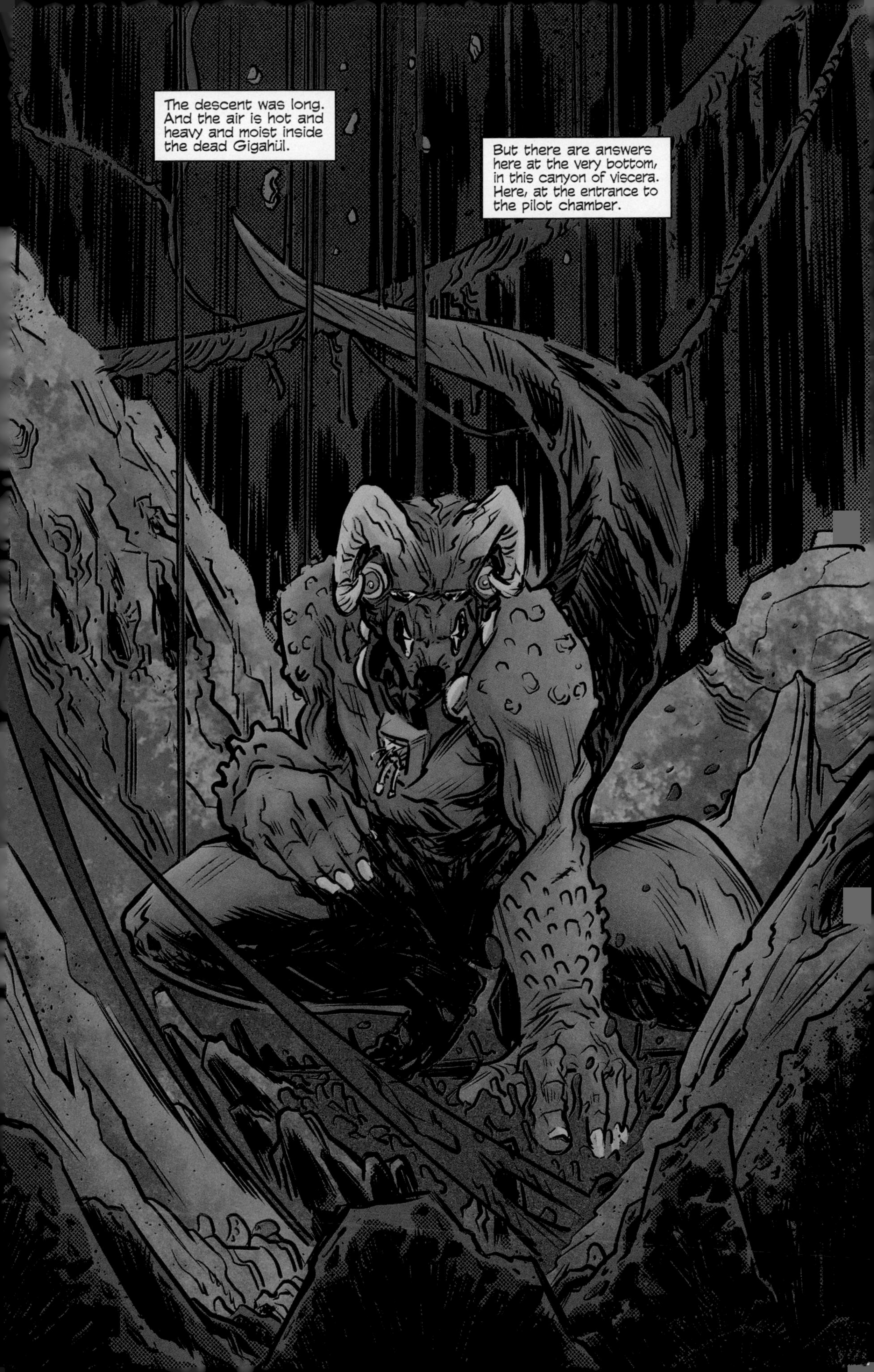
The descent was long. And the air is hot and heavy and moist inside the dead Gigahül.
But there are answers here at the very bottom, in this canyon of viscera. Here, at the entrance to the pilot chamber.

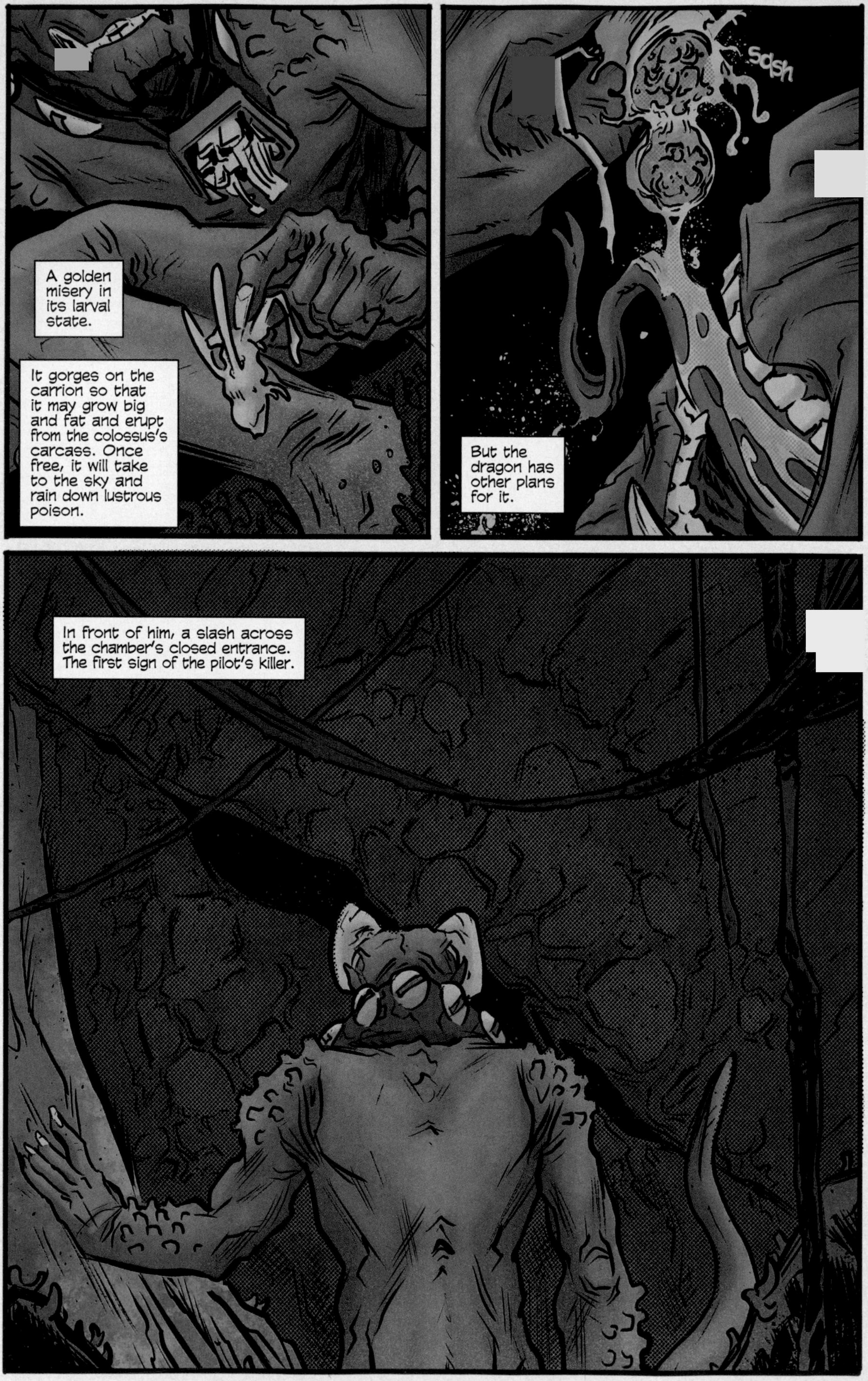

A golden misery in its larval state.
It gorges on the carrion so that it may grow big and fat and erupt from the colossus's carcass. Once free, it will take to the sky and rain down lustrous poison.
Sqsh
But the dragon has other plans for it.
In front of him, a slash across the chamber's closed entrance. The first sign of the pilot's killer.

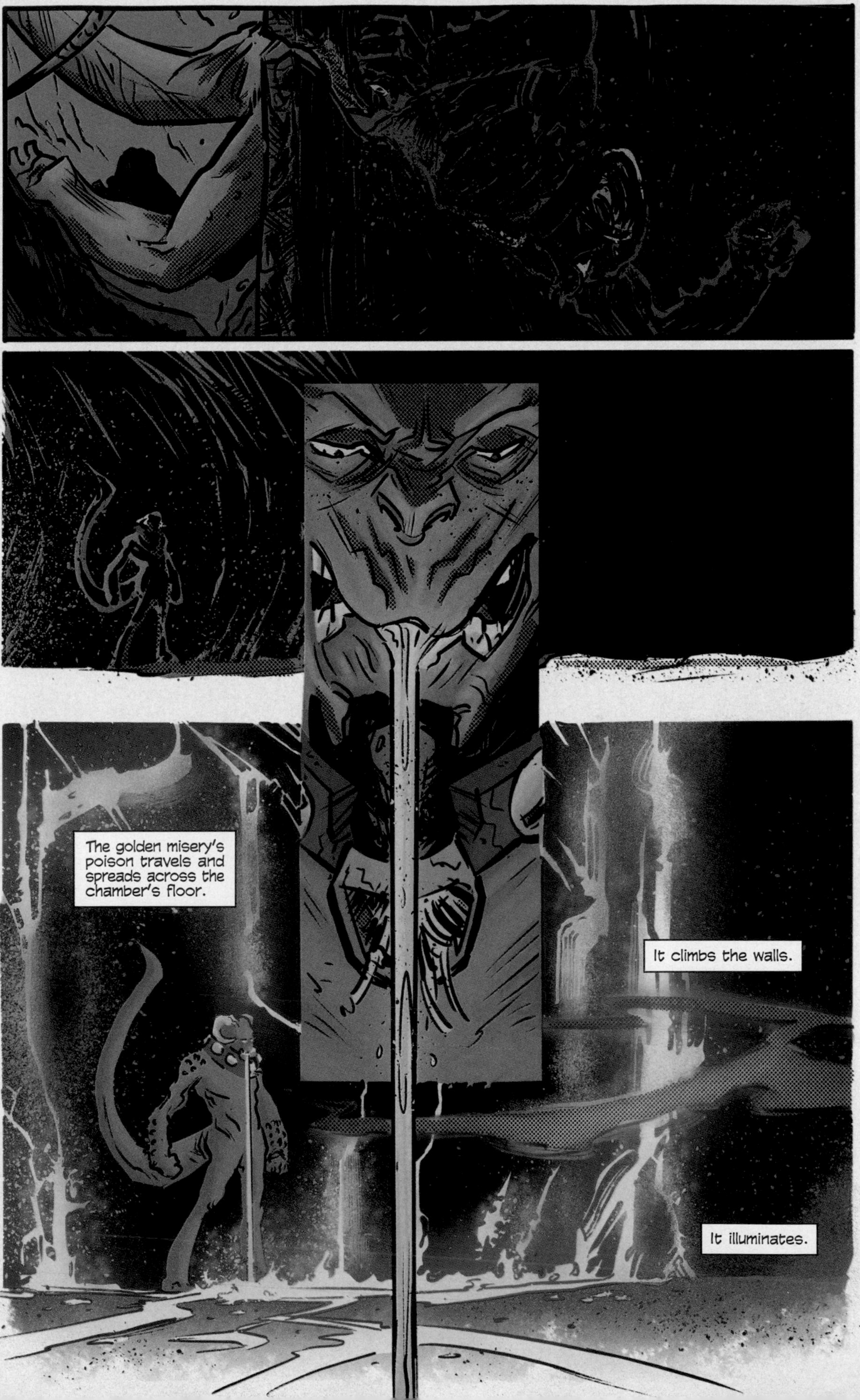
The golden misery's poison travels and spreads across the chamber's floor.
It climbs the walls.
It illuminates.

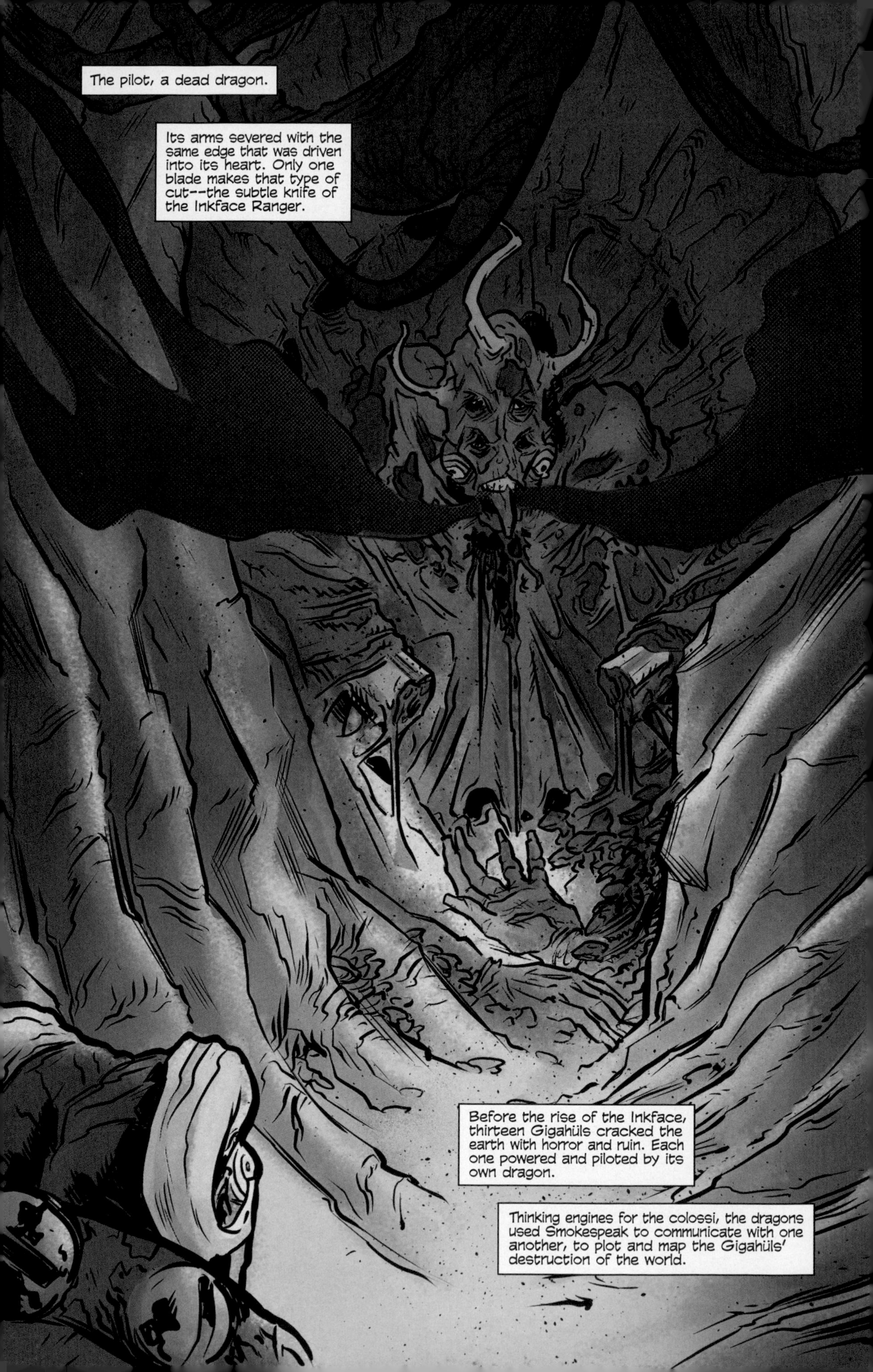

The pilot, a dead dragon.
Its arms severed with the same edge that was driven into its heart. Only one blade makes that type of cut--the subtle knife of the Inkface Ranger.
Before the rise of the Inkface, thirteen Gigahüls cracked the earth with horror and ruin. Each one powered and piloted by its own dragon.
Thinking engines for the colossi, the dragons used Smokespeak to communicate with one another, to plot and map the Gigahüls' destruction of the world.

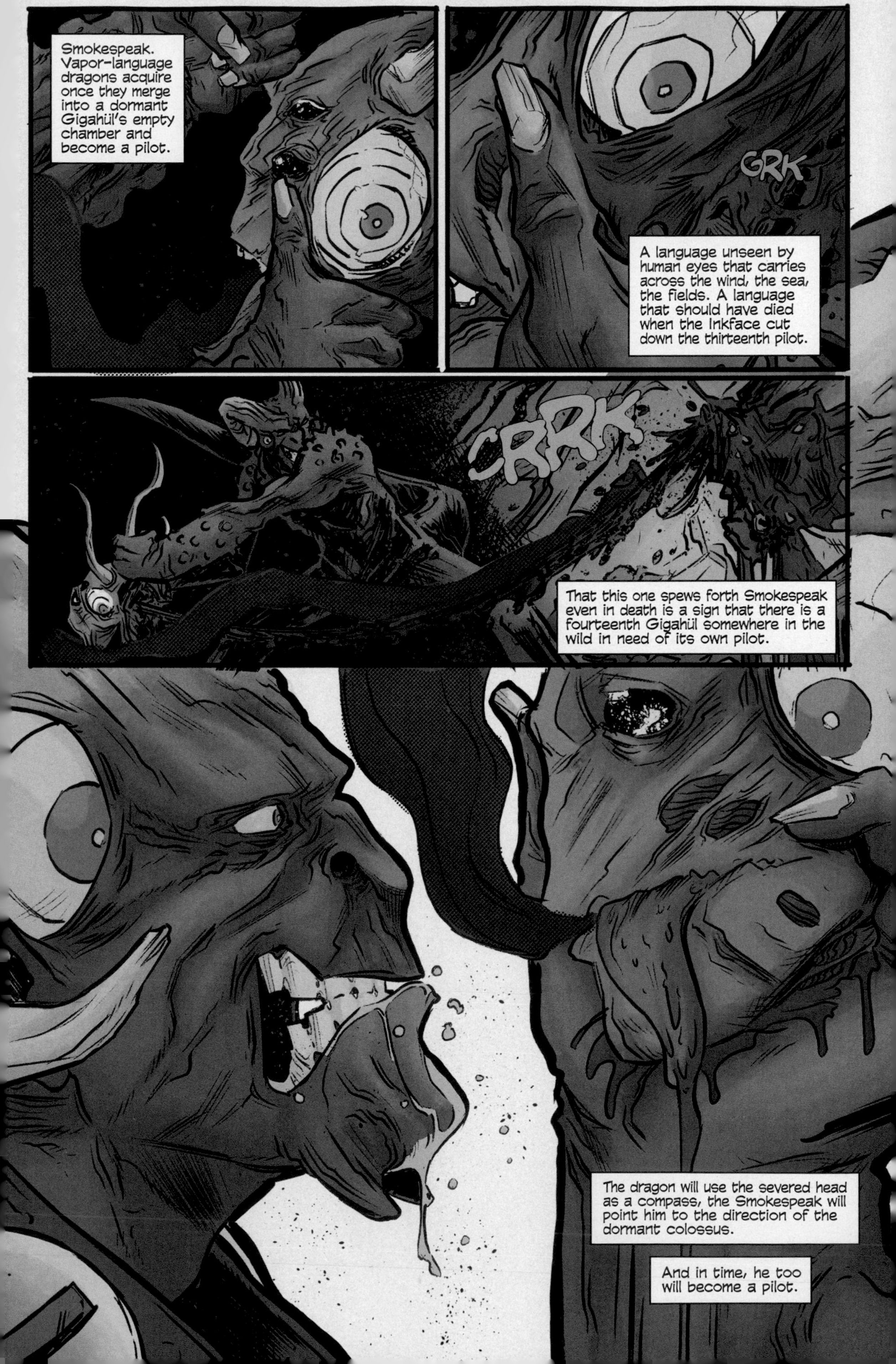
Smokespeak. Vapor-language dragons acquire once they merge into a dormant Gigahül's empty chamber and become a pilot.
GRK
A language unseen by human eyes that carries across the wind, the sea, the fields. A language that should have died when the Inkface cut down the thirteenth pilot.
CRRK
That this one spews forth Smokespeak even in death is a sign that there is a fourteenth Gigahül somewhere in the wild in need of its own pilot.
The dragon will use the severed head as a compass, the Smokespeak will point him to the direction of the dormant colossus.
And in time, he too will become a pilot.

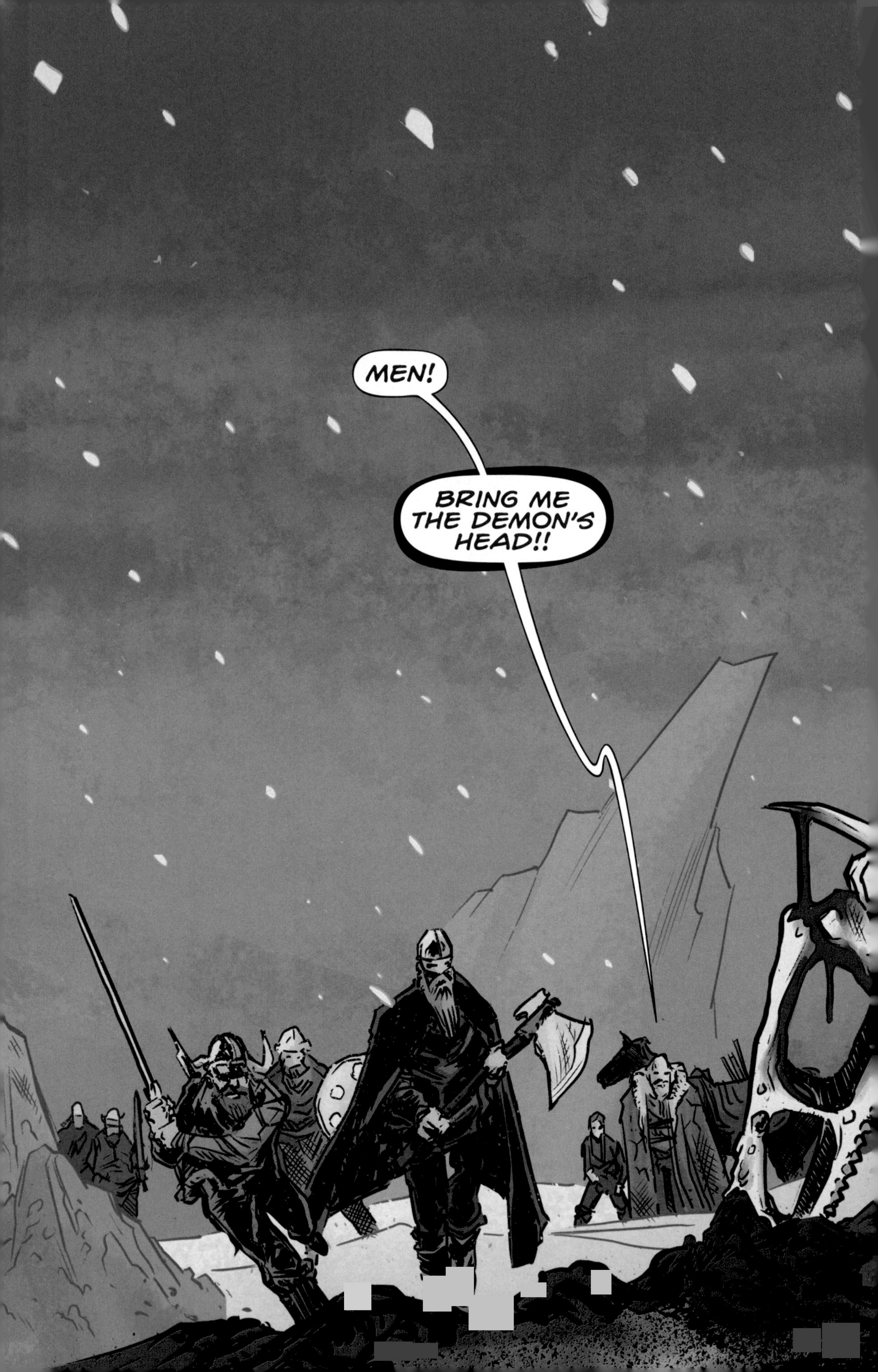
MEN!
BRING ME THE DEMON'S HEAD!!

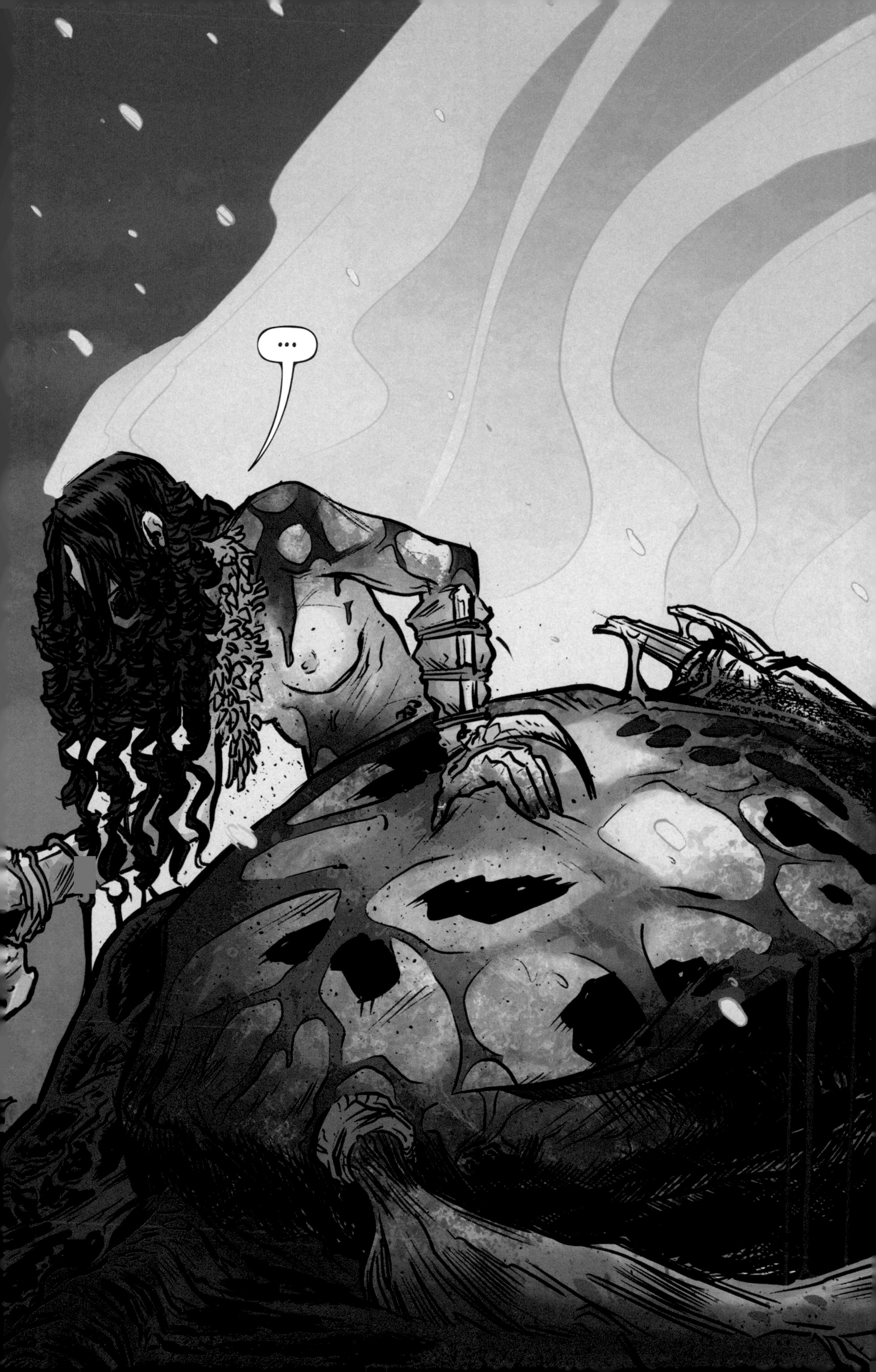
...

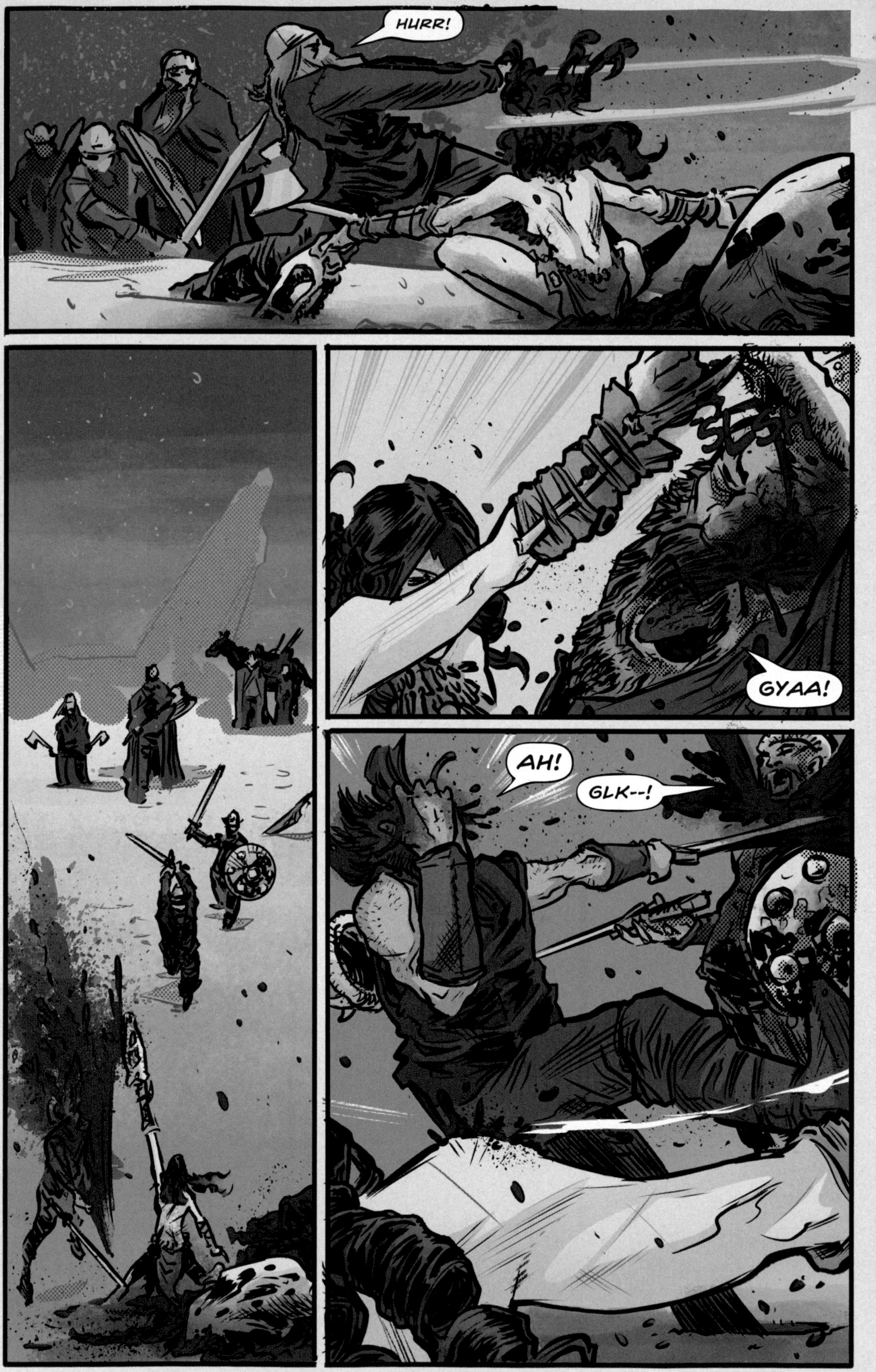
HURR!
SESH
GYAA!
AH!
GLK--!

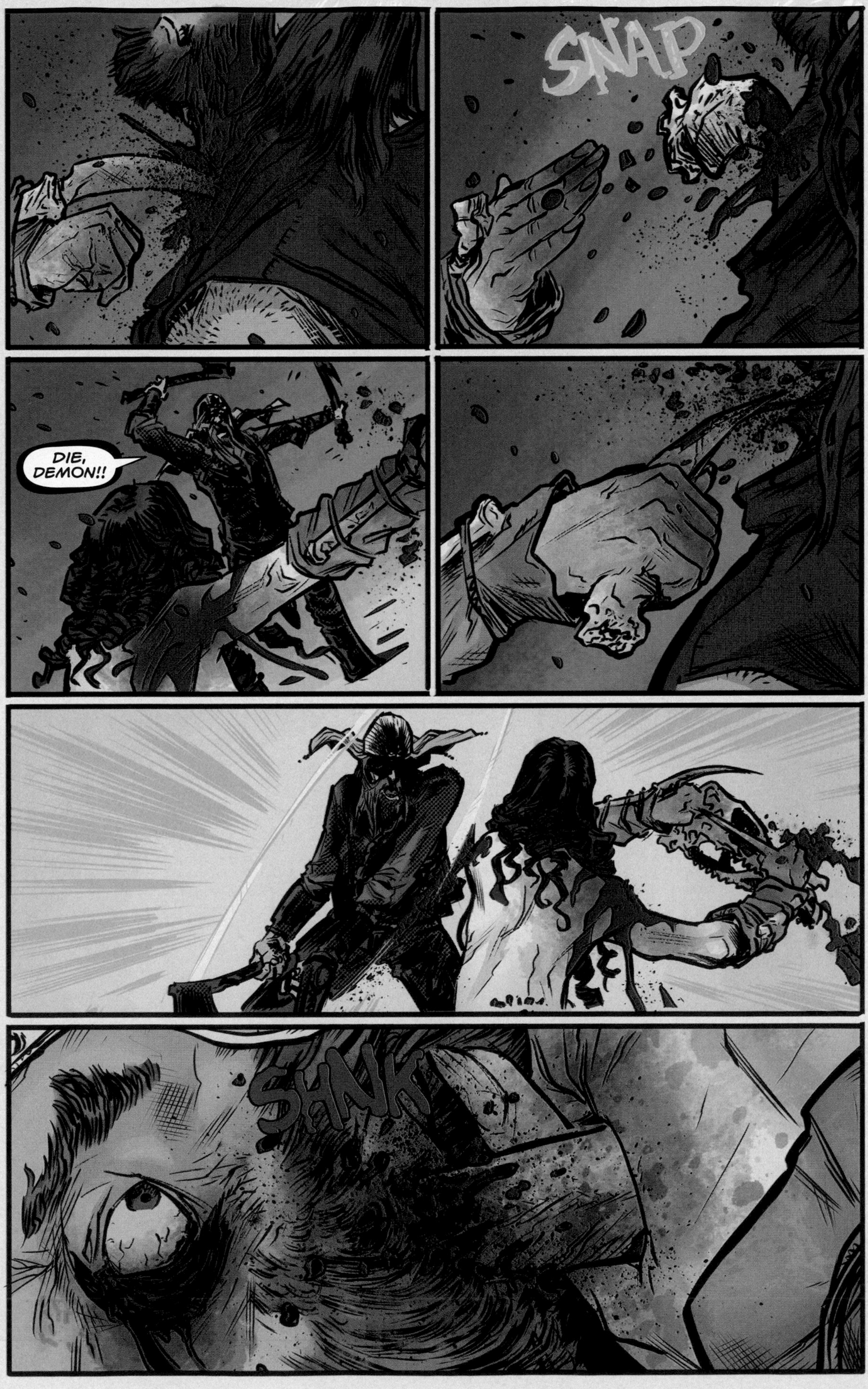
SNAP
DIE, DEMON!!
SHNK

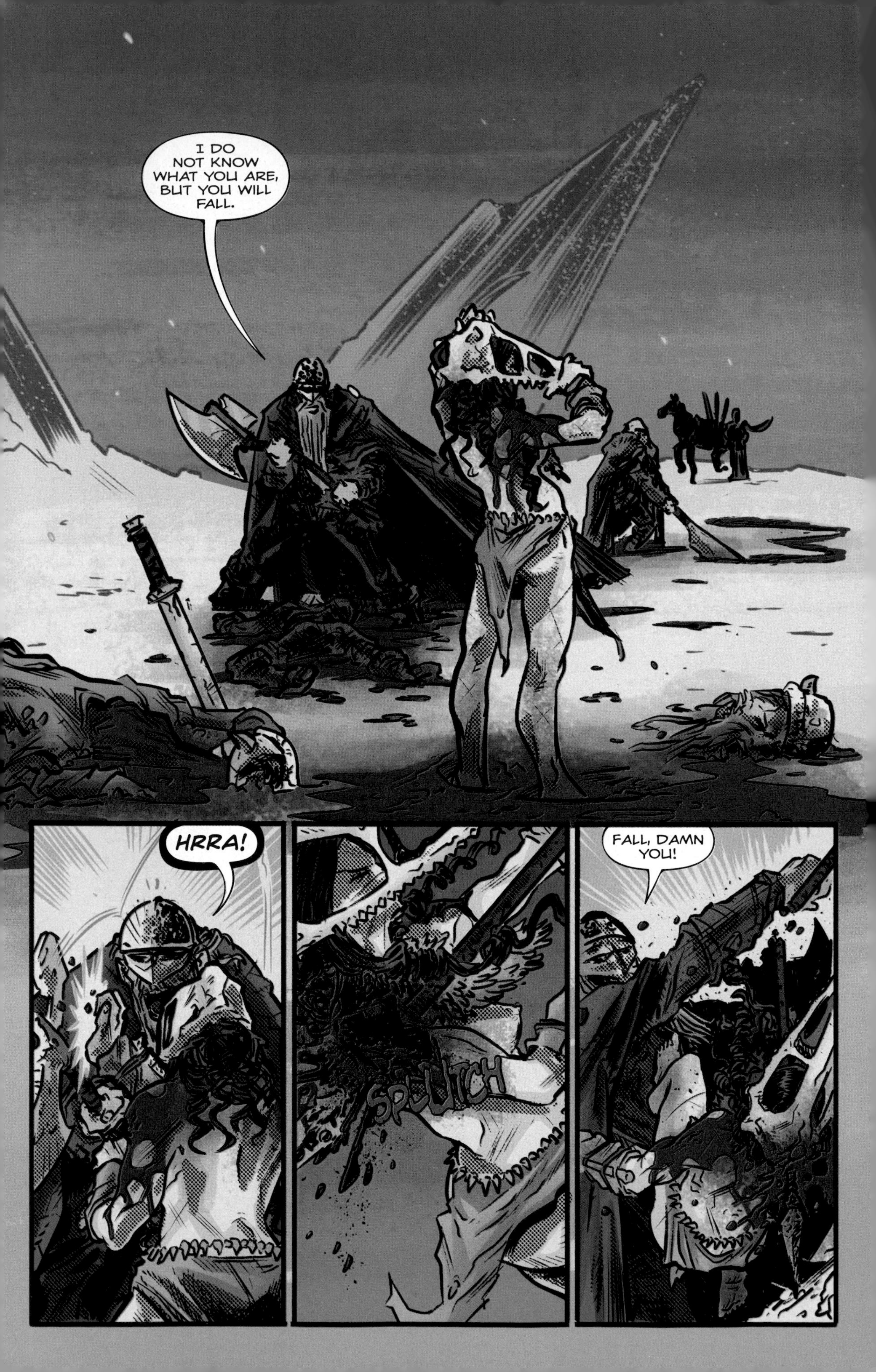
I DO NOT KNOW WHAT YOU ARE, BUT YOU WILL FALL.
HRRA!
SPLUTCH
FALL, DAMN YOU!

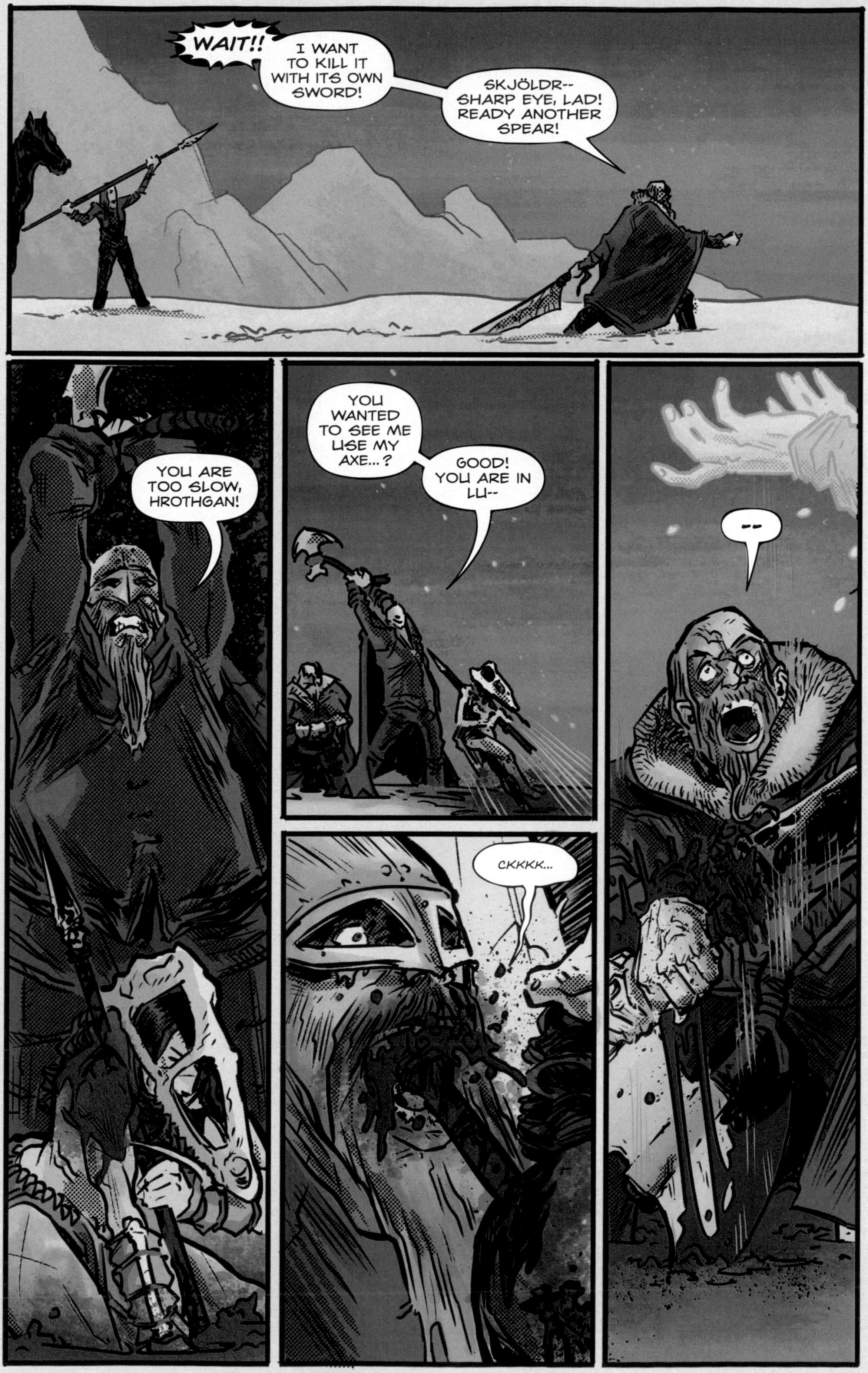
WAIT!!
I WANT TO KILL IT WITH ITS OWN SWORD!
SKJÖLDR-- SHARP EYE, LAD! READY ANOTHER SPEAR!
YOU ARE TOO SLOW, HROTHGAN!
YOU WANTED TO SEE ME USE MY AXE...?
GOOD! YOU ARE IN LU--
CKKKK...
--

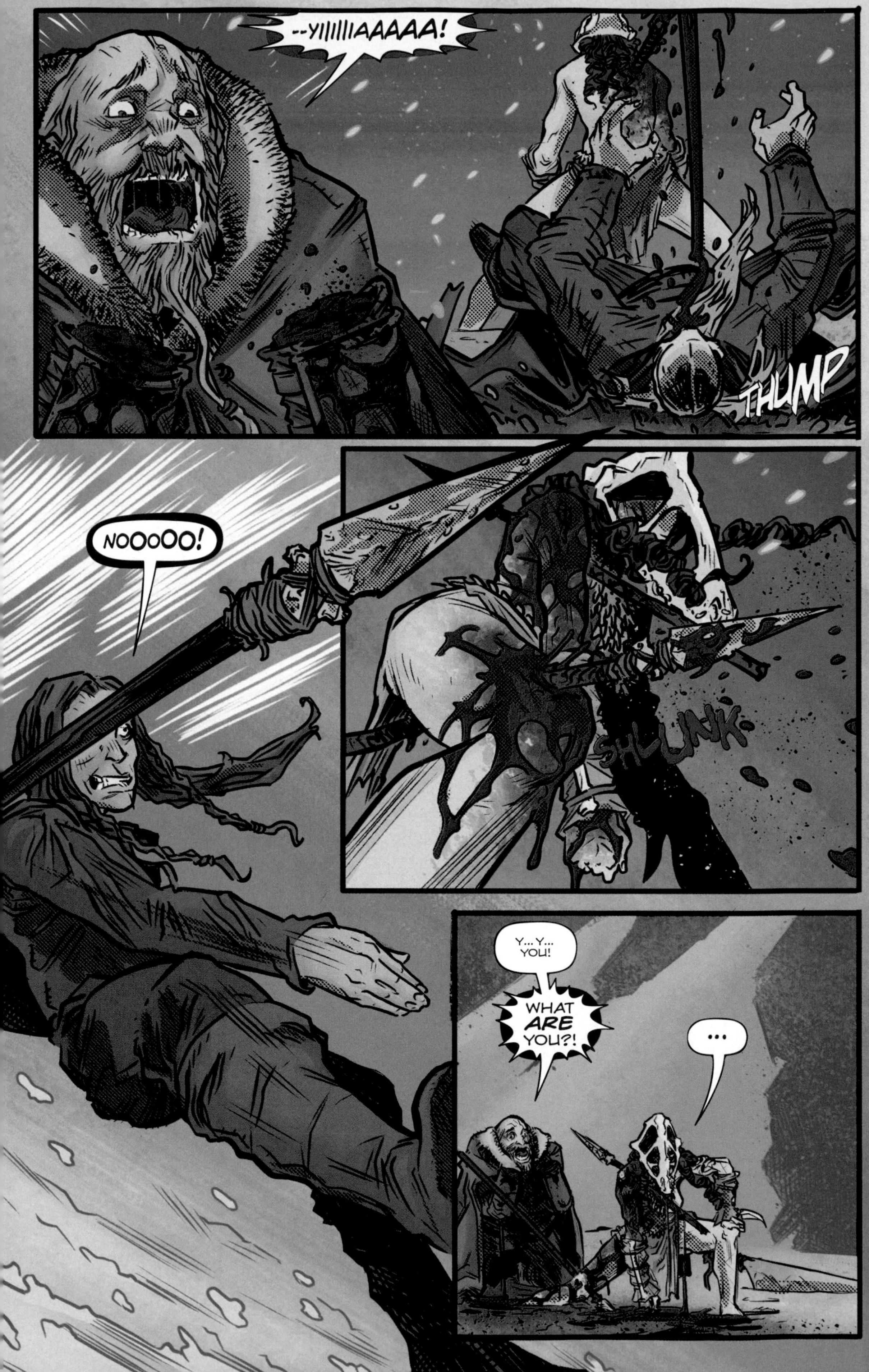
--YIIIIIIAAAAA!
THUMP
NOOOOO!
SHLUNK
Y... Y... YOU!
WHAT ARE YOU?!
...

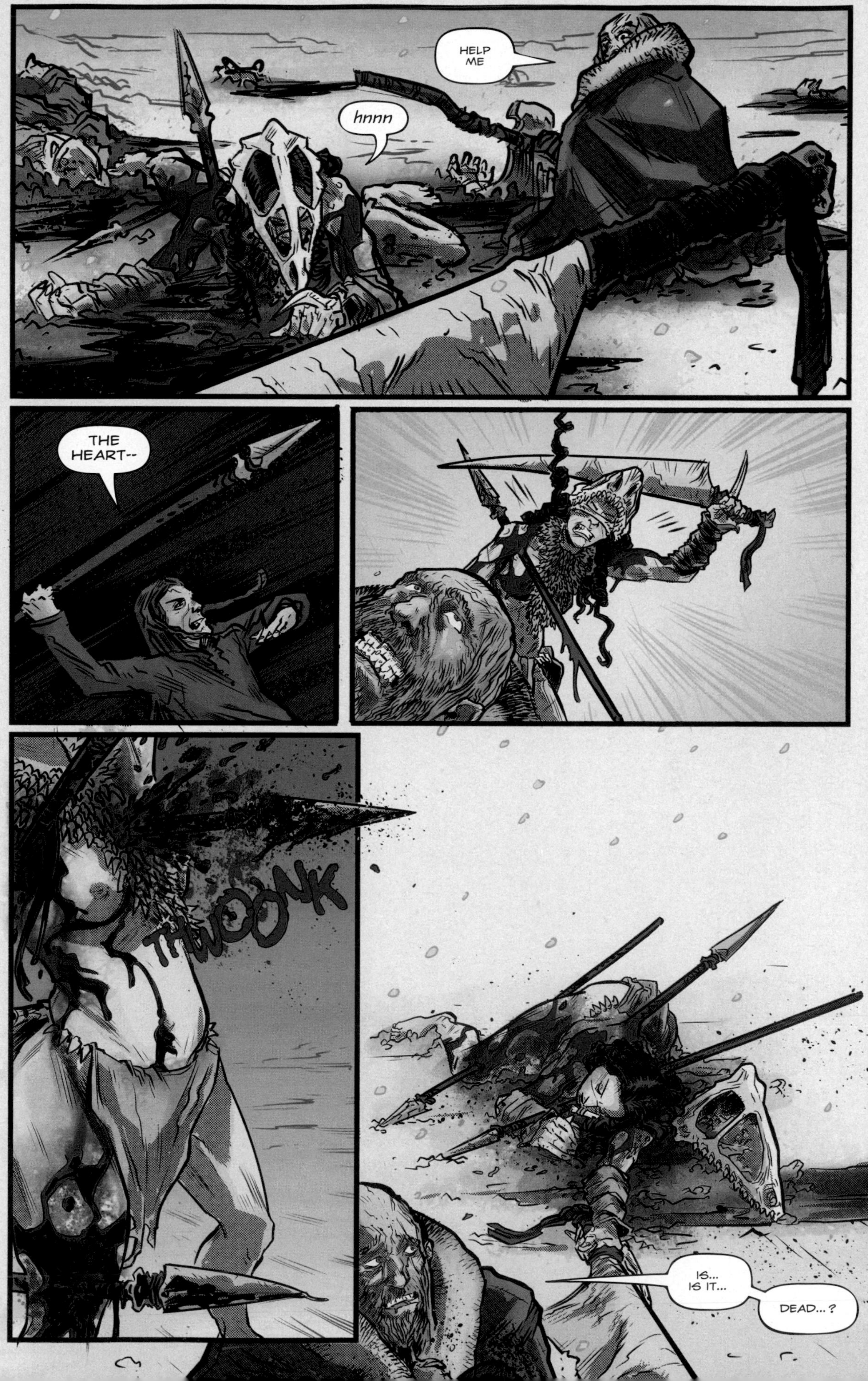
hnnn
HELP ME
THE HEART--
THWOONK
IS... IS IT...
DEAD...?

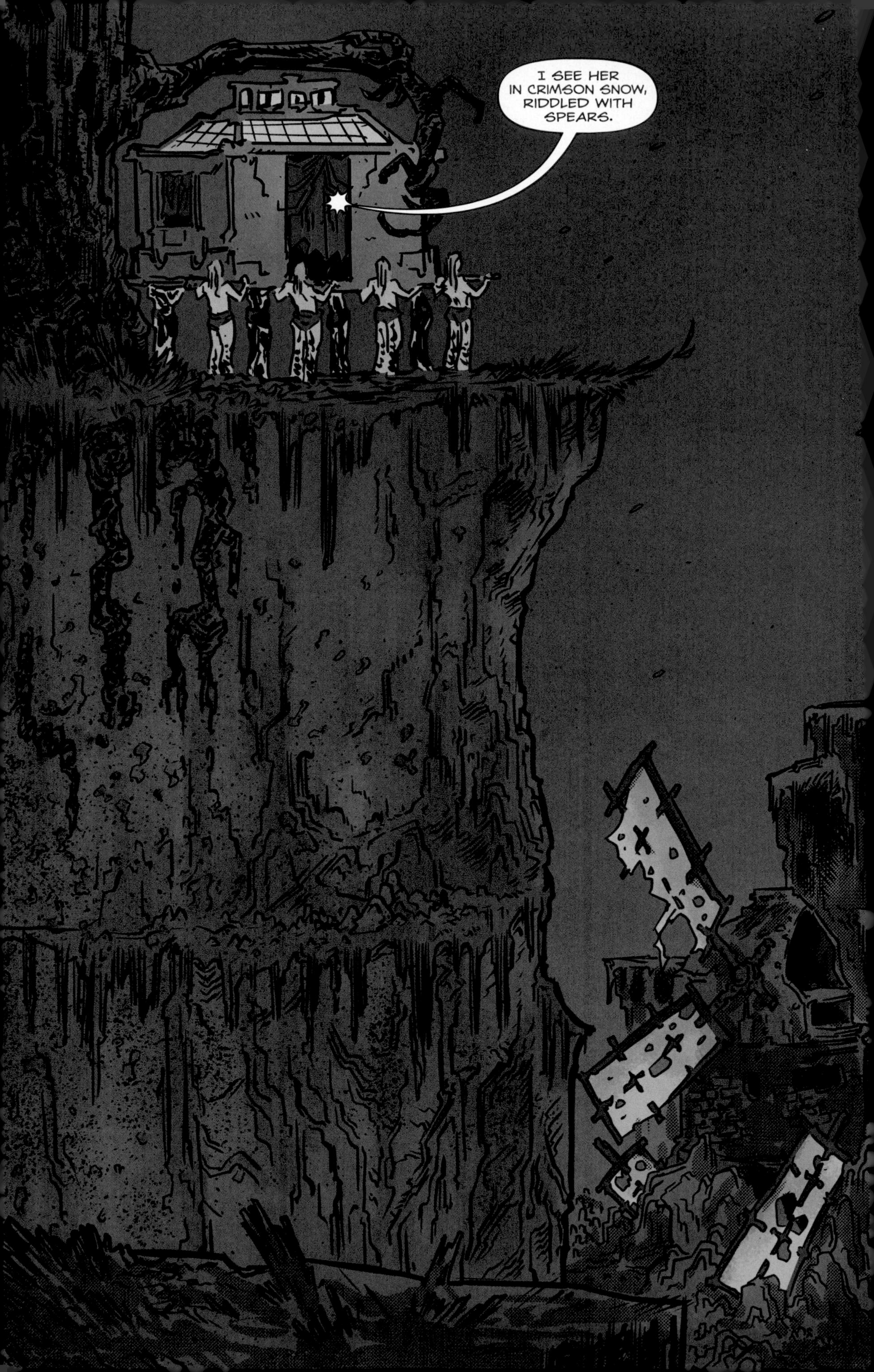
I SEE HER IN CRIMSON SNOW, RIDDLED WITH SPEARS.

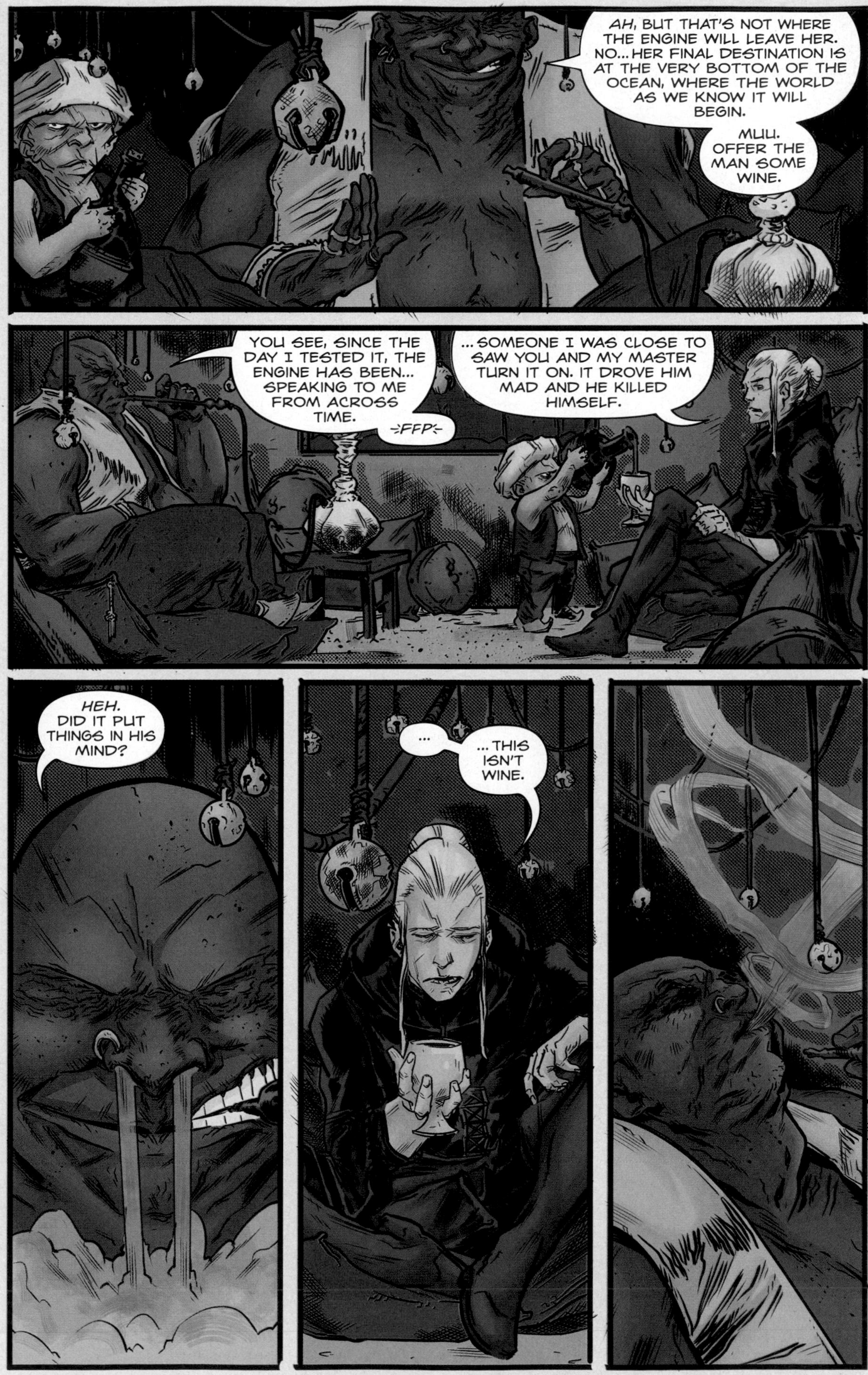
AH, BUT THAT'S NOT WHERE THE ENGINE WILL LEAVE HER. NO... HER FINAL DESTINATION IS AT THE VERY BOTTOM OF THE OCEAN, WHERE THE WORLD AS WE KNOW IT WILL BEGIN.
MUU. OFFER THE MAN SOME WINE.
YOU SEE, SINCE THE DAY I TESTED IT, THE ENGINE HAS BEEN... SPEAKING TO ME FROM ACROSS TIME.
FFP
...SOMEONE I WAS CLOSE TO SAW YOU AND MY MASTER TURN IT ON. IT DROVE HIM MAD AND HE KILLED HIMSELF.
HEH. DID IT PUT THINGS IN HIS MIND?
...
...THIS ISN'T WINE.

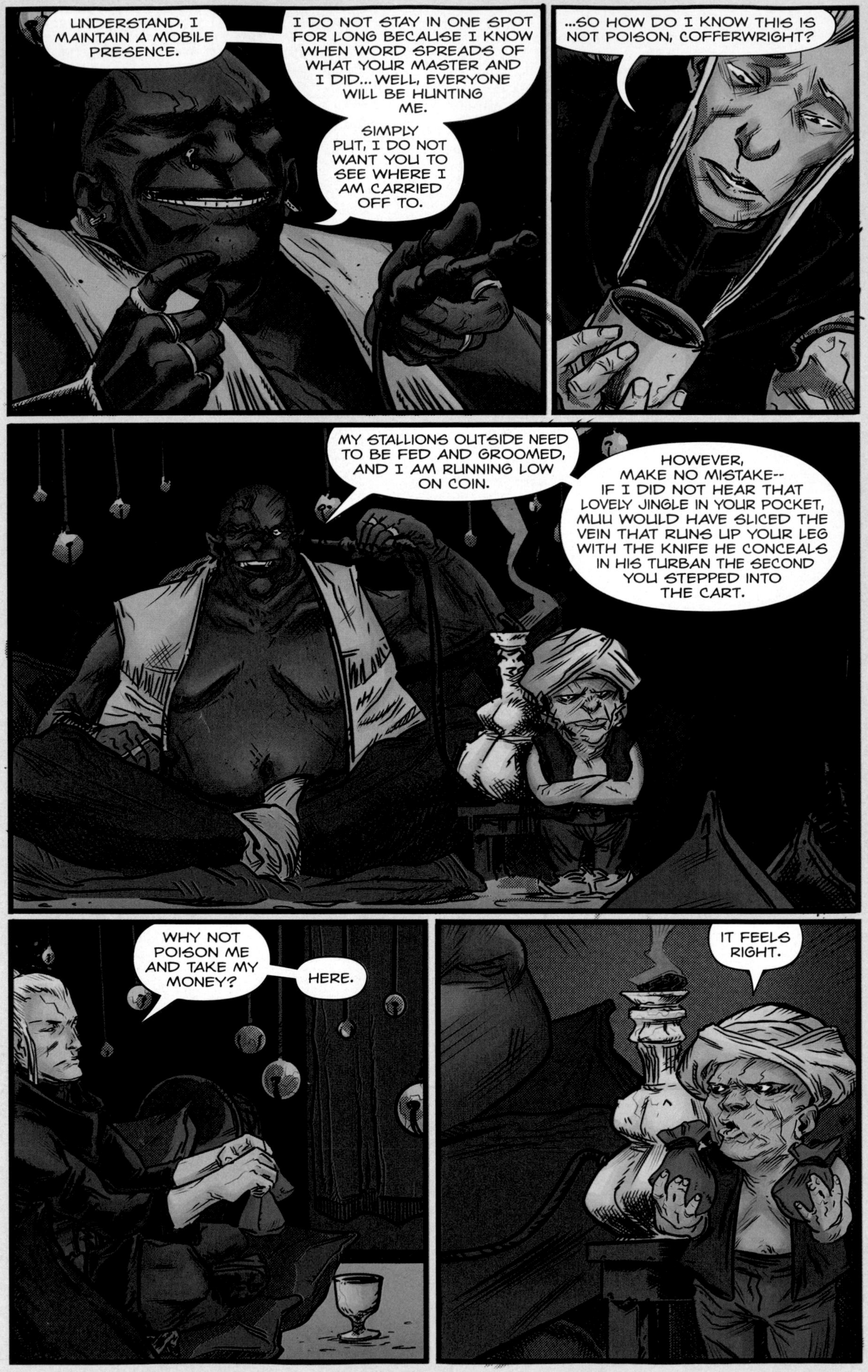
UNDERSTAND, I MAINTAIN A MOBILE PRESENCE.
I DO NOT STAY IN ONE SPOT FOR LONG BECAUSE I KNOW WHEN WORD SPREADS OF WHAT YOUR MASTER AND I DID... WELL, EVERYONE WILL BE HUNTING ME.
SIMPLY PUT, I DO NOT WANT YOU TO SEE WHERE I AM CARRIED OFF TO.
...SO HOW DO I KNOW THIS IS NOT POISON, COFFERWRIGHT?
MY STALLIONS OUTSIDE NEED TO BE FED AND GROOMED, AND I AM RUNNING LOW ON COIN.
HOWEVER, MAKE NO MISTAKE-- IF I DID NOT HEAR THAT LOVELY JINGLE IN YOUR POCKET, MUU WOULD HAVE SLICED THE VEIN THAT RUNS UP YOUR LEG WITH THE KNIFE HE CONCEALS IN HIS TURBAN THE SECOND YOU STEPPED INTO THE CART.
WHY NOT POISON ME AND TAKE MY MONEY?
HERE.
IT FEELS RIGHT.

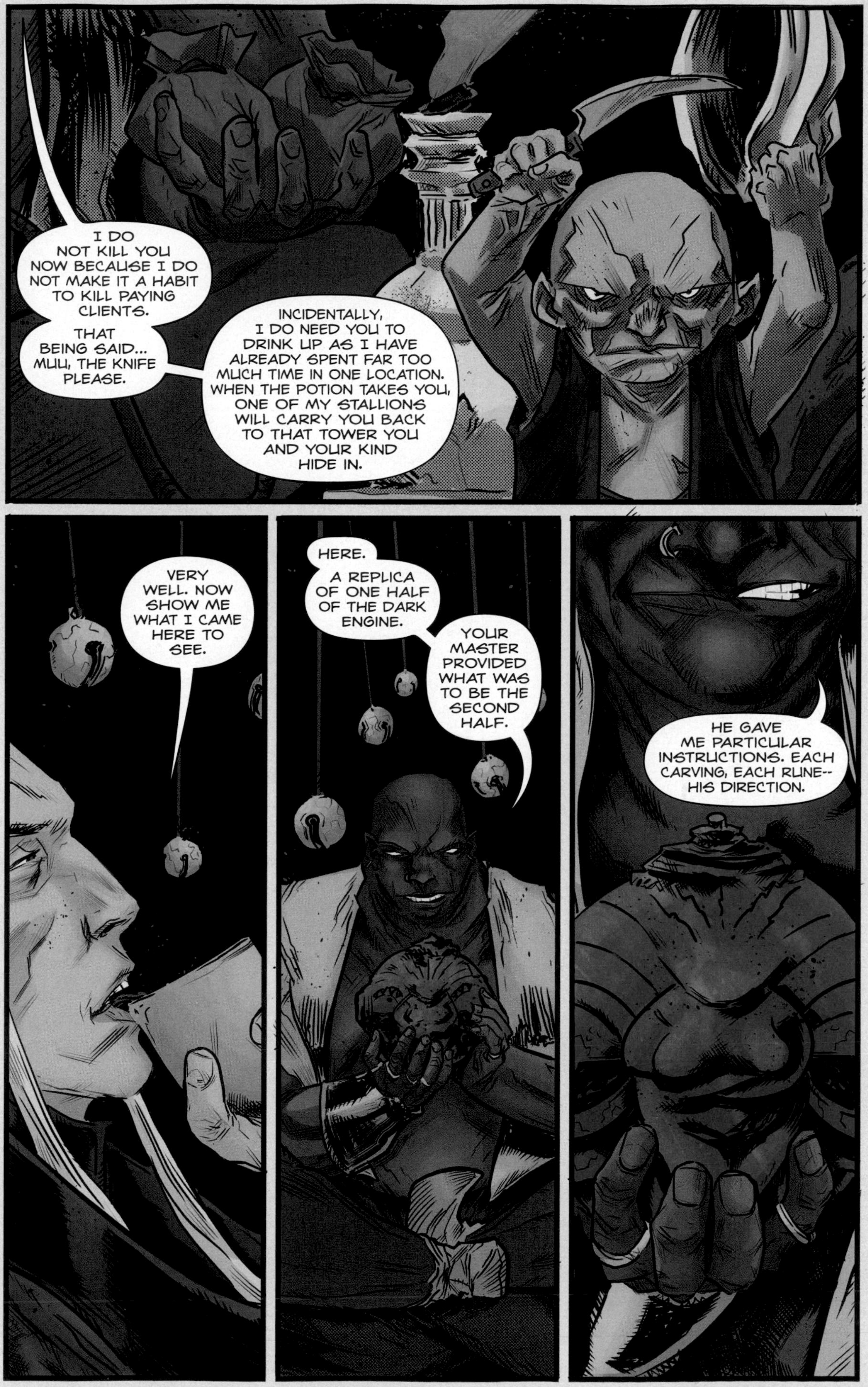
I DO NOT KILL YOU NOW BECAUSE I DO NOT MAKE IT A HABIT TO KILL PAYING CLIENTS.
THAT BEING SAID... MUU, THE KNIFE PLEASE.
INCIDENTALLY, I DO NEED YOU TO DRINK UP AS I HAVE ALREADY SPENT FAR TOO MUCH TIME IN ONE LOCATION. WHEN THE POTION TAKES YOU, ONE OF MY STALLIONS WILL CARRY YOU BACK TO THAT TOWER YOU AND YOUR KIND HIDE IN.
VERY WELL. NOW SHOW ME WHAT I CAME HERE TO SEE.
HERE.
A REPLICA OF ONE HALF OF THE DARK ENGINE.
YOUR MASTER PROVIDED WHAT WAS TO BE THE SECOND HALF.
HE GAVE ME PARTICULAR INSTRUCTIONS. EACH CARVING, EACH RUNE-- HIS DIRECTION.

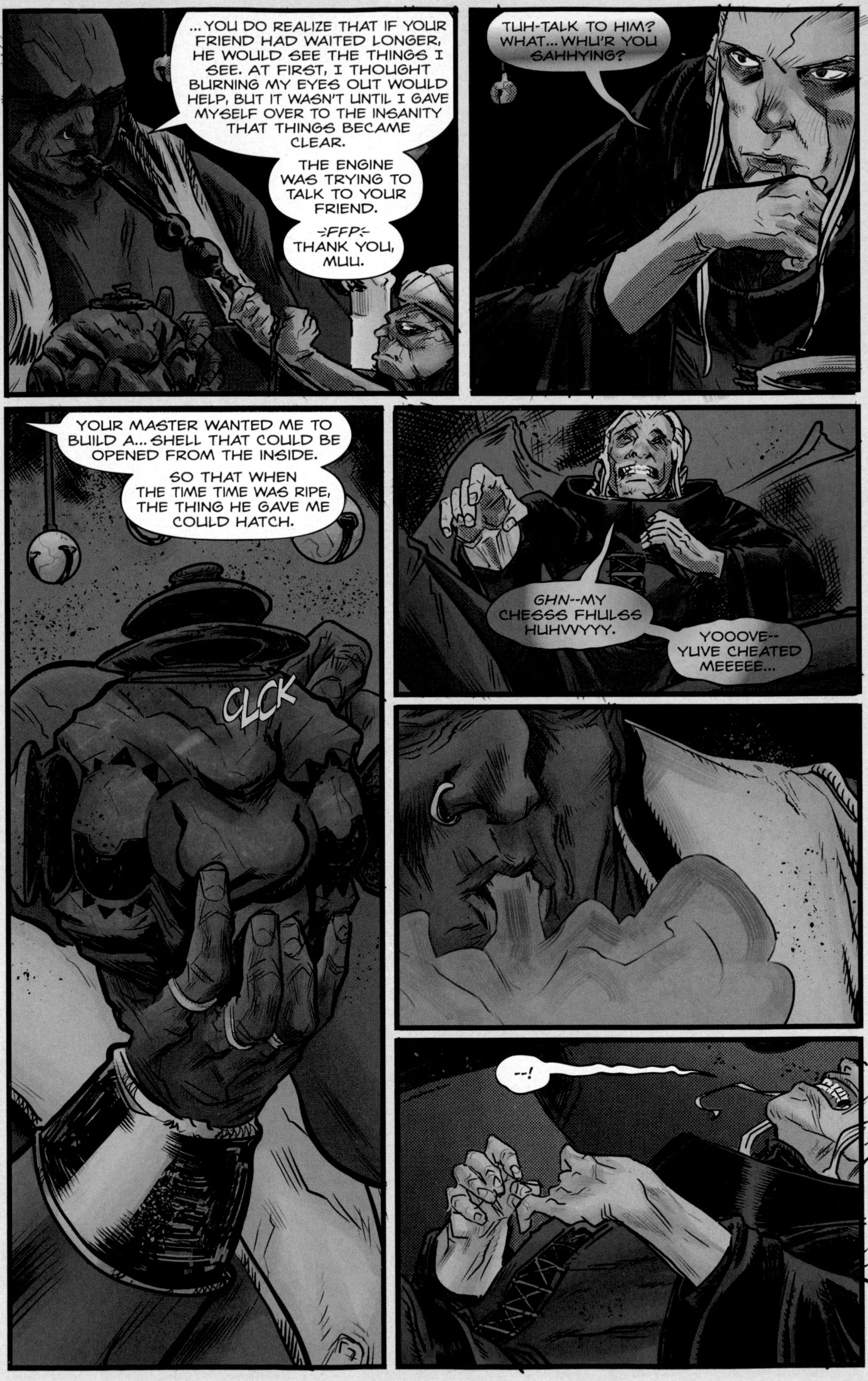
...YOU DO REALIZE THAT IF YOUR FRIEND HAD WAITED LONGER, HE WOULD SEE THE THINGS I SEE. AT FIRST, I THOUGHT BURNING MY EYES OUT WOULD HELP, BUT IT WASN'T UNTIL I GAVE MYSELF OVER TO THE INSANITY THAT THINGS BECAME CLEAR.
THE ENGINE WAS TRYING TO TALK TO YOUR FRIEND.
=FFP=
THANK YOU, MUU.
TUH-TALK TO HIM? WHAT... WHU'R YOU SAHHYING?
YOUR MASTER WANTED ME TO BUILD A... SHELL THAT COULD BE OPENED FROM THE INSIDE.
SO THAT WHEN THE TIME TIME WAS RIPE, THE THING HE GAVE ME COULD HATCH.
CLCK
GHN--MY CHESSS FHULSS HUHWYYY.
YOOOVE-- YUVE CHEATED MEEEEE...
--!

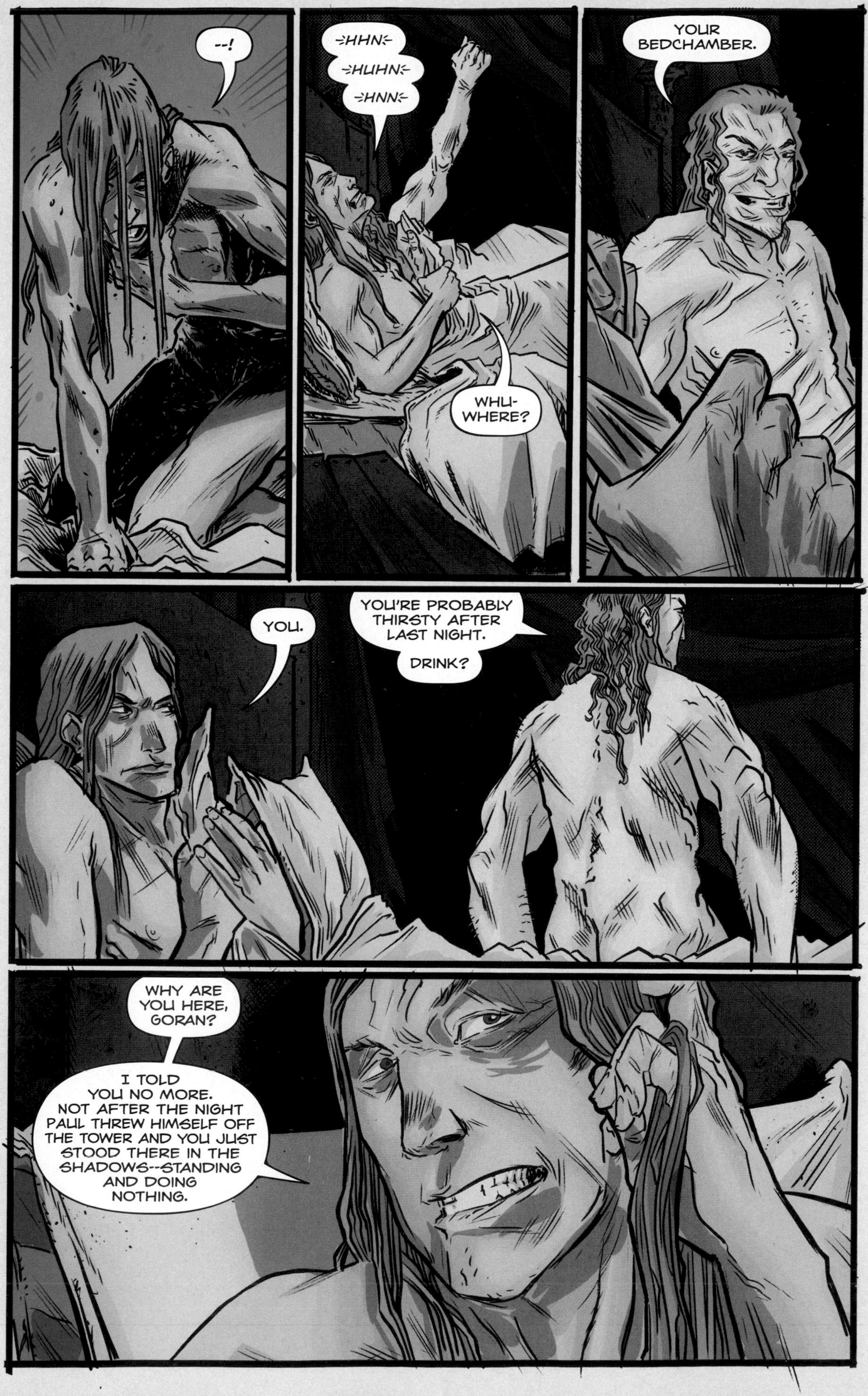
--!
-HHN-
-HUHN-
-HNN-
WHU-WHERE?
YOUR BEDCHAMBER.
YOU.
YOU'RE PROBABLY THIRSTY AFTER LAST NIGHT.
DRINK?
WHY ARE YOU HERE, GORAN?
I TOLD YOU NO MORE. NOT AFTER THE NIGHT PAUL THREW HIMSELF OFF THE TOWER AND YOU JUST STOOD THERE IN THE SHADOWS--STANDING AND DOING NOTHING.

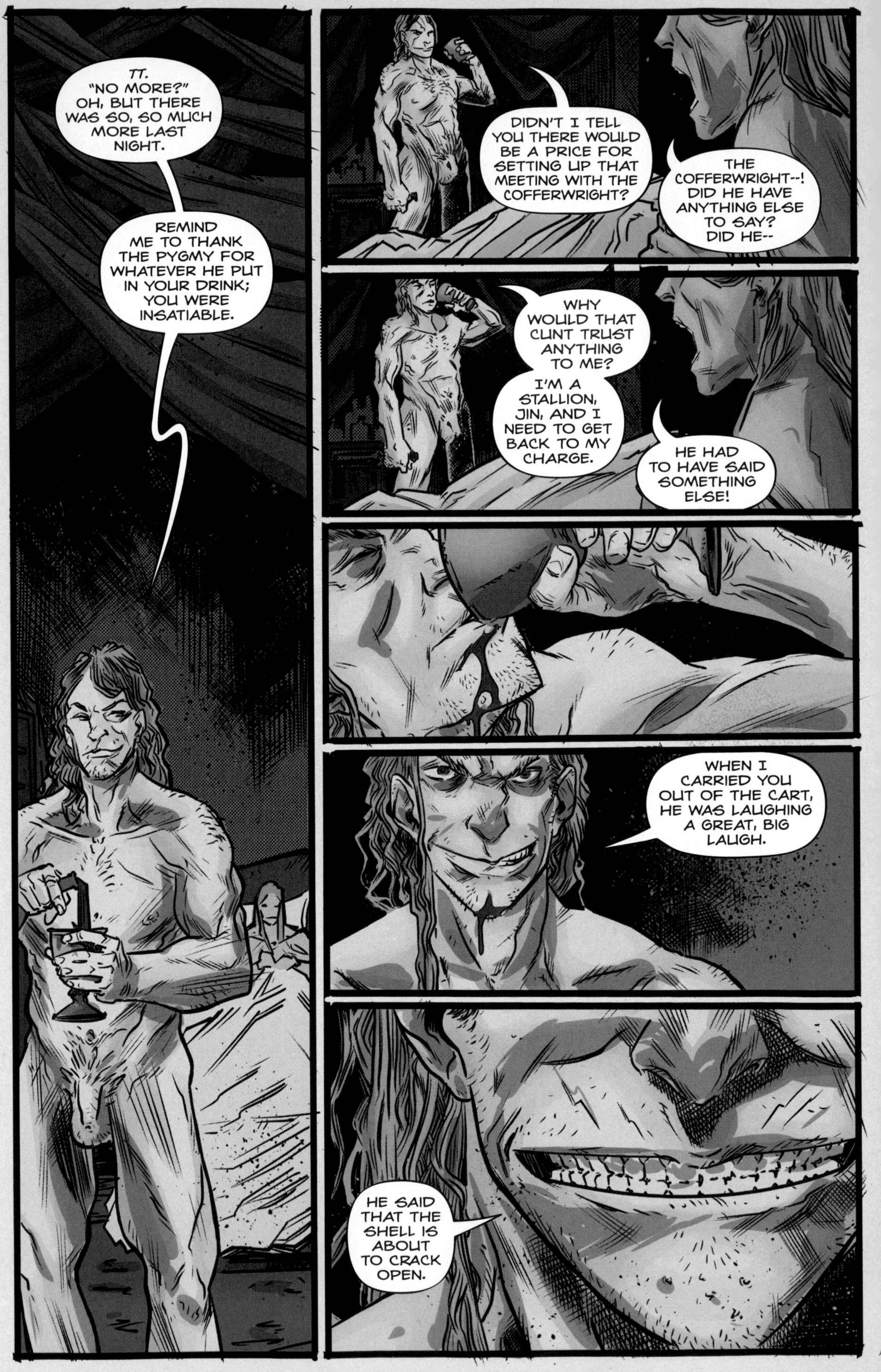
TT. "NO MORE?" OH, BUT THERE WAS SO, SO MUCH MORE LAST NIGHT.
REMIND ME TO THANK THE PYGMY FOR WHATEVER HE PUT IN YOUR DRINK; YOU WERE INSATIABLE.
DIDN'T I TELL YOU THERE WOULD BE A PRICE FOR SETTING UP THAT MEETING WITH THE COFFERWRIGHT?
THE COFFERWRIGHT--! DID HE HAVE ANYTHING ELSE TO SAY? DID HE--
WHY WOULD THAT CUNT TRUST ANYTHING TO ME?
I'M A STALLION, JIN, AND I NEED TO GET BACK TO MY CHARGE.
HE HAD TO HAVE SAID SOMETHING ELSE!
WHEN I CARRIED YOU OUT OF THE CART, HE WAS LAUGHING A GREAT, BIG LAUGH.
HE SAID THAT THE SHELL IS ABOUT TO CRACK OPEN.

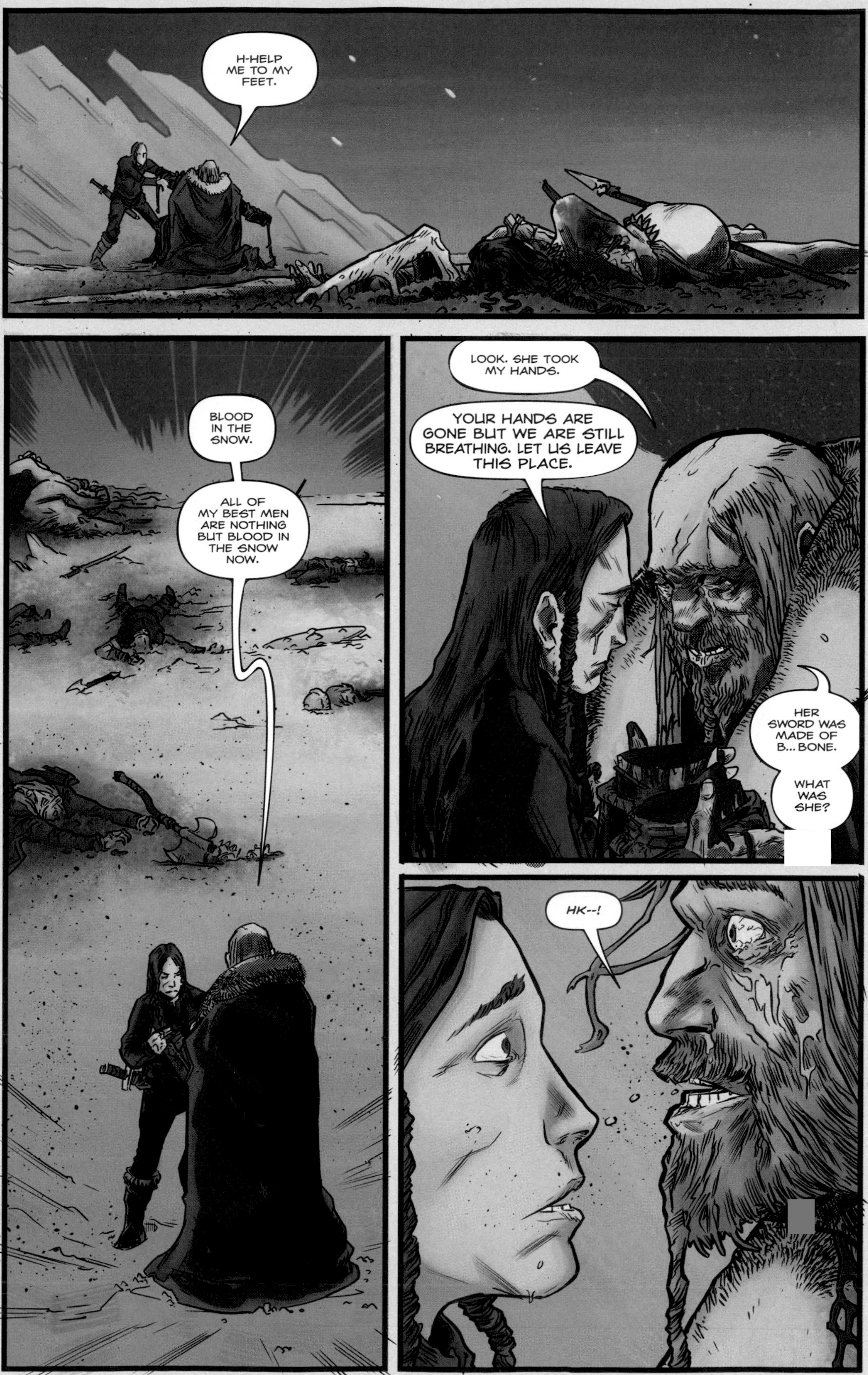
H-HELP ME TO MY FEET.
BLOOD IN THE SNOW.
ALL OF MY BEST MEN ARE NOTHING BUT BLOOD IN THE SNOW NOW.
LOOK. SHE TOOK MY HANDS.
YOUR HANDS ARE GONE BUT WE ARE STILL BREATHING. LET US LEAVE THIS PLACE.
HER SWORD WAS MADE OF B... BONE.
WHAT WAS SHE?
HK--!

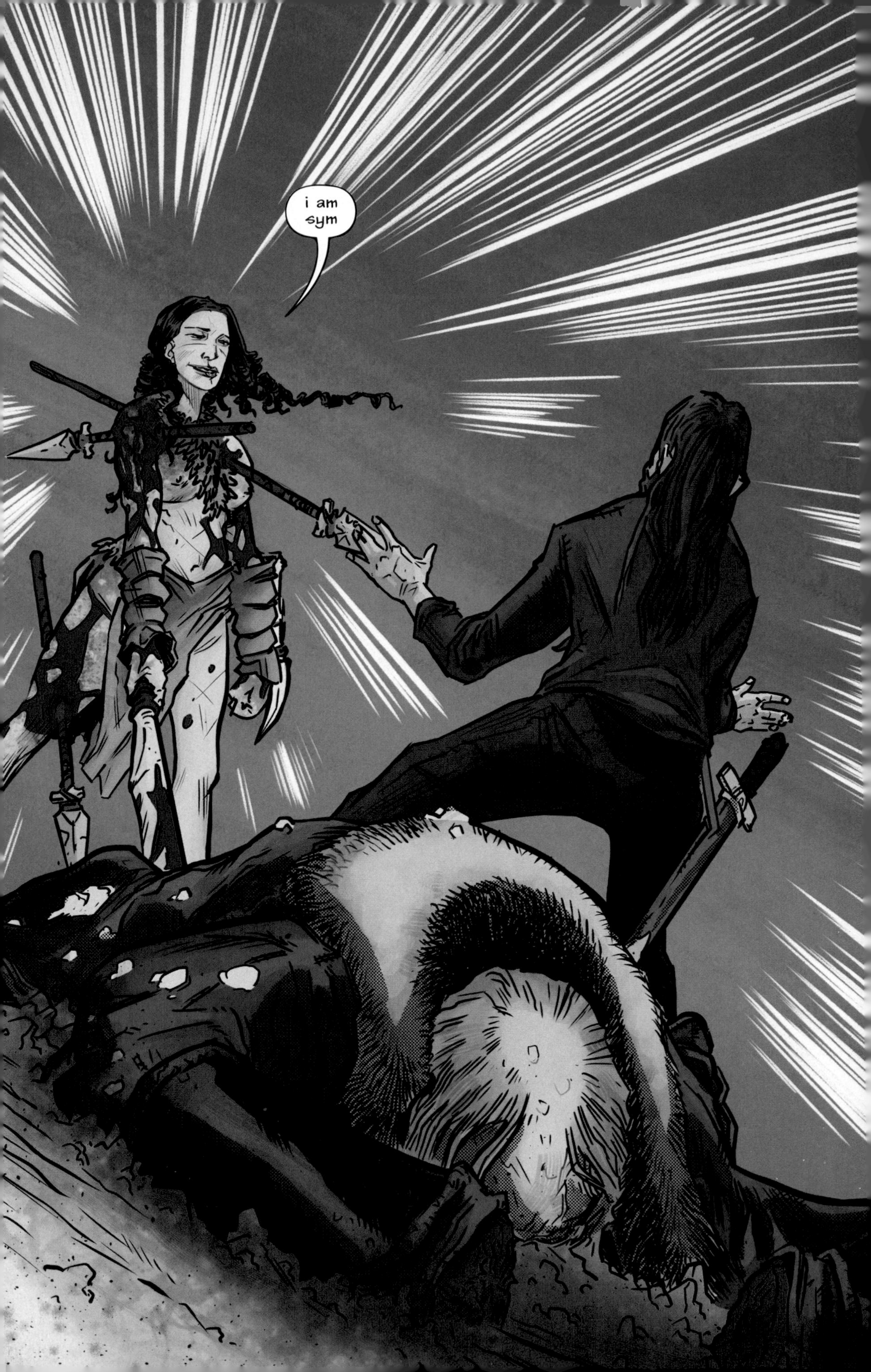
i am sym

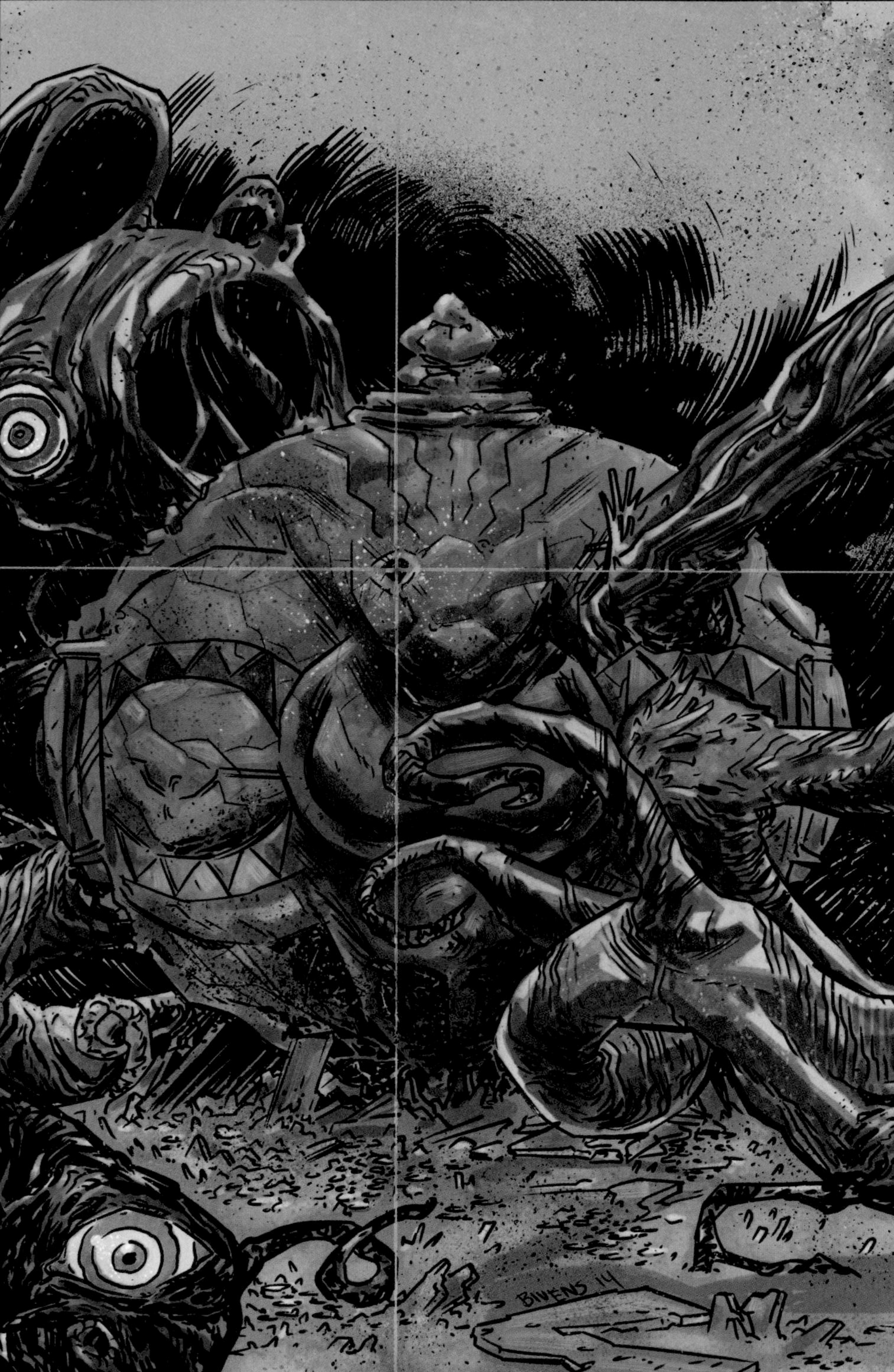
BIVENS '14

CHAPTER FOUR

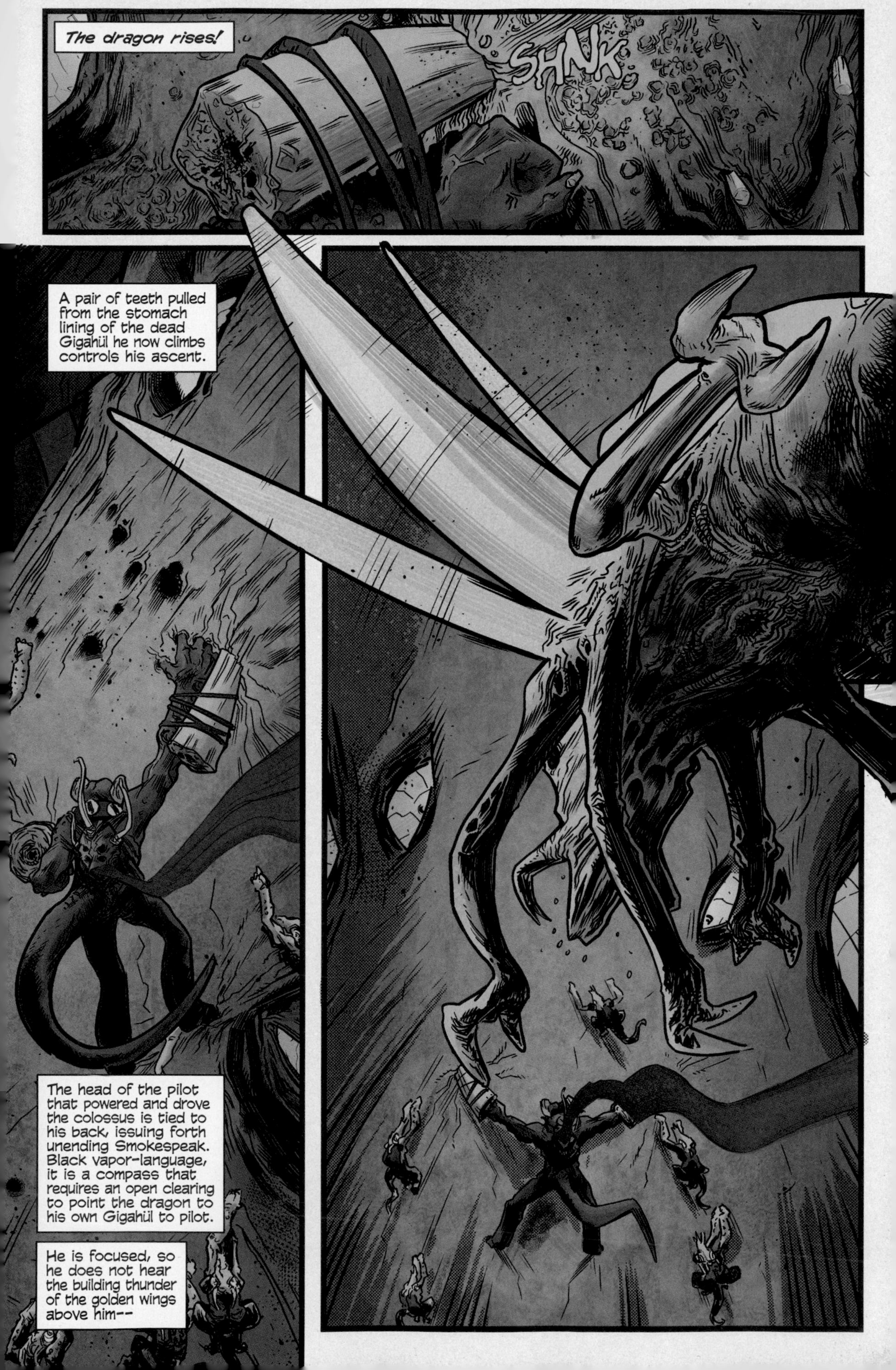
The dragon rises!
SHNK
A pair of teeth pulled from the stomach lining of the dead Gigahül he now climbs controls his ascent.
The head of the pilot that powered and drove the colossus is tied to his back, issuing forth unending Smokespeak. Black vapor-language, it is a compass that requires an open clearing to point the dragon to his own Gigahül to pilot.
He is focused, so he does not hear the building thunder of the golden wings above him--

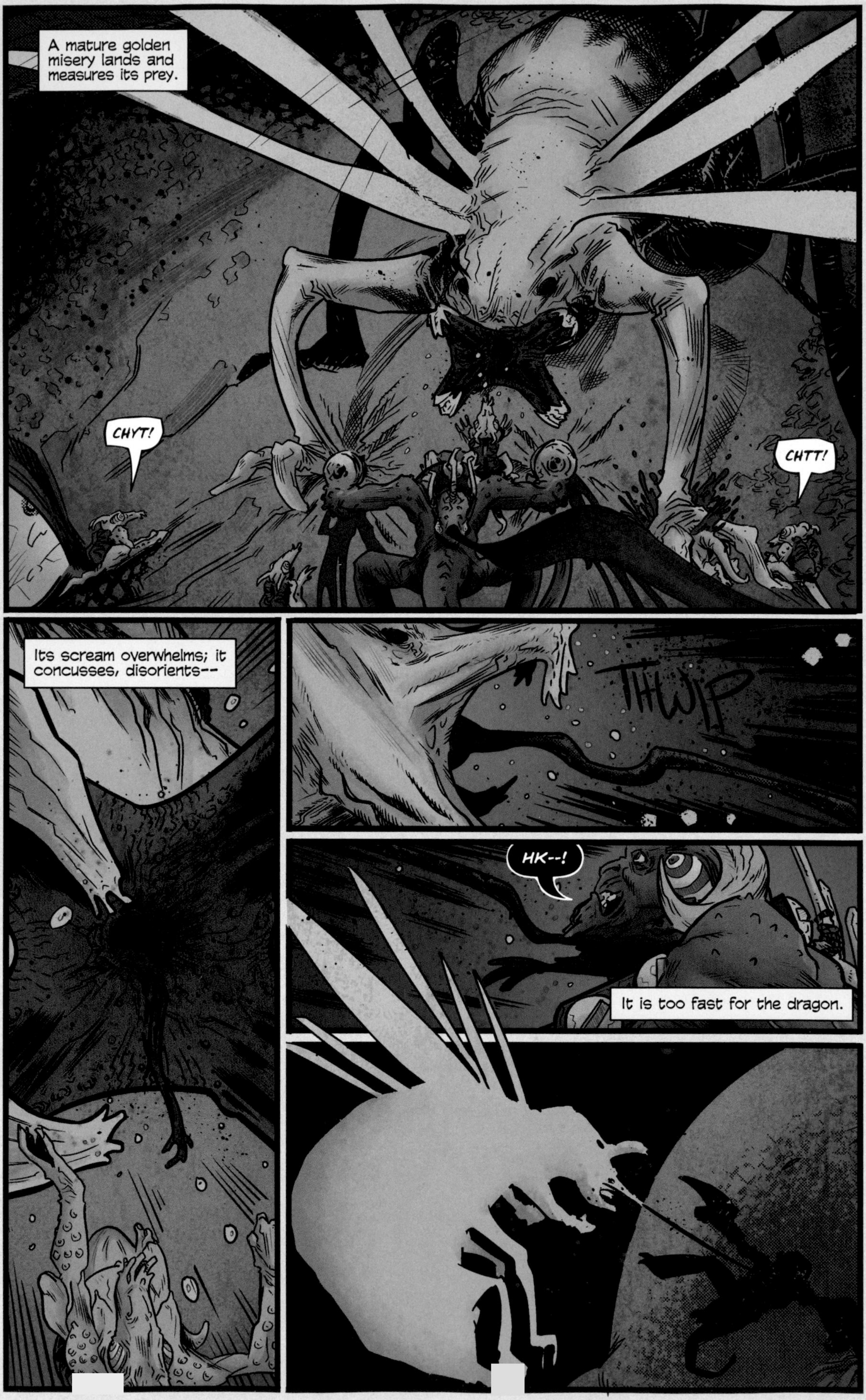
A mature golden misery lands and measures its prey.
CHYT!
CHTT!
Its scream overwhelms; it concusses, disorients--
THWIP
HK--!
It is too fast for the dragon.

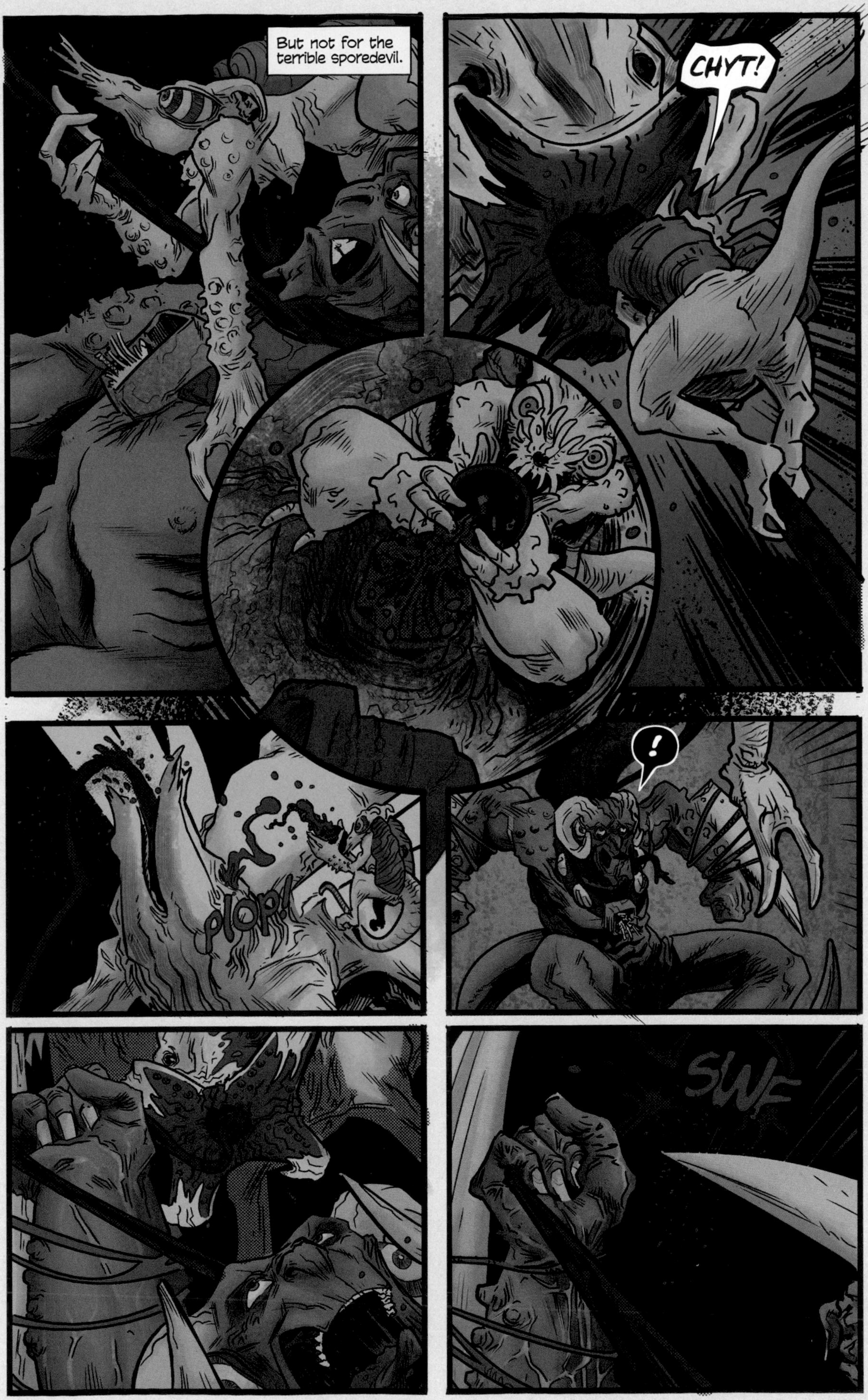
But not for the terrible sporedevil.
CHYT!
PLOP!
!
SWF

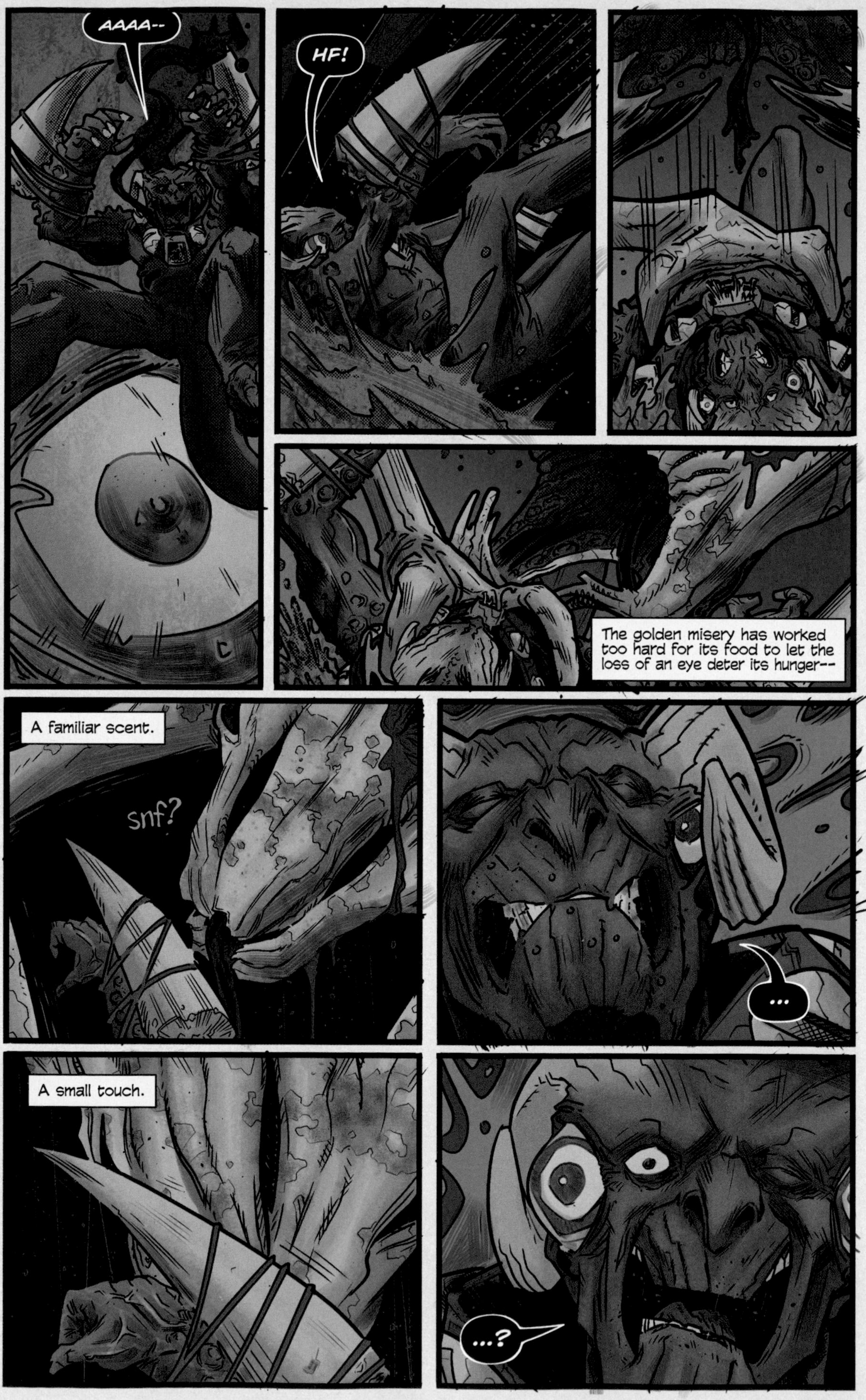
AAAA--
HF!
The golden misery has worked too hard for its food to let the loss of an eye deter its hunger--
A familiar scent.
snf?
...
A small touch.
...?

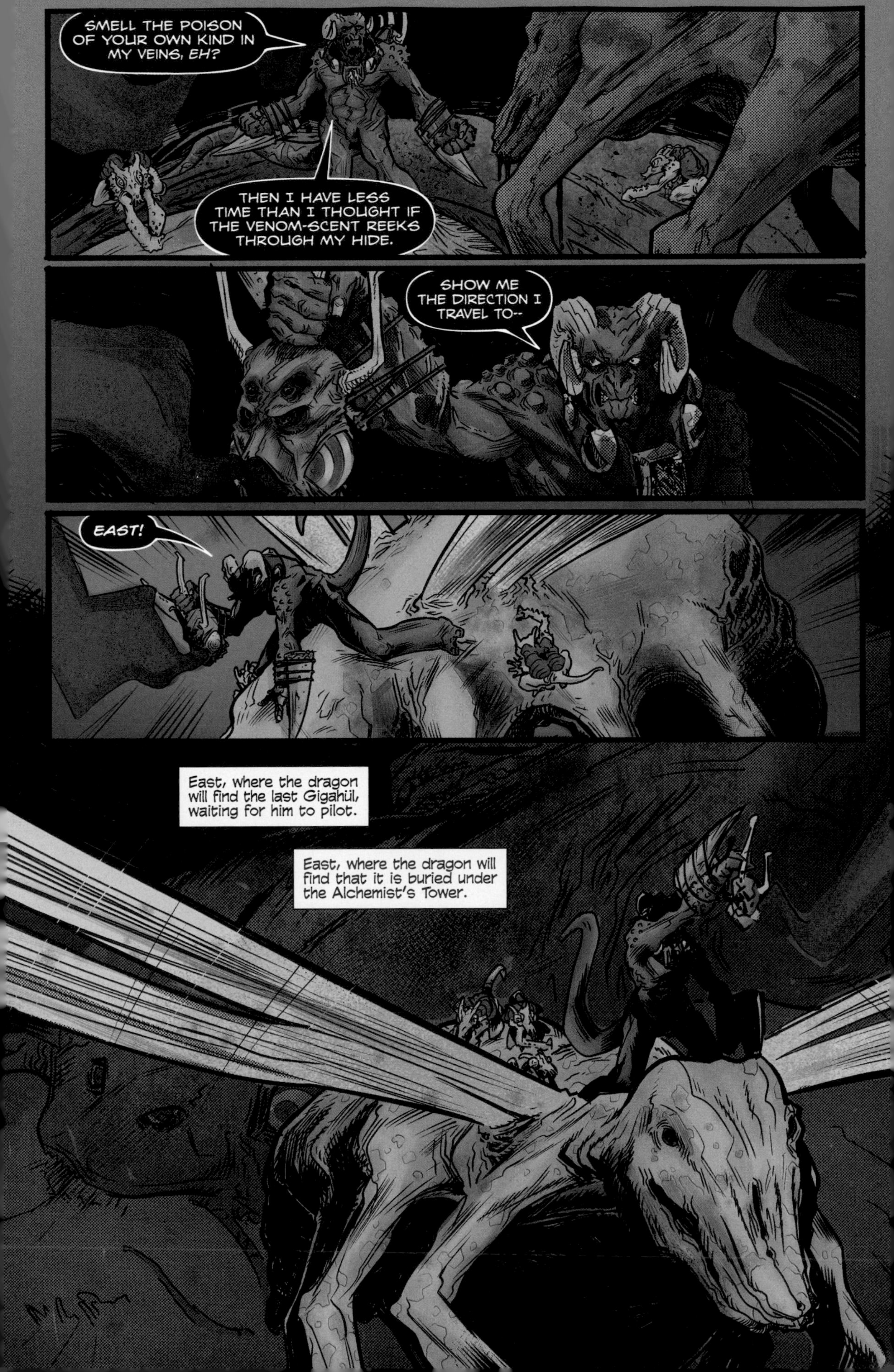
SMELL THE POISON OF YOUR OWN KIND IN MY VEINS, EH?
THEN I HAVE LESS TIME THAN I THOUGHT IF THE VENOM-SCENT REEKS THROUGH MY HIDE.
SHOW ME THE DIRECTION I TRAVEL TO--
EAST!
East, where the dragon will find the last Gigahül, waiting for him to pilot.
East, where the dragon will find that it is buried under the Alchemist's Tower.

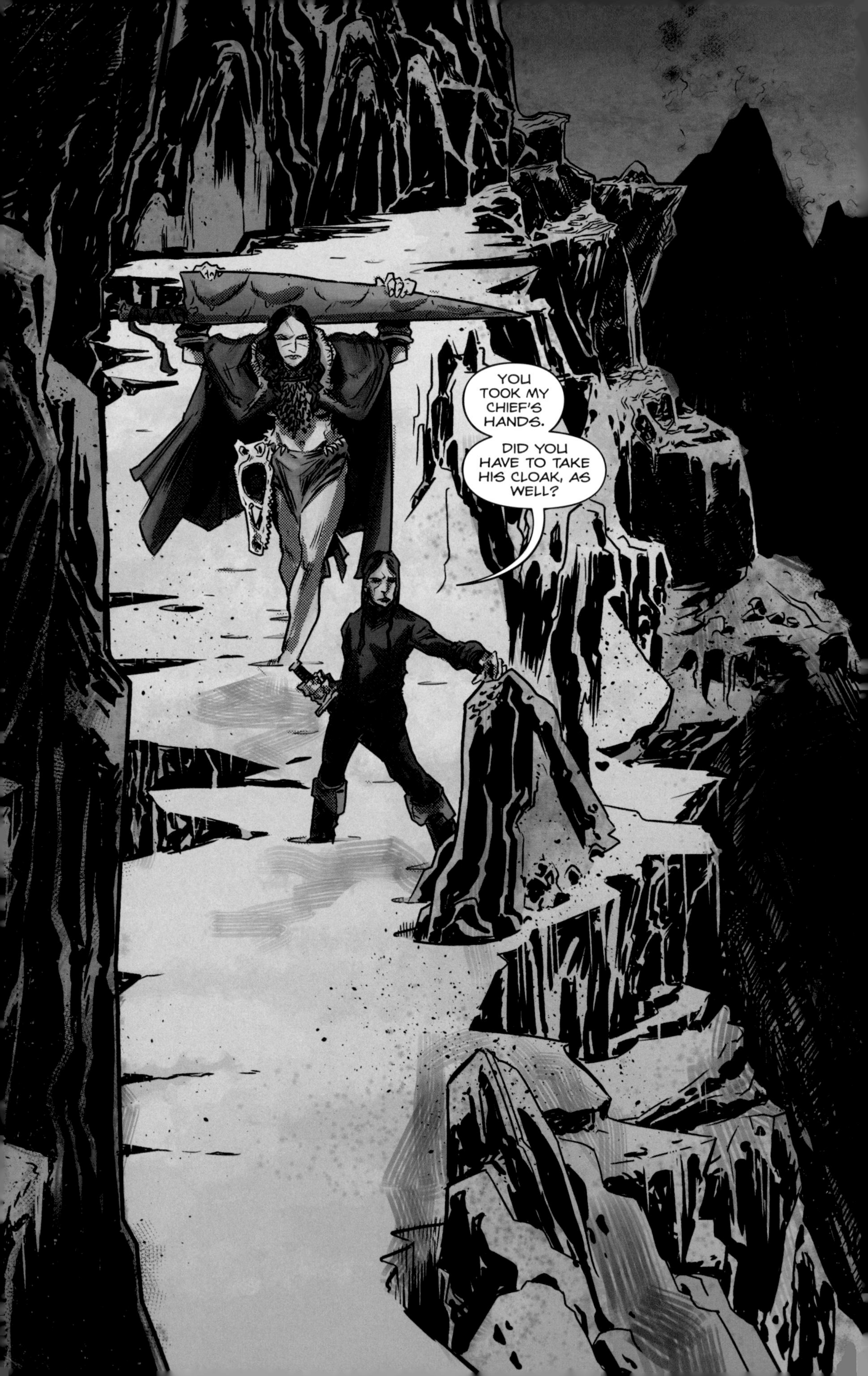
YOU TOOK MY CHIEF'S HANDS.
DID YOU HAVE TO TAKE HIS CLOAK, AS WELL?

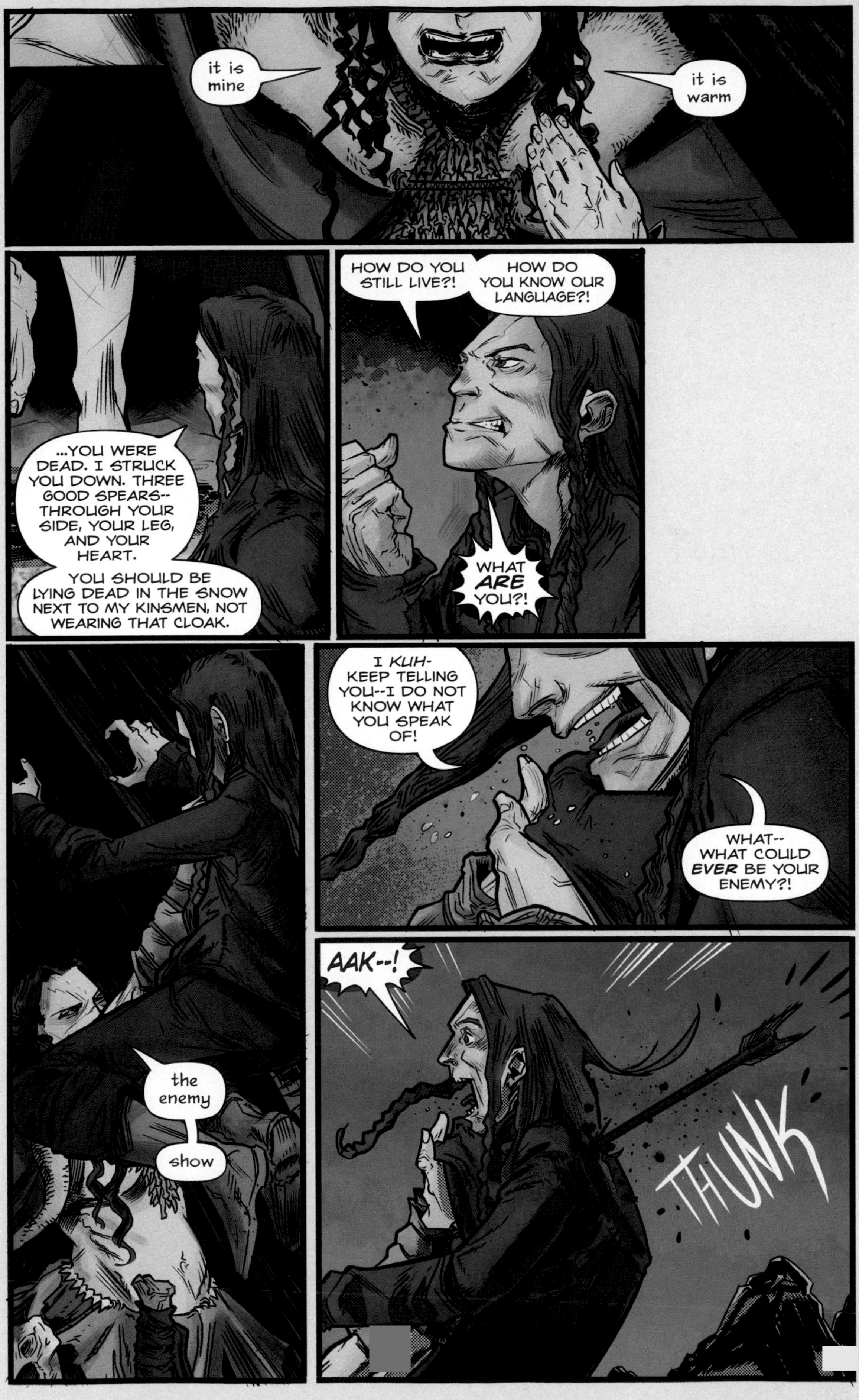

it is mine
it is warm
...YOU WERE DEAD. I STRUCK YOU DOWN. THREE GOOD SPEARS--THROUGH YOUR SIDE, YOUR LEG, AND YOUR HEART.
YOU SHOULD BE LYING DEAD IN THE SNOW NEXT TO MY KINSMEN, NOT WEARING THAT CLOAK.
HOW DO YOU STILL LIVE?!
HOW DO YOU KNOW OUR LANGUAGE?!
WHAT *ARE* YOU?!
the enemy
show
I *KUH*-KEEP TELLING YOU--I DO NOT KNOW WHAT YOU SPEAK OF!
WHAT--WHAT COULD *EVER* BE YOUR ENEMY?!
AAK--!
THUNK

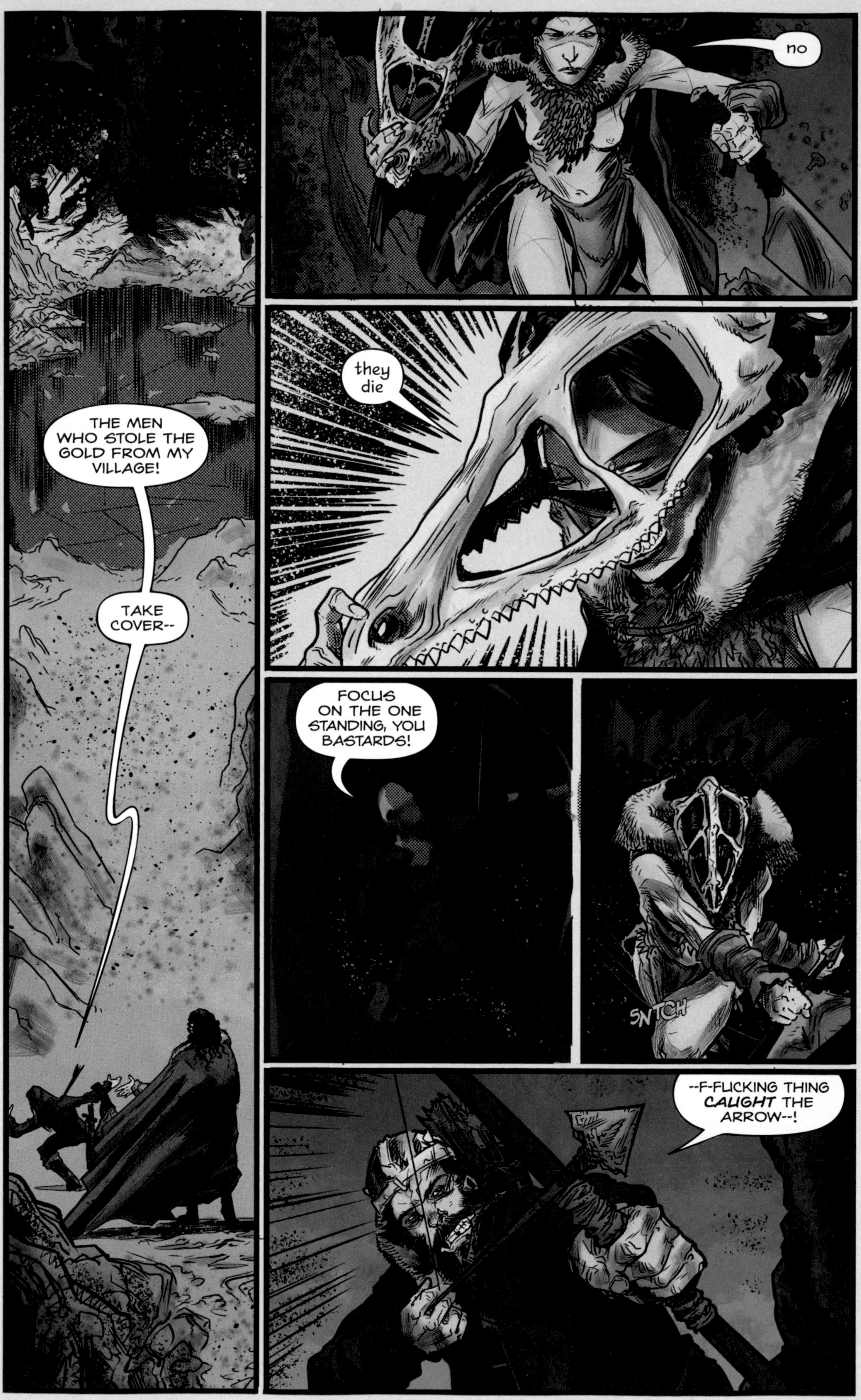
THE MEN WHO STOLE THE GOLD FROM MY VILLAGE!
TAKE COVER--
no
they die
FOCUS ON THE ONE STANDING, YOU BASTARDS!
SNTCH
--F-FUCKING THING CAUGHT THE ARROW--!

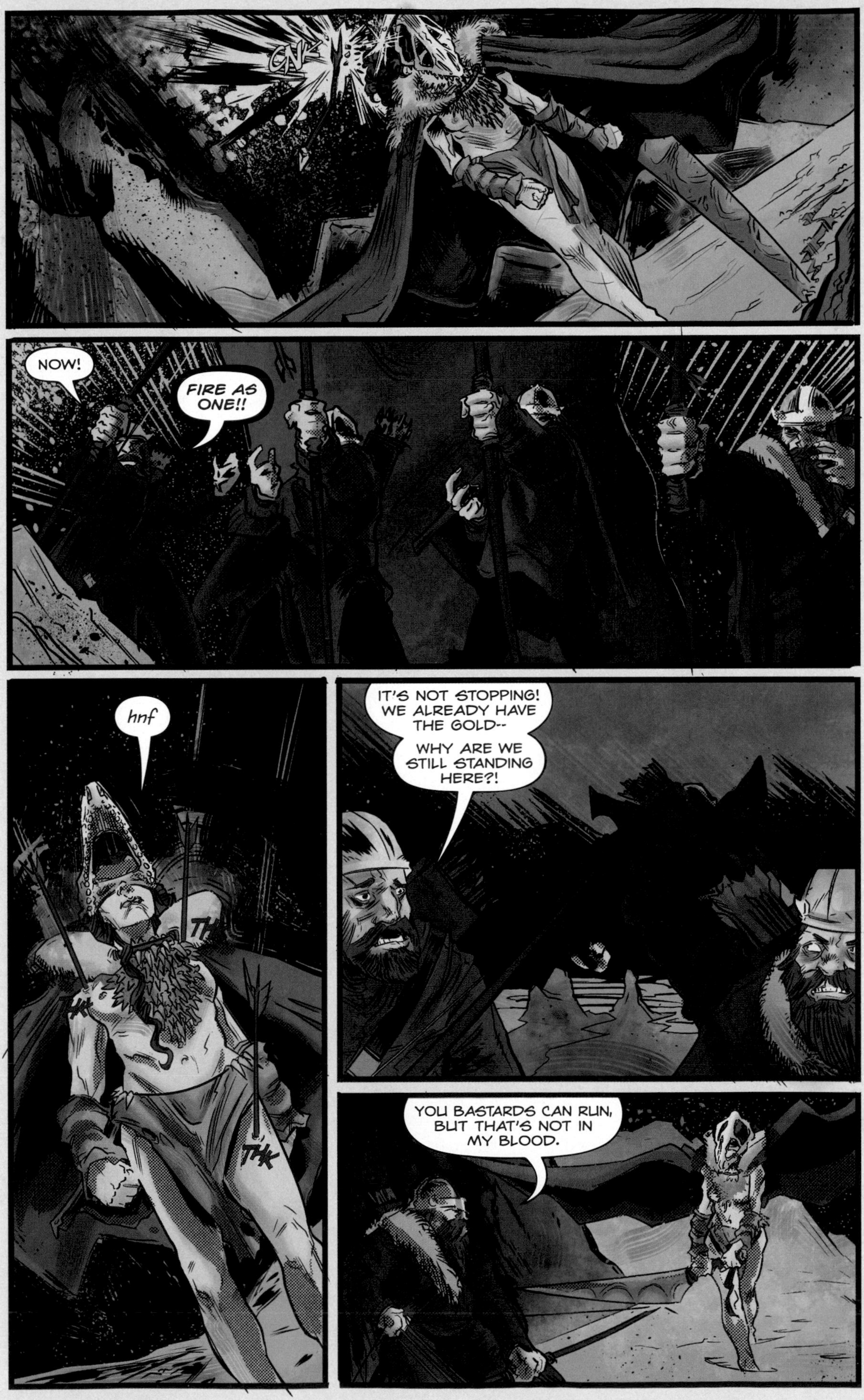
CNK
NOW!
FIRE AS ONE!!
hnf
THK
THK
THK
IT'S NOT STOPPING! WE ALREADY HAVE THE GOLD--
WHY ARE WE STILL STANDING HERE?!
YOU BASTARDS CAN RUN, BUT THAT'S NOT IN MY BLOOD.

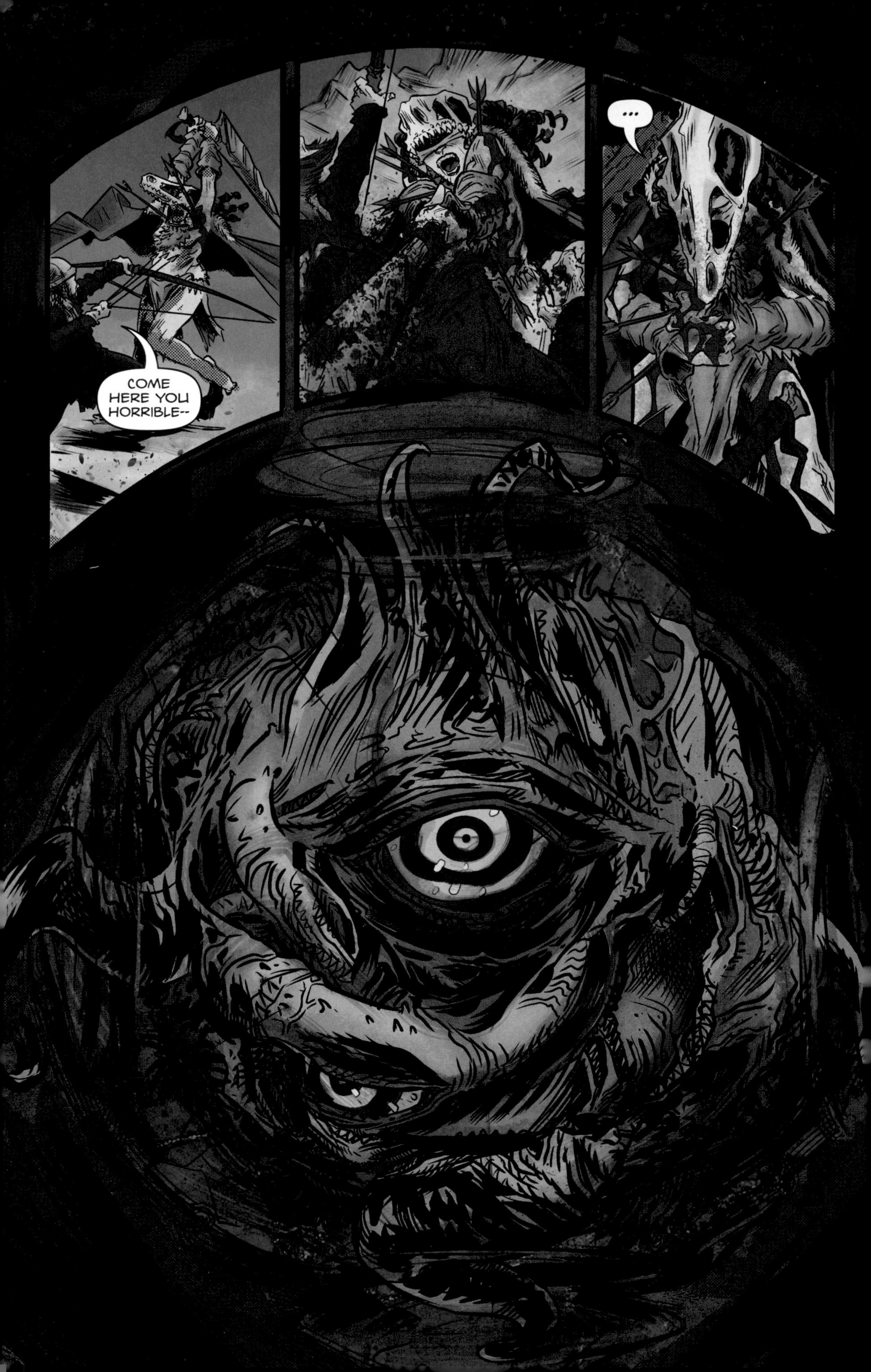
COME HERE YOU HORRIBLE--
...

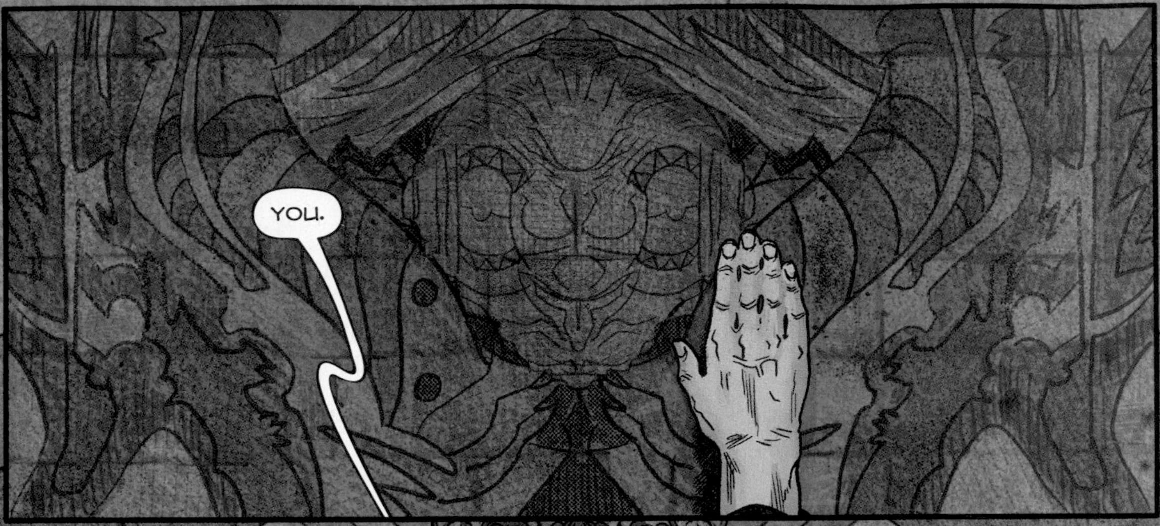
YOU.

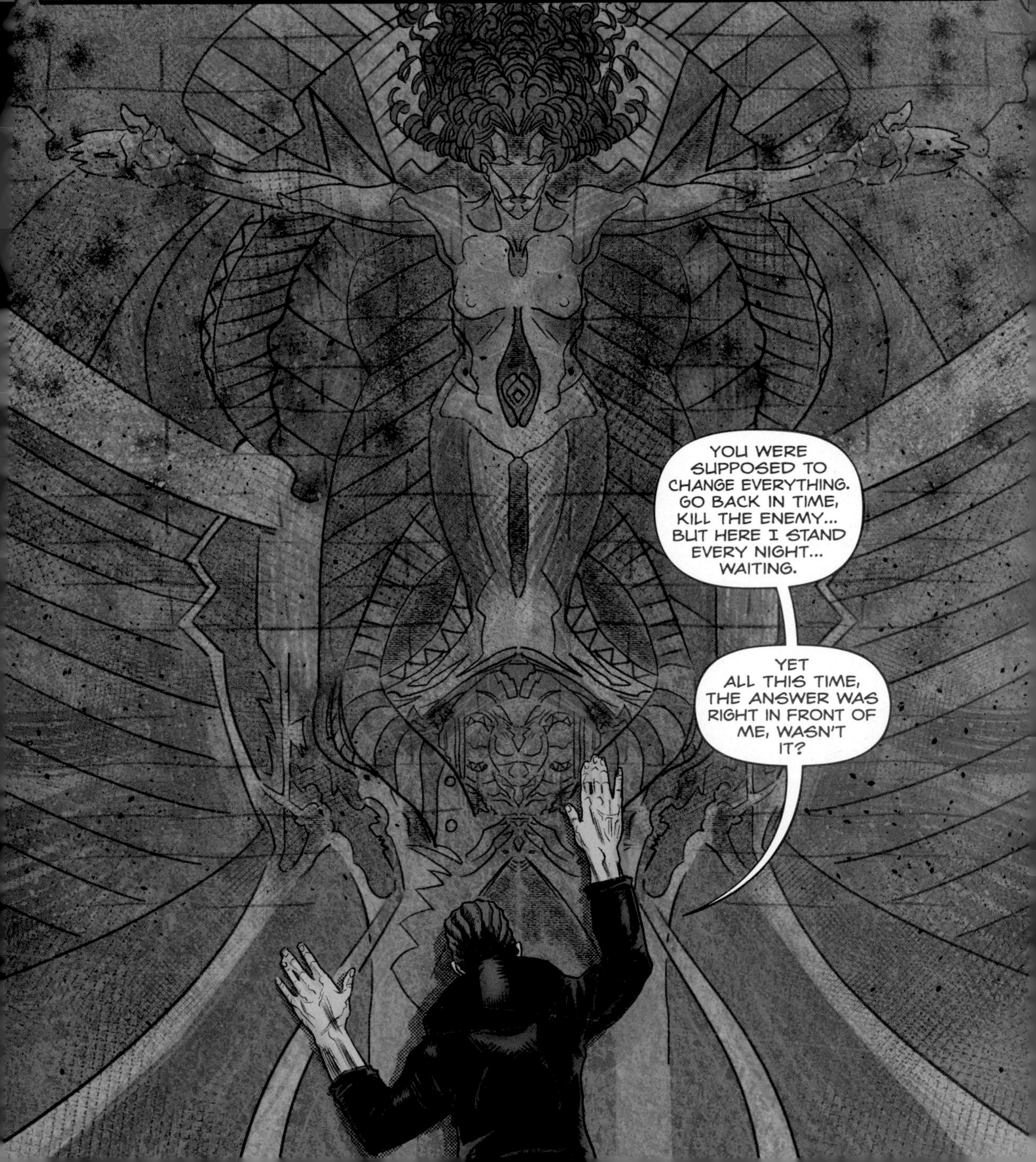
YOU WERE SUPPOSED TO CHANGE EVERYTHING. GO BACK IN TIME, KILL THE ENEMY... BUT HERE I STAND EVERY NIGHT... WAITING.
YET ALL THIS TIME, THE ANSWER WAS RIGHT IN FRONT OF ME, WASN'T IT?

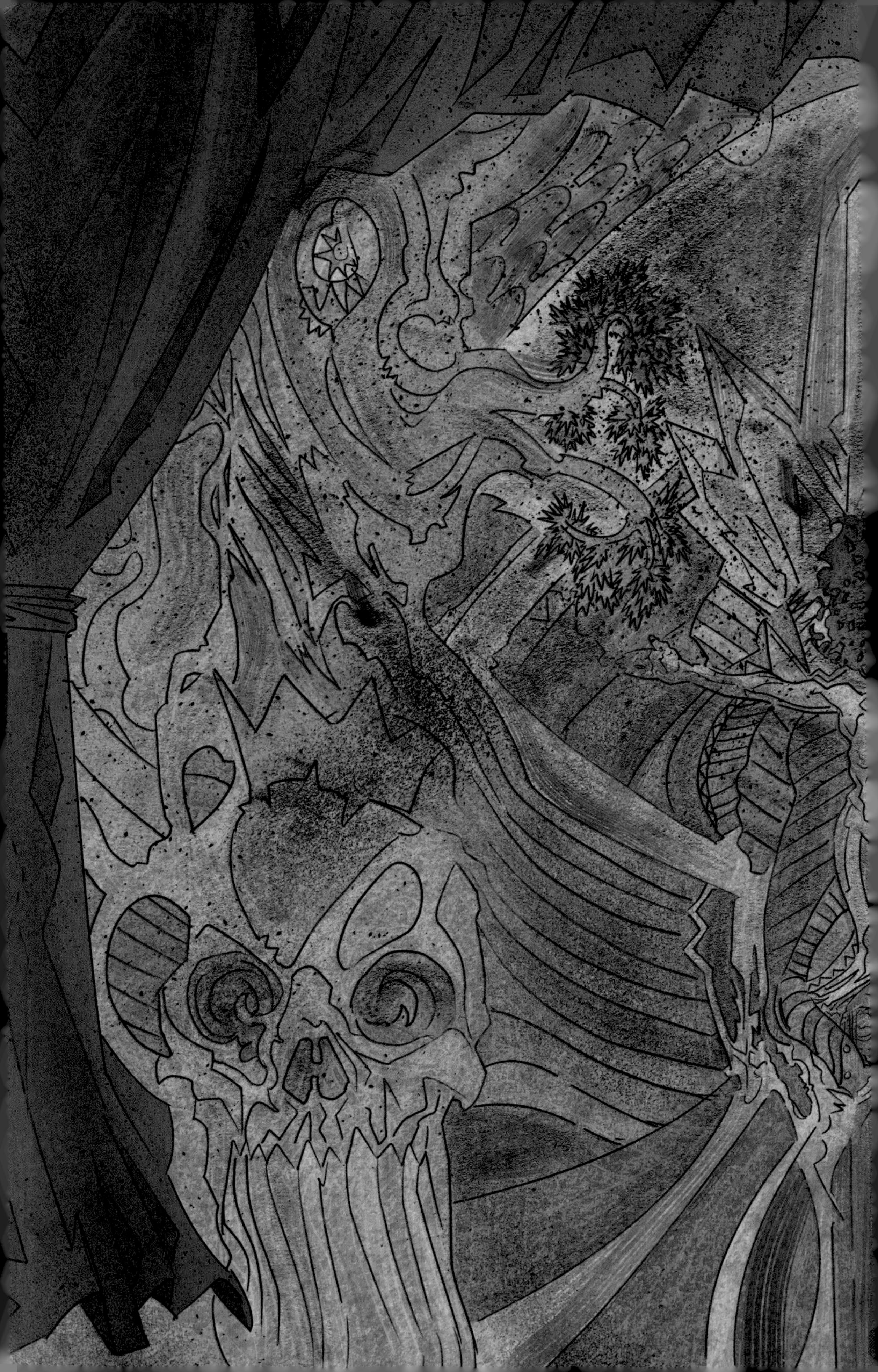

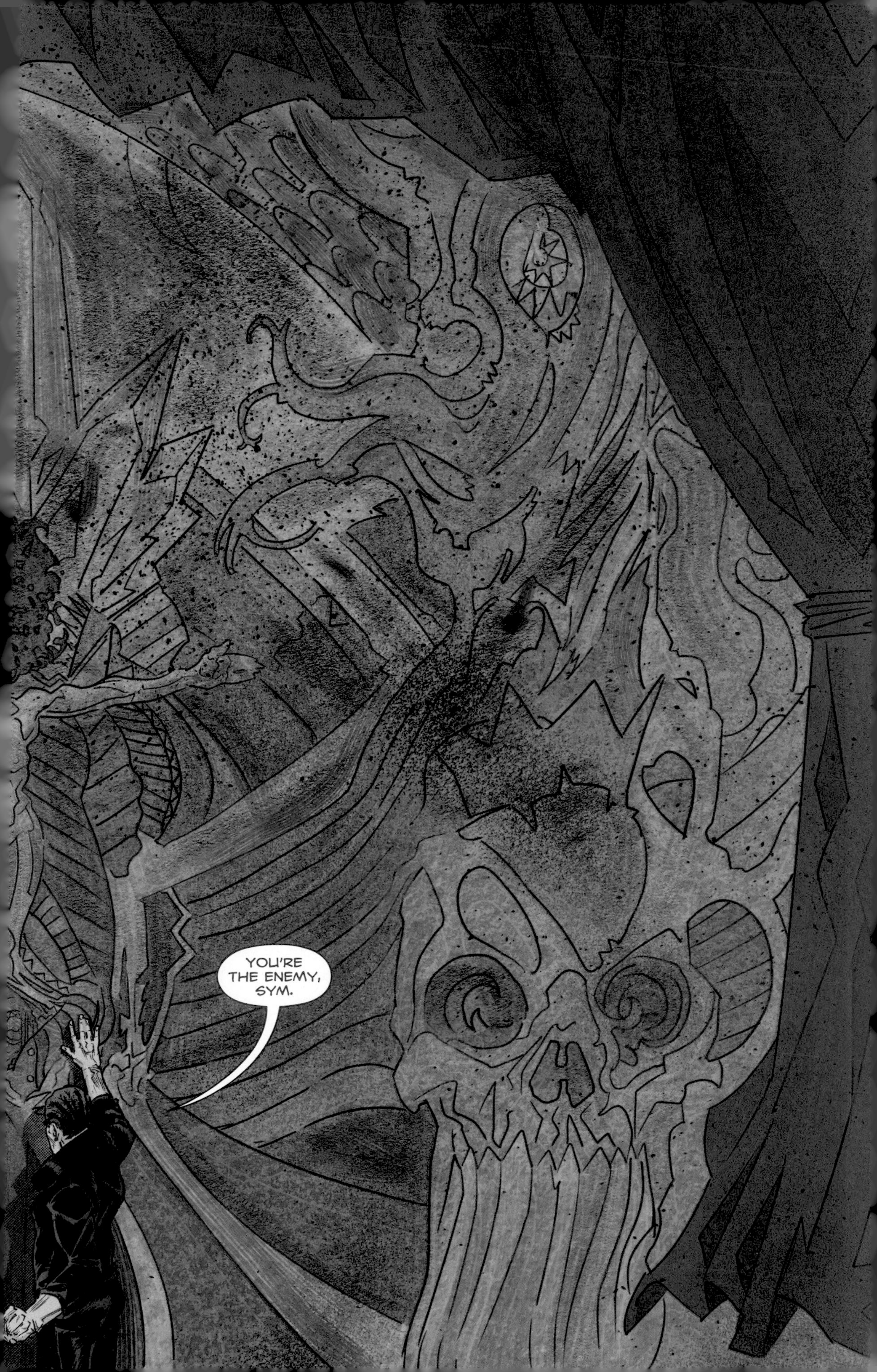
YOU'RE THE ENEMY, SYM.

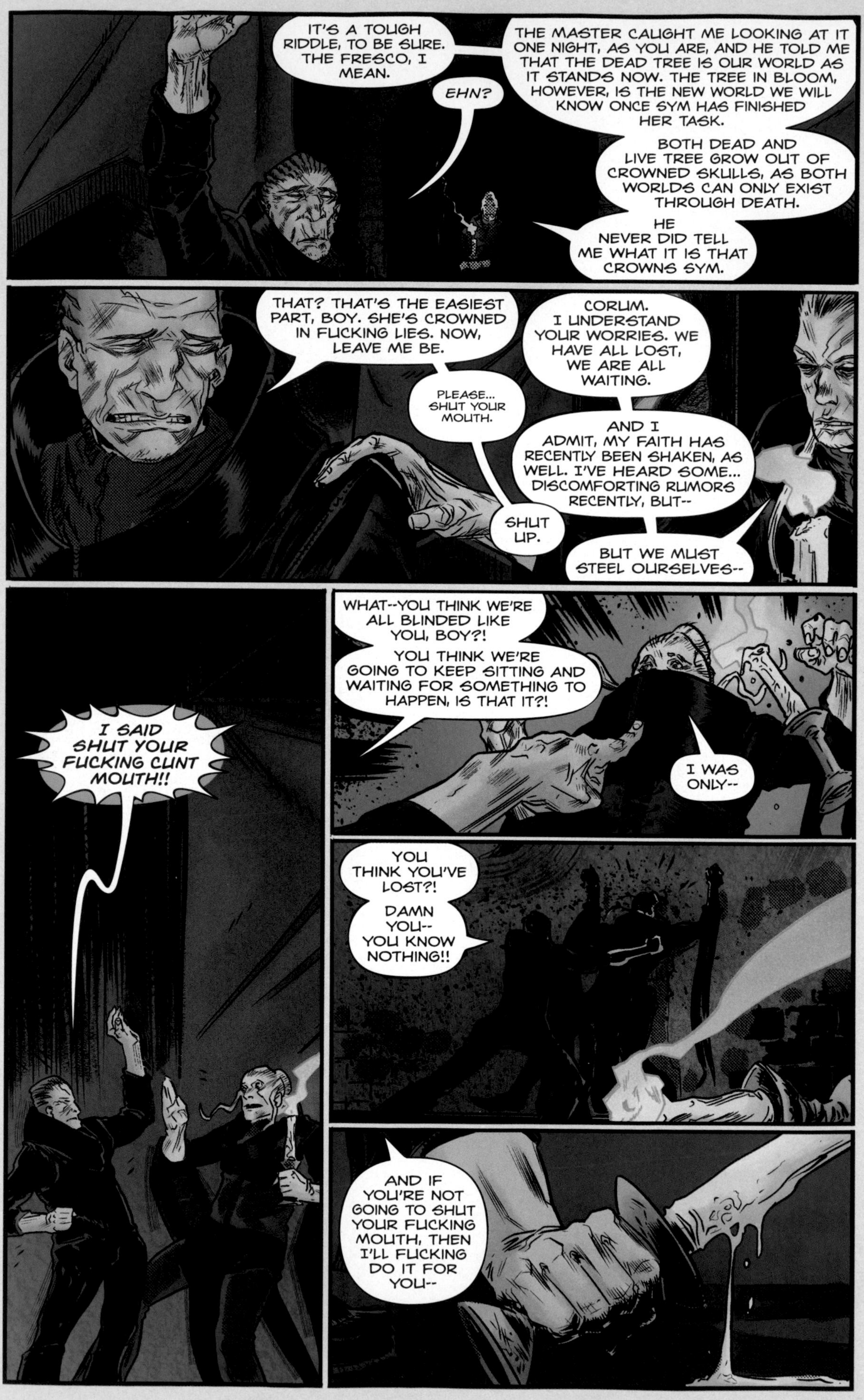
IT'S A TOUGH RIDDLE, TO BE SURE. THE FRESCO, I MEAN.
EHN?
THE MASTER CAUGHT ME LOOKING AT IT ONE NIGHT, AS YOU ARE, AND HE TOLD ME THAT THE DEAD TREE IS OUR WORLD AS IT STANDS NOW. THE TREE IN BLOOM, HOWEVER, IS THE NEW WORLD WE WILL KNOW ONCE SYM HAS FINISHED HER TASK.
BOTH DEAD AND LIVE TREE GROW OUT OF CROWNED SKULLS, AS BOTH WORLDS CAN ONLY EXIST THROUGH DEATH.
HE NEVER DID TELL ME WHAT IT IS THAT CROWNS SYM.
THAT? THAT'S THE EASIEST PART, BOY. SHE'S CROWNED IN FUCKING LIES. NOW, LEAVE ME BE.
CORUM. I UNDERSTAND YOUR WORRIES. WE HAVE ALL LOST, WE ARE ALL WAITING.
PLEASE... SHUT YOUR MOUTH.
AND I ADMIT, MY FAITH HAS RECENTLY BEEN SHAKEN, AS WELL. I'VE HEARD SOME... DISCOMFORTING RUMORS RECENTLY, BUT--
SHUT UP.
BUT WE MUST STEEL OURSELVES--
I SAID SHUT YOUR FUCKING CUNT MOUTH!!
WHAT--YOU THINK WE'RE ALL BLINDED LIKE YOU, BOY?!
YOU THINK WE'RE GOING TO KEEP SITTING AND WAITING FOR SOMETHING TO HAPPEN, IS THAT IT?!
I WAS ONLY--
YOU THINK YOU'VE LOST?!
DAMN YOU-- YOU KNOW NOTHING!!
AND IF YOU'RE NOT GOING TO SHUT YOUR FUCKING MOUTH, THEN I'LL FUCKING DO IT FOR YOU--

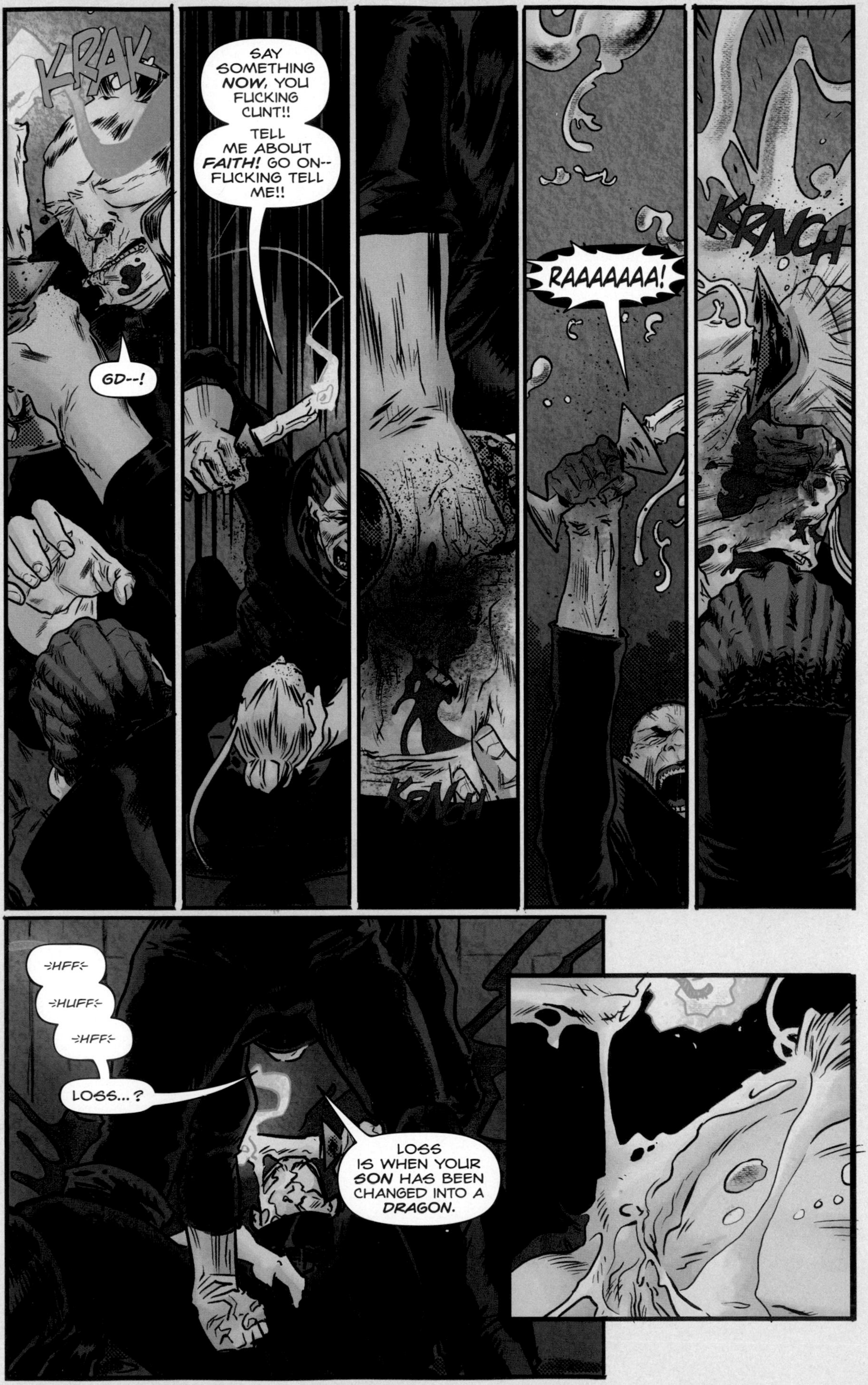
KRAK
GD--!
SAY SOMETHING NOW, YOU FUCKING CUNT!!
TELL ME ABOUT FAITH! GO ON-- FUCKING TELL ME!!
KRNCH
RAAAAAAA!
KRNCH
-HFF-
-HUFF-
-HFF-
LOSS...?
LOSS IS WHEN YOUR SON HAS BEEN CHANGED INTO A DRAGON.

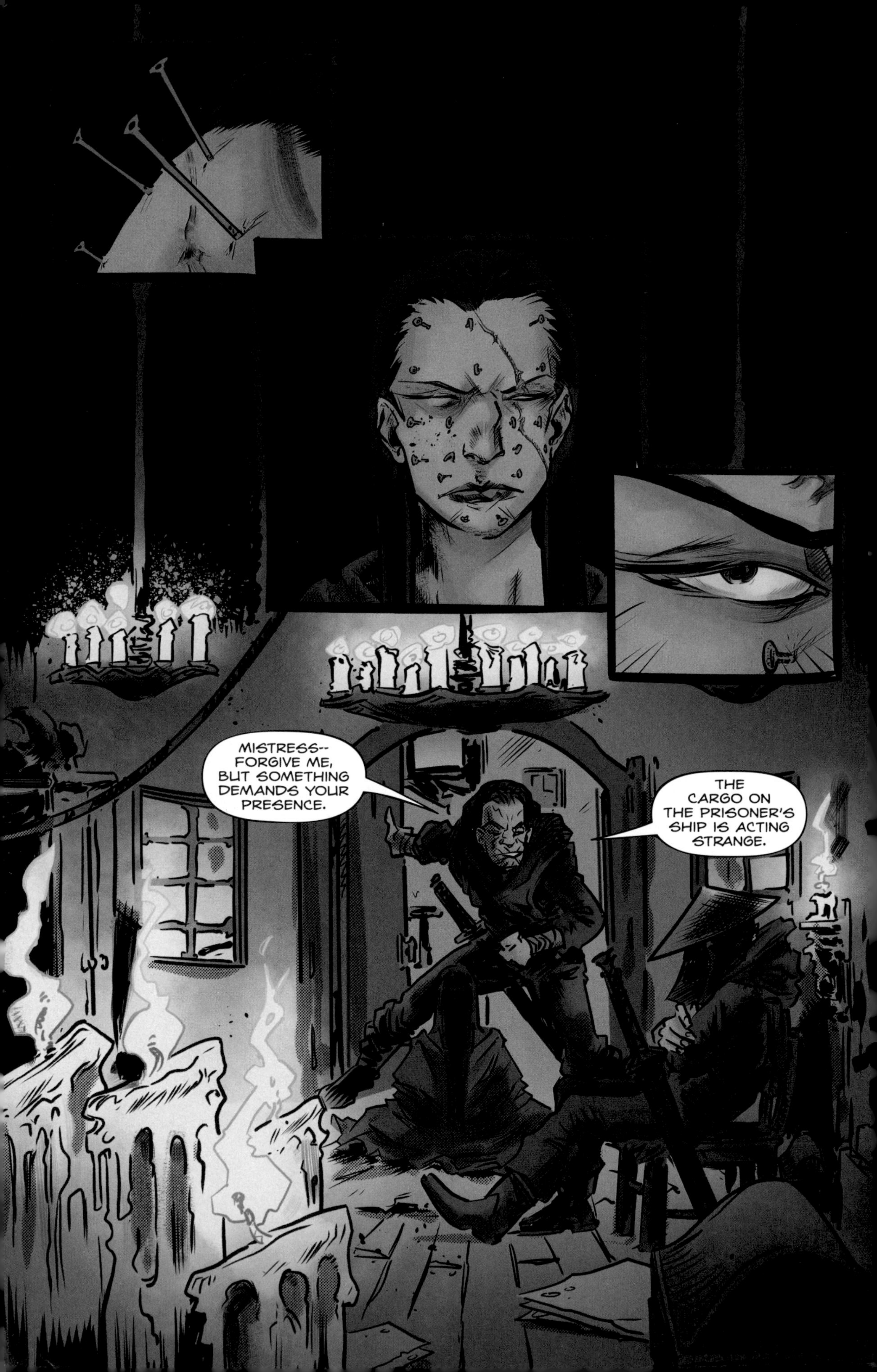
MISTRESS--
FORGIVE ME,
BUT SOMETHING
DEMANDS YOUR
PRESENCE.
THE
CARGO ON
THE PRISONER'S
SHIP IS ACTING
STRANGE.

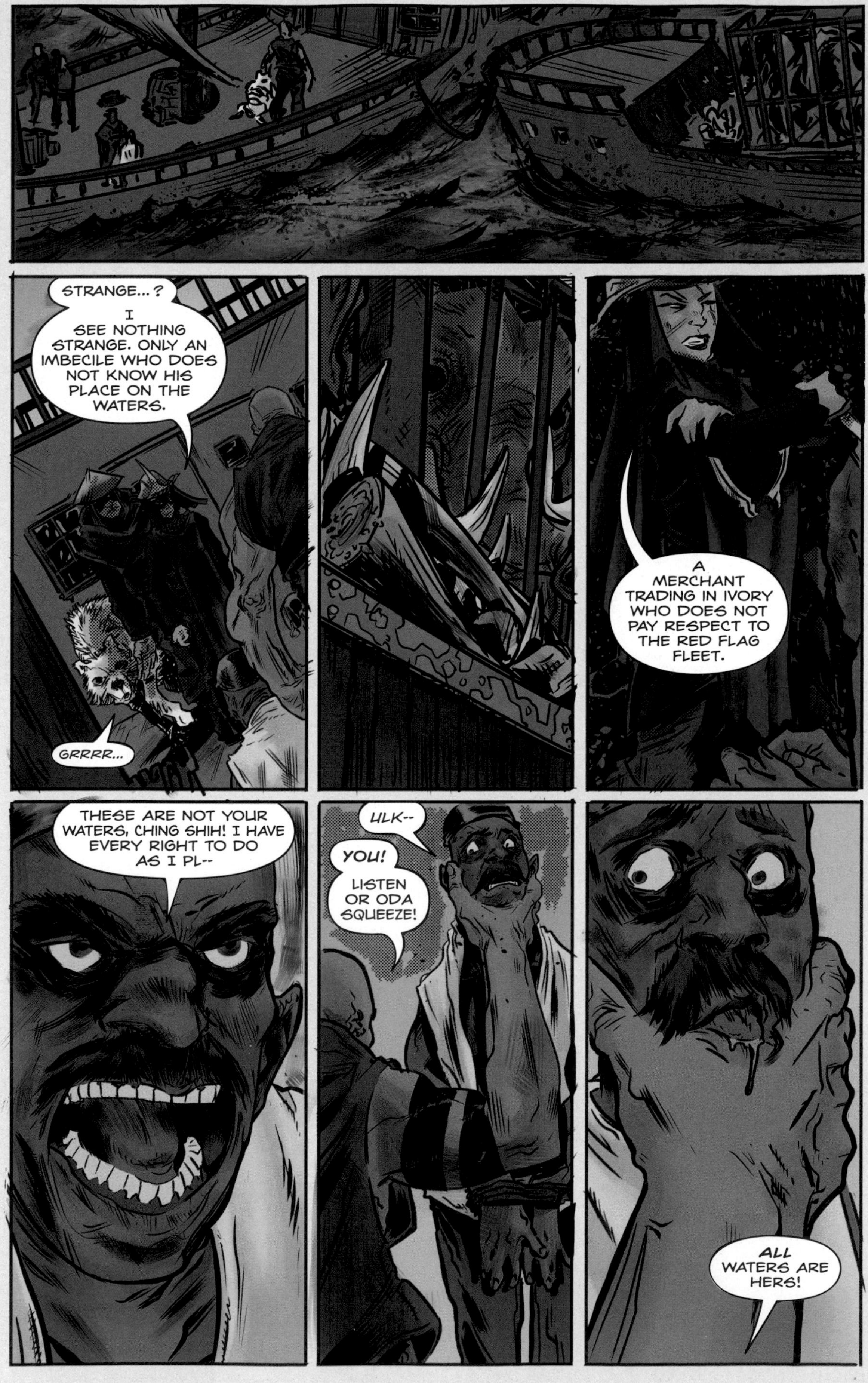
STRANGE...?
I SEE NOTHING STRANGE. ONLY AN IMBECILE WHO DOES NOT KNOW HIS PLACE ON THE WATERS.
GRRRR...
A MERCHANT TRADING IN IVORY WHO DOES NOT PAY RESPECT TO THE RED FLAG FLEET.
THESE ARE NOT YOUR WATERS, CHING SHIH! I HAVE EVERY RIGHT TO DO AS I PL--
ULK--
YOU!
LISTEN OR ODA SQUEEZE!
ALL WATERS ARE HERS!

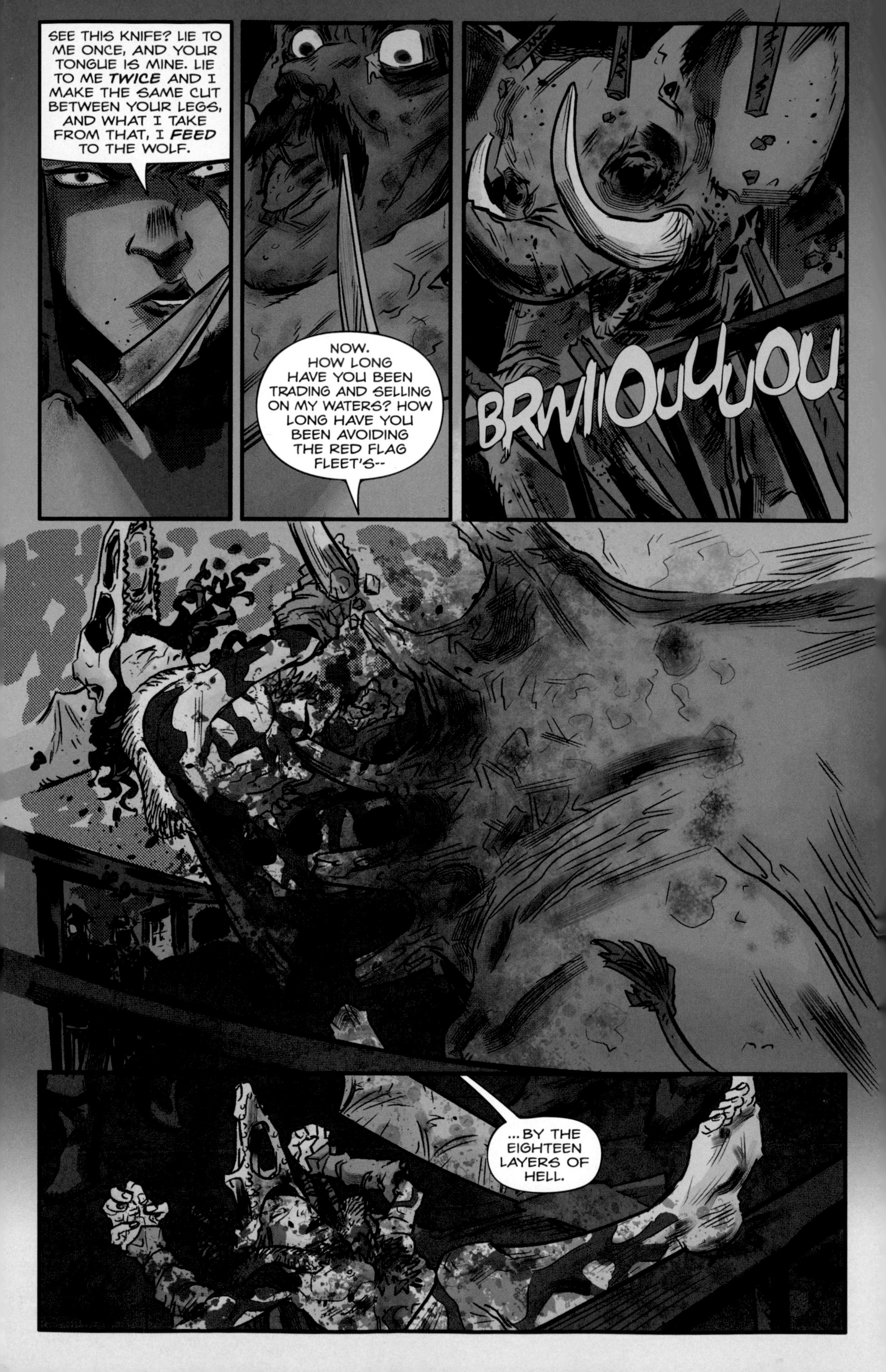
SEE THIS KNIFE? LIE TO ME ONCE, AND YOUR TONGUE IS MINE. LIE TO ME *TWICE* AND I MAKE THE SAME CUT BETWEEN YOUR LEGS, AND WHAT I TAKE FROM THAT, I *FEED* TO THE WOLF.
NOW. HOW LONG HAVE YOU BEEN TRADING AND SELLING ON MY WATERS? HOW LONG HAVE YOU BEEN AVOIDING THE RED FLAG FLEET'S--
BRWIIOUUUUOU
...BY THE EIGHTEEN LAYERS OF HELL.

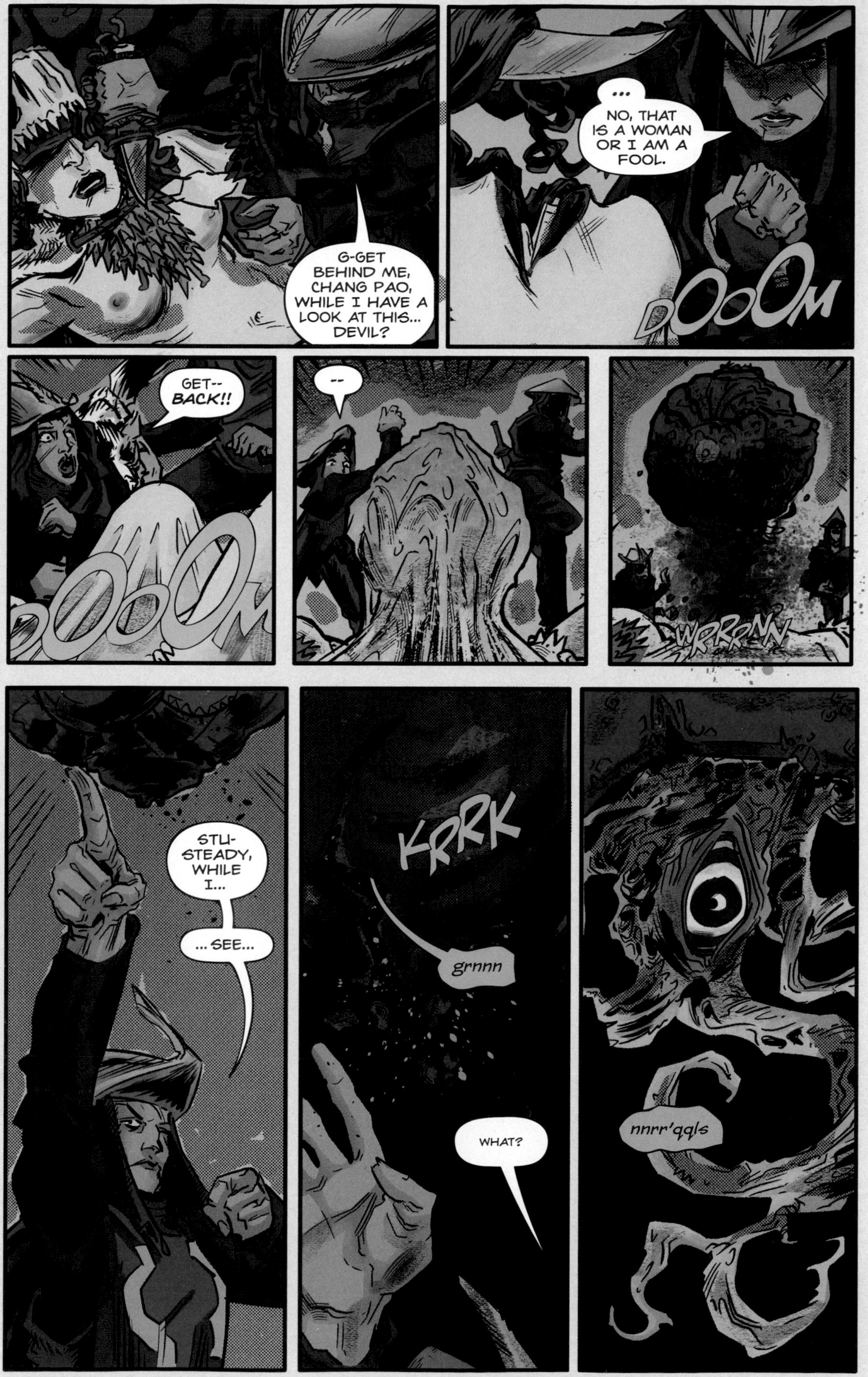
G-GET BEHIND ME, CHANG PAO, WHILE I HAVE A LOOK AT THIS... DEVIL?
...
NO, THAT IS A WOMAN OR I AM A FOOL.
DOOOOM
GET-- BACK!!
DOOOOM
--
WRRRNN
STU- STEADY, WHILE I...
... SEE...
KRRK
grnnn
WHAT?
nnrr'qqls

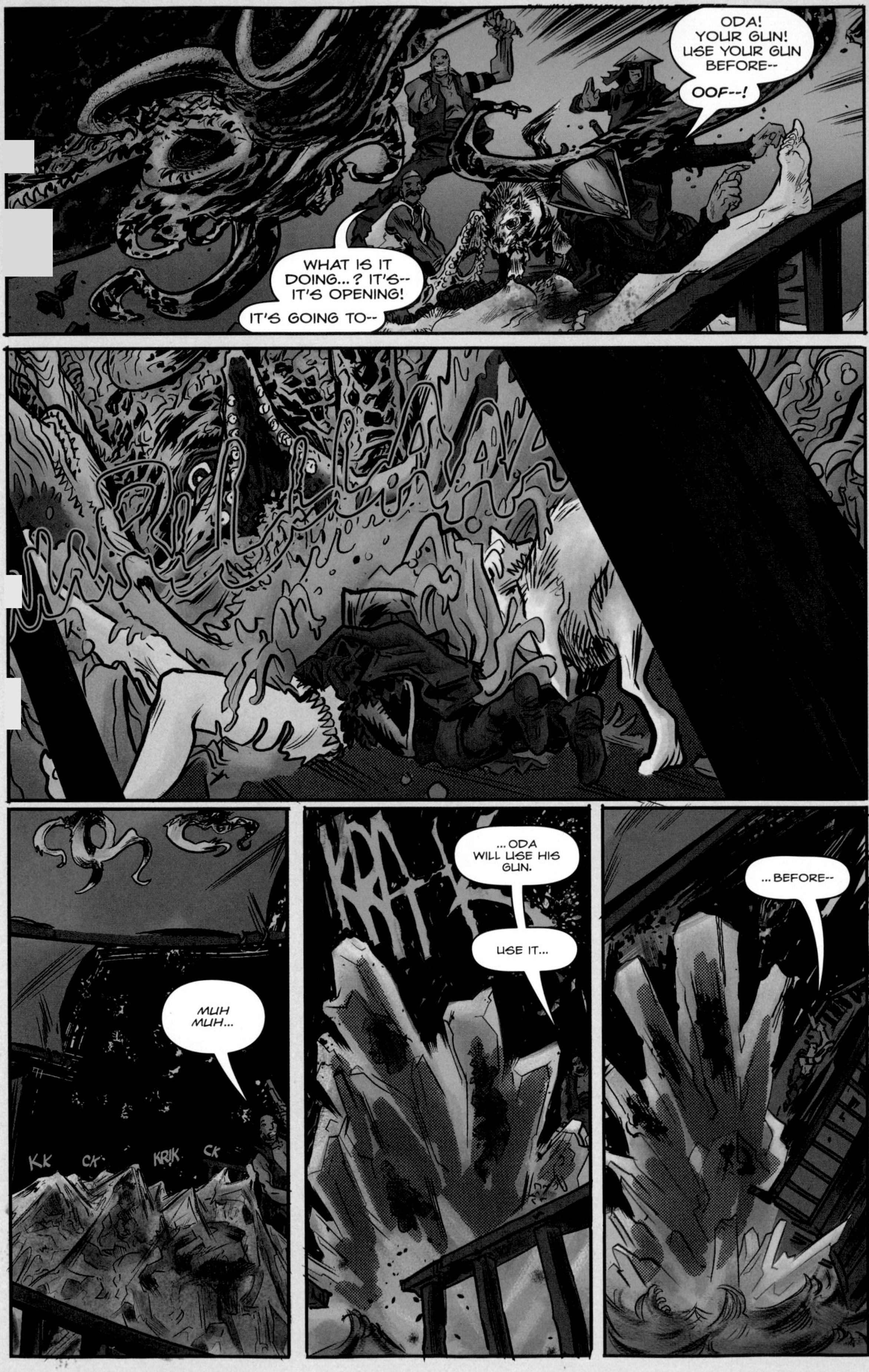
ODA! YOUR GUN! USE YOUR GUN BEFORE--
OOF--!
WHAT IS IT DOING...? IT'S-- IT'S OPENING!
IT'S GOING TO--
MUH MUH...
KK CK KRIK CK
...ODA WILL USE HIS GUN.
USE IT...
...BEFORE--

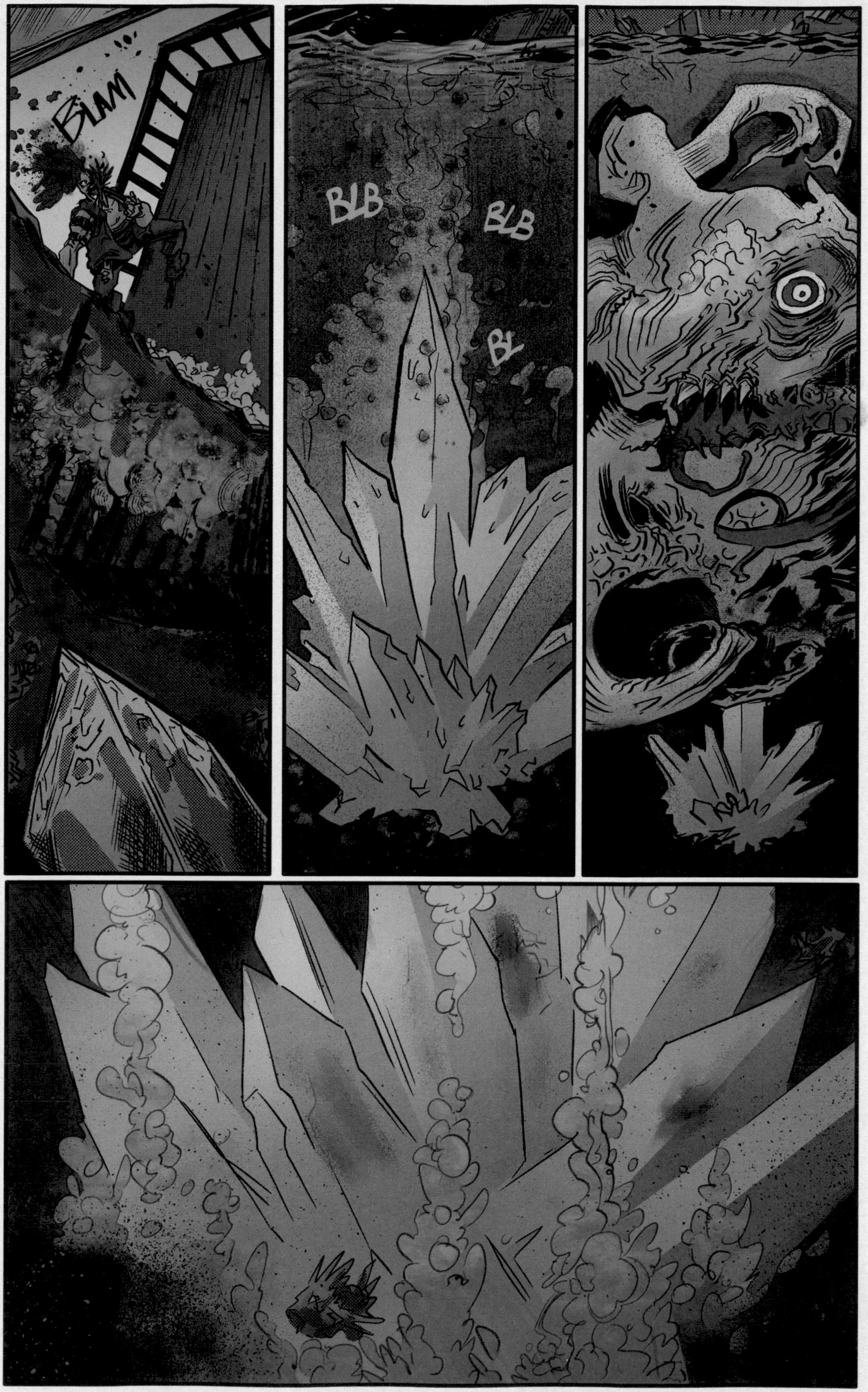
BLAM
BLB
BLB
BL

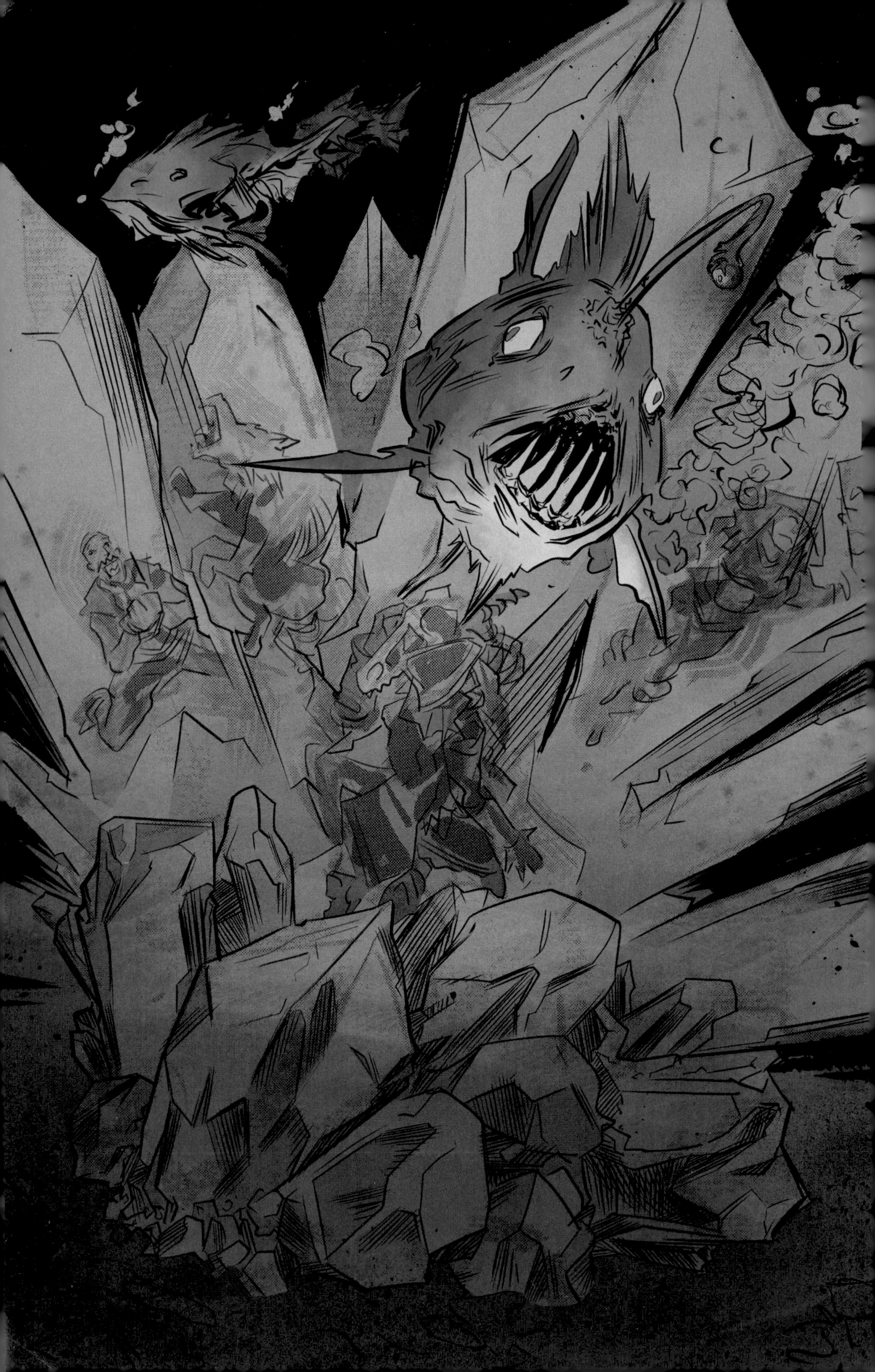

DARK ENGINE

COMING SOON
VOLUME 2: SHADOW OF THE IVORY WOLF

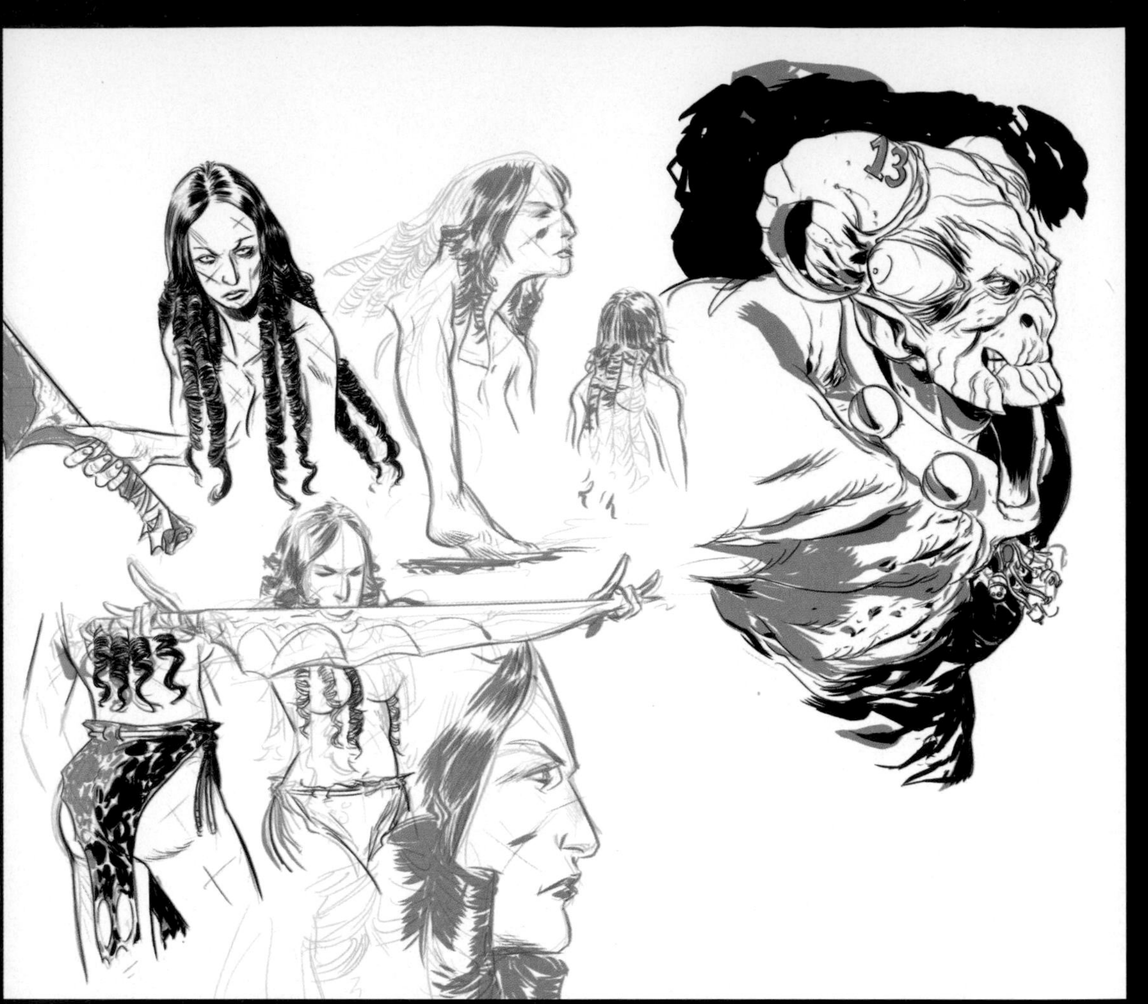
13
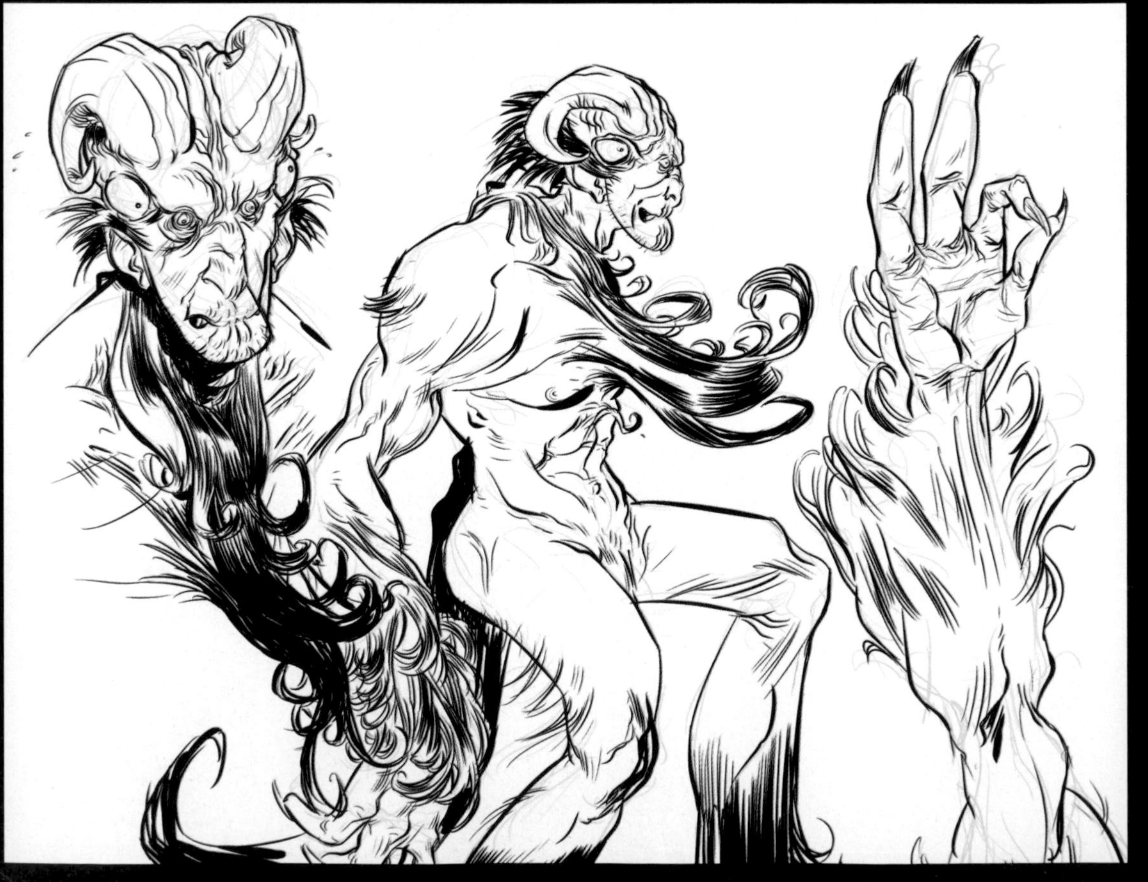

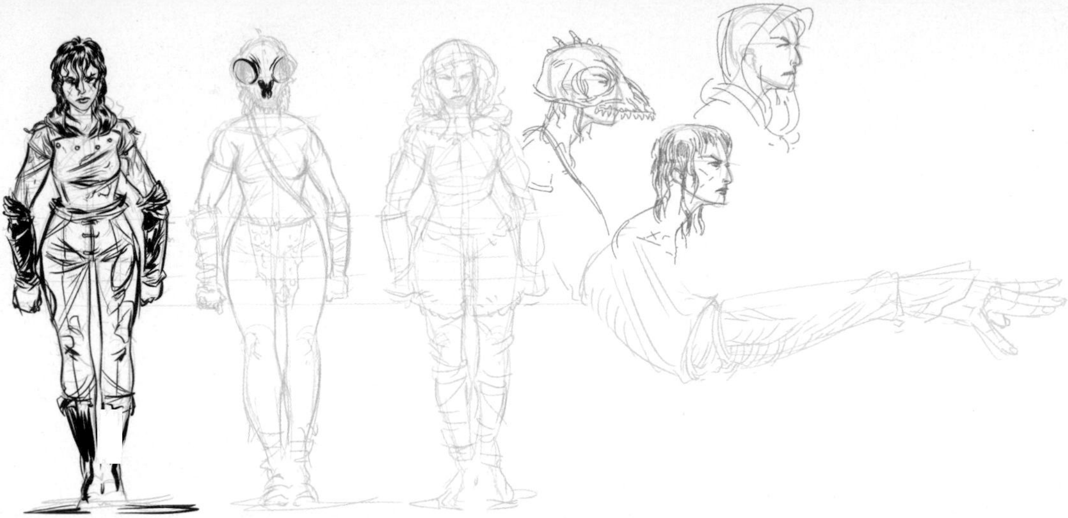
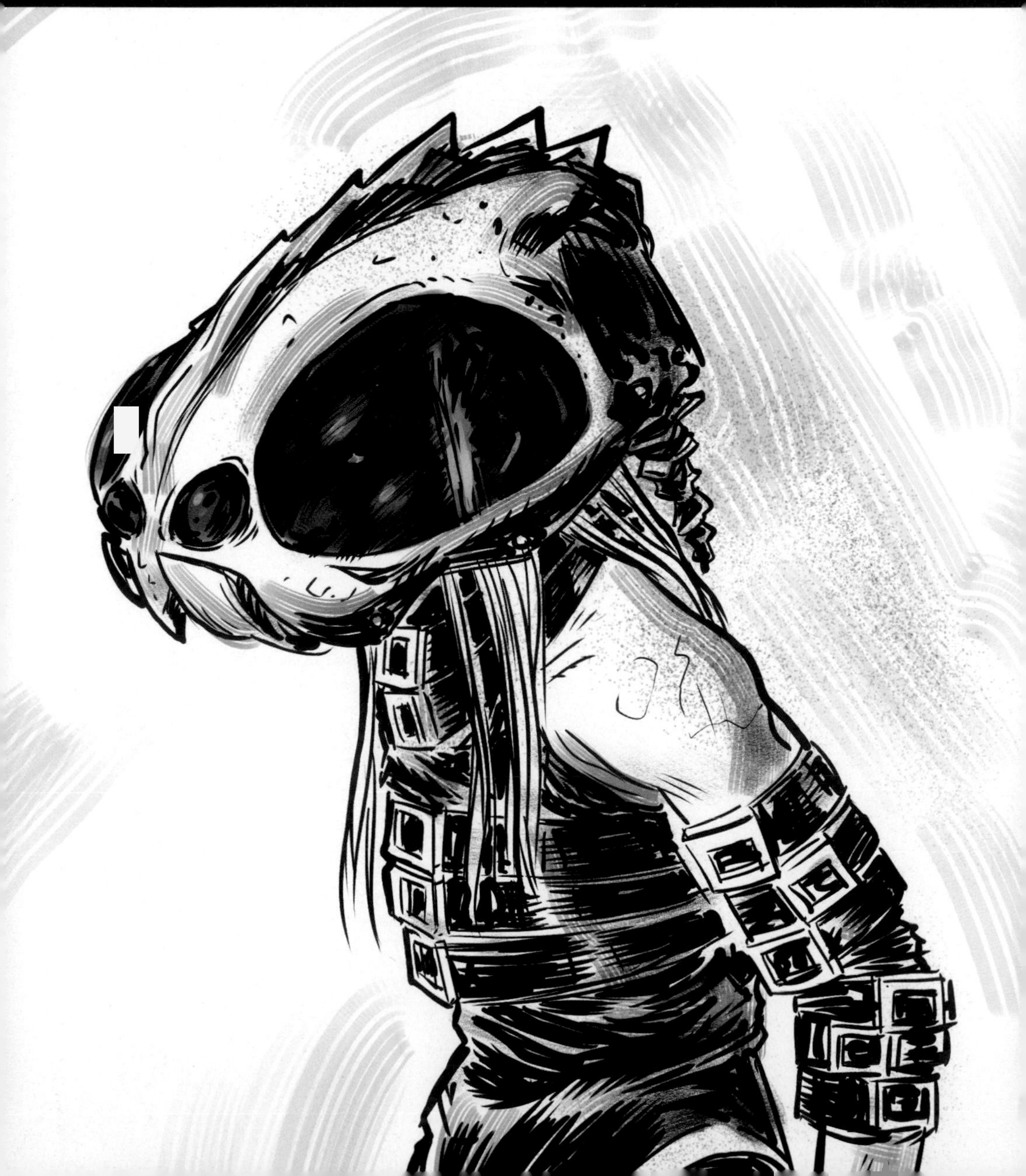

BORN BY THE SAND, NOW LIVING BY THE SEA, RYAN BURTON MAKES HIS WAY THROUGH LIFE BY DREAMING THINGS UP AND TYING THEM DOWN IN INK. A WIFE, TWO KIDS, AND BEAUTIFUL CLOUDS INSIDE HIS HEAD KEEP A SONG IN HIS HEART AND A DEVIL IN HIS STEP. ONCE A SCOUNDREL, HE WAS MADE HONEST BY THE SAME PERSON WHOM THIS STORY IS DEDICATED TO—HIS OWN (DARK) ENGINE, ELIZABETH.

JOHN BIVENS WAS A CONVENTIONAL BOY UNTIL HE HEARD ABOUT FACEBOOK... AT WHICH TIME HE ATTEMPTED TO MAKE A BOOK OUT OF FACES. THE COURT REQUIRED HIM TO SPEND TIME IN A HOSPITAL WHERE HE LEARNED ARTS AND CRAFTS, THEN CAME DARK ENGINE. HAVING OVERLOOKED JOHN'S PAST CRIMES, HE NOW HAS THE LOVE AND SUPPORT OF HIS WONDERFUL WIFE MALLORY.